Early Settlement in Berkshire:
Mesolithic–Roman Occupation Sites in the Thames and Kennet Valleys

by I. Barnes, W.A. Boismier, R.M.J. Cleal,
A.P. Fitzpatrick, and M.R. Roberts

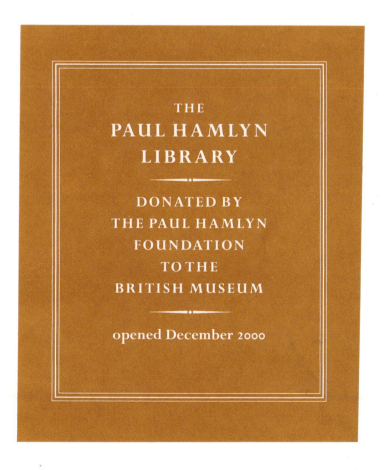

Reconstruction of the Dunston Park settlement, by Julian Cross

Early Settlement in Berkshire:
Mesolithic–Roman Occupation Sites in the Thames and Kennet Valleys

by I. Barnes, W.A. Boismier, R.M.J. Cleal,
A.P. Fitzpatrick, and M.R. Roberts

with contributions from
Paul Booth, A.J. Clapham, C. Cox, Peter Crew, Janet Egerton, Steve Ford,
Clive Gamble, P.A. Harding, F.M.A. Healy, R. Montague,
Jacqueline I. McKinley, L.N. Mepham, Elaine L. Morris,
and Mark Robinson

illustrations by
Simon Chew, Linda Coleman, Julian Cross, Serena Garrett,
S.E. James, Karen Nichols and Linda Stacey

Wessex Archaeology Report No. 6

Wessex Archaeology/Oxford Archaeological Unit
1995

Published 1995 by the Trust for Wessex Archaeology Ltd
Portway House, Old Sarum Park, Salisbury, England, SP4 6EB

British Library Cataloguing in Publication Data
A catalogue record for this book is available from the British Library

ISBN 1–874350–12–4
ISSN 0965–5778

Produced by Wessex Archaeology
Printed by Derry & Son Ltd, Nottingham

Series Editor: Julie Gardiner
Assistant Editor: Melanie Gauden

The publishers wish to acknowledge with gratitude
grants from Beazer Homes, Bryant Homes, English
Heritage, Luff Development, Summerleaze Ltd, and
Trencherwood Homes towards the cost of publishing
this volume

Front cover: Dunston Park, Bronze Age round-house 1128 under excavation, looking south
Back cover: Weir Bank Stud Farm, Bray, north terminal of ditch 819, part of Middle Bonze Age enclosure 925

Contents

1. Neolithic and Bronze Age Settlement at Weir Bank Stud Farm, Bray,
by I. Barnes and R.M.J. Cleal

2. An Analysis of Worked Flint Artefact Concentrations from Maidenhead Thicket, Maidenhead, *by W.A. Boismier*

3. An Early Iron Age Settlement at Dunston Park, Thatcham,
by A.P. Fitzpatrick, I. Barnes, and R.M.J. Cleal

List of Figures

List of Plates

List of Tables

Contents of Microfiche

Acknowledgments

Weir Bank Stud Farm, Bray
The initial evaluation was managed by S.J. Lobb and directed in the field by C.A. Butterworth with the assistance of S. Tatler. The excavation strategy was devised by S.J. Lobb of Wessex Archaeology and P. Chadwick, then County Archaeological Officer for Berkshire. The fieldwork was managed and directed by I. Barnes with the assistance of R. Brook. In addition J. Graham, T. Sammes, and T. Jones, all members of the Maidenhead Archaeological and Historical Society, gave their time voluntarily. The help of the gravel pit site manager, Ron Barlow, was invaluable in the smooth undertaking of the excavations. The site archives are presently held at Wessex Archaeology's offices in Salisbury It is hoped to deposit these and the artefacts with Reading Museum. The post-excavation was managed by A.P. Fitzpatrick and the report written by I. Barnes and R.M.J. Cleal. The project was commissioned and funded by Summerleaze Ltd.

Maidenhead Thicket
The data was analysed using the SPSSX subprogram NONPAR CORR (SPSS Inc. 1986) on the University of Cambridge's IBM 3084 mainframe computer. Special thanks are owed by the author to R. Rippengal for his generously offered expertise in running SPSSX at Cambridge and on the use of the ZED line editor. Particular thanks are owed to S. Ford for the generous loan of a copy of his unpublished thesis.

The fieldwork was undertaken by M. Trott (stage I) and P. Harding (stage II) assisted by N. Adam, J. Lancley, and S. Tatler. The project was managed throughout by R. Newman, the author of the stage II project design. Wessex Archaeology are grateful to P. Chadwick for all his help and support and to S. Trow of Eng lish Heritage for his assistance at the post-excavation phase. The entire project was financed by English Heritage.

Dunston Park
The project was commissioned and supported by Trencherwood Homes (South Eastern) Limited and the authors are grateful to A.K. George and R.D. Goodenough for their assistance. Thanks are also due to Mr Janaway, the landowner, for his help during the evaluation and to Mr Lynam of the Barton Willmore Planning Partnership for his assistance in establishing the project. Dr J.D Hill, St Edmund's, Cambridge University and D. S. McOmish (Royal Commission on the Historic Monuments of England) kindly commented on the draft report, while S. Chadwick Hawkes (University of Oxford) kindly made information available in advance of her own publications.

The project was supervised in the field by I. Barnes, with the assistance of P.A. Harding in 1991 and was managed initially by Susan Lobb and subsequently by A.P. Fitzpatrick. The finds are presently held at the offices of Wessex Archaeology and will be deposited at Newbury Museum in due course.

Park Farm, Binfield
The Oxford Archaeological Unit would like to thank Bryant Homes, Beazer Homes, and Luff developments for funding fieldwork, post-excavation analysis, and publication. Tim Allen and Frances Healy commented on an earlier version of the text. The final version has been edited by Ellen McAdam and Frances Healy. Paul Booth is grateful to Jane Timby for help with Silchester ware and to Kevin Crouch for general discussion of the pottery traditions of the Middle Thames Valley. The archive will be deposited in Reading Museum.

Abstract

Four sites situated in the Thames and Kennet Valleys of Berkshire are discussed. These range in date from the Mesolithic to the Romano-British period.

An archaeological evaluation ahead of gravel extraction on the River Thames floodplain at Wier Bank Stud Farm, Bray, Maidenhead, in 1989 identified an area of Middle Bronze Age occupation. Subsequent excavations, covering an area of 2.24 ha, during the spring of 1991, revealed evidence of settlement dating from the earlier Neolithic to the Roman periods. The Neolithic and later Iron Age–Romano-British use of the site was on a small scale, the major use of the area being represented by a number of ditches, most of which formed part of a field system dating to the Middle Bronze Age. These ditches may have been utilised over a long period and were associated with small areas of Middle Bronze Age occupation. A triple-ditch feature also contained Middle Bronze Age pottery and other material. A round-house and other associated features appeared to form a late stage in the use of the area, at a time when the field system may have been already abandoned or approaching the end of its use.

Worked flint artefacts were recovered during a two stage evaluation undertaken at Maidenhead Thicket in 1990. Three concentrations of later Neolithic/Early Bronze Age flintwork were analysed, indicating that the southern and central clusters were the remains of limited artefact quarry or extraction sites while the northern cluster was probably the remains of a residential site. Spatial analysis identified a number of significant artefact class associations and the broads positions of intra-site activity areas for the three concentrations. The artefact concentrations are discussed in relation to larger regional distribution of broadly contemporaneous flint concentrations and isolated findspots known from the area.

Following a systematic evaluation, the first phase of excavations at Dunston Park examined an unenclosed Early Iron Age settlement of 7th century BC date. Evidence for Bronze Age and Romano-British activity, and a medieval field system was also recovered. One round-house could certainly be attributed to the Early Iron Age settlement and the distribution of finds within it was clearly restricted to one side. The associated cereals and querns, a crucible, a spindle-whorl, and flint and pottery suggest some of the activities undertaken by the occupants of the house.

An appendix reports on a 7th century BC pit group with ironsmithing debris found in the evaluation at Cooper's Farm. The group provides some of the earliest well dated evidence for ironworking in the region.

Investigations were undertaken in advance of the construction of housing, a hotel, a golf course, and a road at Park Farm Binfield, following on from an archaeological assessment of approximately 85 ha carried out the previous year. Three areas were selected for more intensive examination.

Area E was the site of a small rural settlement, occupied from perhaps the 1st century BC to the 2nd century AD and consisting of a nucleus of houses surrounded, and eventually enclosed, by two areas of enclosures. It is unusual in being located on London Clay, in the high frequency of loomweights among the finds, and in the quantity of oak charcoal recovered. The organisation and function of the site and its place in the local settlement hierarchy are discussed.

Areas B and A/M both contained Mesolithic flint scatters. Fieldwalking, test-pitting, and sieving methods are described and their results assessed, the technology and typology of the collection are described, and the scatters are placed in the context of contemporaneous regional settlement.

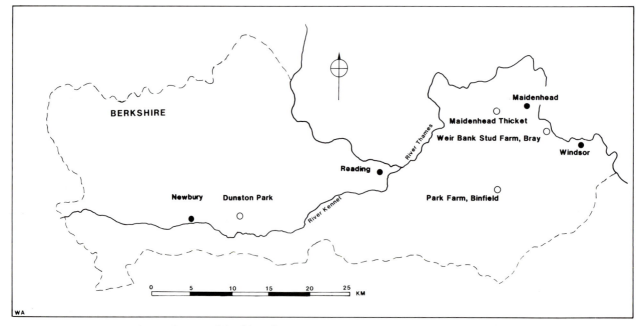

Figure 1   Location of sites discussed in this volume

1. Neolithic and Bronze Age Settlement at Weir Bank Stud Farm, Bray

by I. Barnes and R.M.J. Cleal

with contributions from A.J. Clapham, C. Cox, Janet Egerton, Clive Gamble, Jacqueline I. McKinley, R. Montague, and Elaine L. Morris

1 Introduction

In 1989 a planning application was submitted to Berkshire County Council by Summerleaze Ltd to extract gravel from approximately 7 hectares of land near Weir Bank Stud Farm at Bray (centred on SU 9095 7900), to the south-east of Maidenhead (Fig. 2). Aerial photographs showed the application area to be covered with cropmarks indicating the presence of enclosures, ditches, and pits (Figs 3 and 4). Consequently, Berkshire County Council required an assessment of the archaeological deposits prior to the completion of a Section 52 agreement (under the *Town and Country Planning Act*) as part of the planning application. Wessex Archaeology was commissioned by Summerleaze Ltd to undertake the assessment which was carried out in 1989, and the subsequent excavations which were undertaken in 1991.

Geological and Topographical Background

The site was 350 m south-west of the present course of the River Thames on the western bank of the floodplain. The drift geology comprised floodplain gravel (Geological Survey 1981). The land in the area is generally flat, lying at *c.* 22 m OD and is for the most part cultivated; the site itself was under a crop of spring onions at the start of the evaluation. A low ridge, little more than a metre higher than the rest of the field, ran north-east–south-west along the centre of the field.

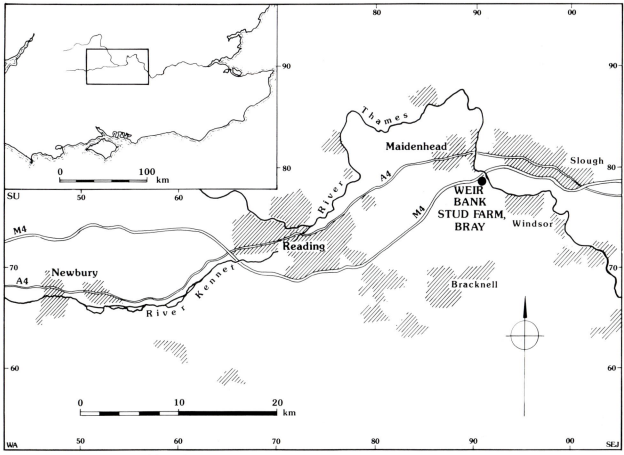

Figure 2   Bray: general location map

2

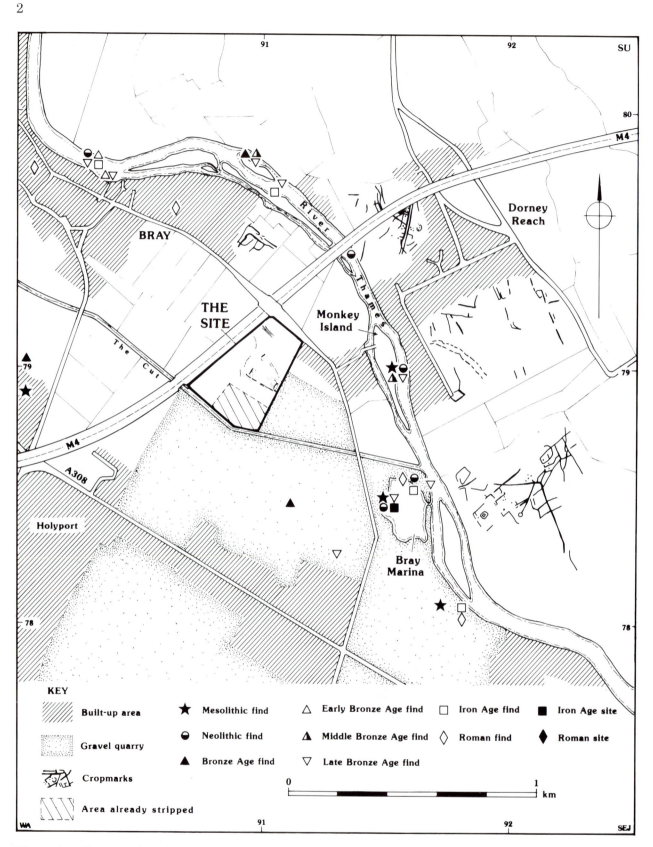

KEY

▨	Built-up area	★	Mesolithic find	△	Early Bronze Age find	□ Iron Age find ■ Iron Age site
⣿	Gravel quarry	◓	Neolithic find	▲	Middle Bronze Age find	◇ Roman find ◆ Roman site
	Cropmarks	▲	Bronze Age find	▽	Late Bronze Age find	
	Area already stripped					

Figure 3   Bray: archaeological sites and findspots in the local area

Archaeological Background

Much evidence of archaeological activity has been recovered from the area surrounding the site (Fig. 3) and also from nearby stretches of the River Thames. Earlier gravel extraction at Bray Marina and in other gravel pits to the south, along with the construction of the M4 motorway to the west, brought to light a wide diversity of material, dating from the Mesolithic to recent centuries. But although earlier gravel extraction has shown

Plate 1   Bray: aerial photograph of the site under cereal crop, 27 July 1975. North is to the bottom of the plate. (NMR 882 frame 95. © Royal Commission on the Historical Monuments of England. Crown Copyright)

the surrounding area to have been rich in artefacts (information from Sites and Monuments Record (SMR)), there has been little investigation of the evidence for settlement in the area.

2 Aerial Photographic Assessment, by C. Cox

This assessment of the aerial photographic evidence is based on a run of three consecutive oblique monochrome photographs taken by the Royal Commission on the Historical Monuments of England Air Photographs Unit on July 27th 1975 (882/93–95, NGR Index No. SU9178/6) (Plate 1).

Interpretation and mapping were carried out at 1:2500 scale following procedures described by Palmer and Cox (1993). The print run, although oblique, allowed stereoscopic examination at x1.5 magnification. All rectification was carried out using AERIAL 4.2 software (Haigh forthcoming) and mean error values for control point matching were less than ± 2.0 m.

The assessment area was under a ripening cereal crop at the time of photography. Buried ditches and other cut and natural features were causing positive cropmarks. The ditches were not in this case revealed by colour or tonal differences but, as with earthworks, the marks were visible due to shadow and highlight effects caused by differential crop growth revealed by early morning sunlight. This effect of 'upstanding'

4

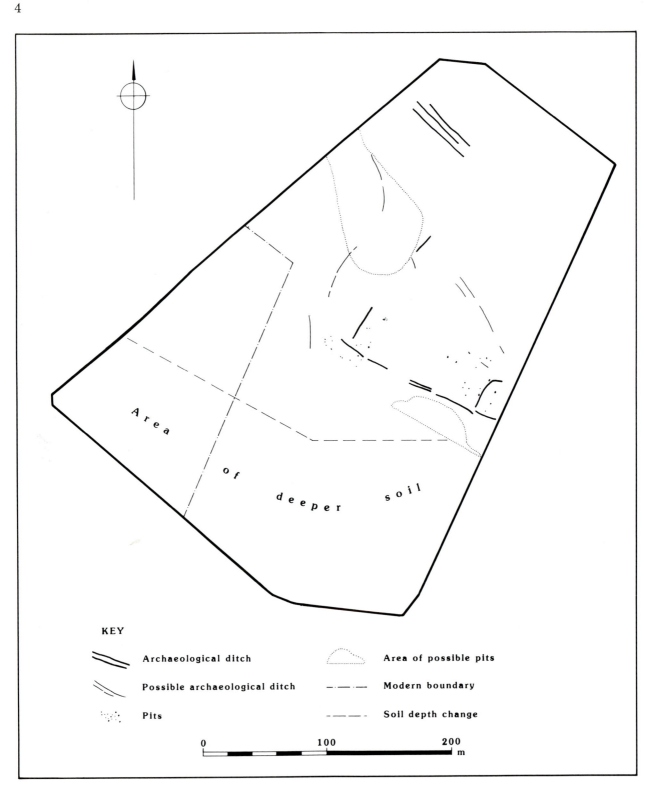

KEY

Archaeological ditch		Area of possible pits	
Possible archaeological ditch	—·—·—	Modern boundary	
Pits	—·——·—	Soil depth change	

0   100   200
                              m

Figure 4   Bray: transcription of aerial photographic evidence

cropmarks has been noted on many occasions (eg, Riley 1987, 31). The obliquely angled sunlight showed those features which lay perpendicular to its direction. Features lying in the same direction as the sunlight did not show well on this occasion, even under stereoscopic examination. Long shadows also obscured some parts of the assessment area; the true extent of the site may not have been recorded on the available photographs.

A triple ditched linear feature could be seen within the north-western part of the assessment area. To the south-east, part of a probable enclosure with associated single and double ditches was visible. There are some areas of densely spaced pits or other cut features which in some cases are indistinguishable from natural features. Where these features are particularly amor-

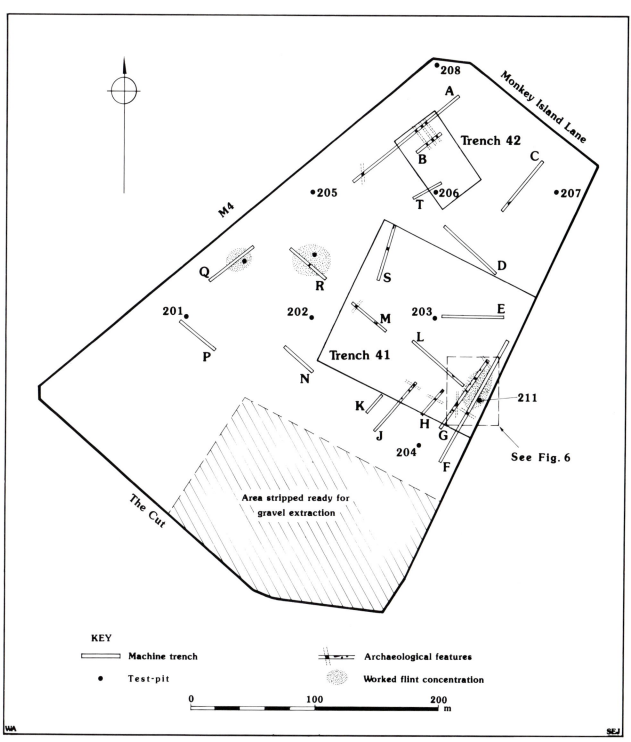

Figure 5   Bray: site plan of the evaluation

phous or numerous, they have been shown as a general area in Figure 4.

The aerial evidence corresponds well to, and is augmented by, the excavation evidence. As expected, particularly when interpreting ditched sites showing as cropmarks, excavation revealed more ditches and many more small cut features than could be interpreted from the aerial evidence alone, which hints at, but does not fully reveal, the type and extent of the site. Some of the ditches showing on the aerial photographs as slight,

possibly archaeological, features were not identified in excavation (Fig. 8). The excavated round-house, 491, was certainly not identifiable from the available photographs, and could only be suggested via interpretation in retrospect of excavation. The length of shadow cast by the modern field boundary hedge may have obscured any cropmarked indication of the ditch 915 running parallel to it, which was not visible on the photographs. Major ditches 558 and 819 were also not visible. The multi-phase nature of the site identified by excavation was not apparent solely from the available aerial evidence.

The edges of the bank deposits were discernible under the stereoscope, and a slight increase in soil depth could be inferred from a darkening in the general tone of the crop over the south-western part of the area, which may possibly mask further archaeological features. The 1:10,000 general plan shows parallel linear ditches in the south-western sector. These were not identifiable on the aerial photographs examined.

3 The Evaluation

The evaluation (Wessex Archaeology site W312), was commissioned after the initial planning application, and undertaken in September 1989 (Farwell 1989). Eighteen machine trenches and 11 hand dug test-pits were excavated (Fig. 5), covering 2.05% of the application area.

The work confirmed the existence of archaeological deposits across the application area, particularly in the areas of cropmark concentrations. As well as ditches associated with the cropmarks a number of pits, post-holes, and hollows were also identified. Many of the features appeared to have been badly plough-damaged. Where pottery was recovered from features it was predominantly of Middle Bronze Age date. Other finds included a sarsen saddle quern, animal bones, and worked flints largely of Bronze Age character, indicating that the site constituted a settlement. A minority element in the flint collection was identifiable as of Mesolithic or Neolithic date. It was also noted that there were three surface concentrations of prehistoric worked flint (Fig. 5) which did not correlate with any particular grouping of excavated features identified in the evaluation.

A trench was also excavated through the low bank which ran along the centre of the site. No features were found in the trench and the bank was interpreted at that time as a natural feature.

4 Excavation Research Design

Following the evaluation Berkshire County Council, in conjunction with English Heritage, identified two areas, totalling 2.5 ha, of archaeological interest for detailed examination (Figs 5, 8). Two aims were specified: to assess the nature and spatial distribution of the worked flint assemblage identified as surviving in the topsoil, and to recover information from the Middle Bronze Age occupation to enhance understanding of the economy and function of the site. The excavation design included the excavation of test-pits across one of the flint concentrations, the stripping by machine of the two areas of greatest archaeological interest, and the excavation of the better-preserved features within those areas.

Because many of the features excavated in the evaluation had proved to be shallow, and the whole site was known to be plough-damaged, priority for excavation was assigned to those features which could be expected to yield substantial groups of artefacts and faunal remains, such as the larger pits and ditches. In addition to this, a watching brief was to cover those areas of the site outside the two areas specified as of archaeological interest.

5 Pre-Excavation Survey Results

An array of 40 test-pits (Trenches 1–40) 0.50 x 0.50 m in size, spaced 5 m apart, was hand excavated through the topsoil across a worked flint concentration identified during the evaluation (Fig. 6).

In 27 of the test-pits the topsoil — a dark yellowish brown loam — overlay a subsoil comprising a reddish-brown sandy silt with occasional subrounded flint pebbles. In the remaining 13 pits topsoil directly overlay the gravel. There was no variation in artefact numbers between test-pits excavated onto subsoil and those excavated directly onto gravel. Thirty-seven pieces (436 g) of worked flint, including four cores, two scrapers, and a blade, all generally of Middle Bronze Age type, were recovered from 20 of the test-pits (Fig. 6). The maximum number of pieces of worked flint recovered from any individual test-pit was five and no specific pattern in the distribution was evident. Only three pieces (59 g) of burnt flint were found, coming from two test-pits. In addition, three small sherds (9 g) of undiagnostic Roman coarseware pottery were found in adjacent test-pits.

The frequency of artefacts recovered was very low, even though the test-pit spoil was carefully sorted. The recovered amounts per pit were, in general, similar to those found in the evaluation test-pits. On comparison with the subsequently excavated underlying features the initially noted surface flint concentration correlated with the position of a Middle Bronze Age enclosure, 926. A slight increase in frequency of finds towards the northern corner of the test-pit array coincided with the position of ditch 917, a component of the enclosure, from which much worked flint was recovered. Likewise it was assumed that the Romano-British pottery derived from underlying pit, 283, dated to this period.

6 Excavation Results

Two areas (Figs 5, 7) were stripped by machine: Trench 41, 147 x 152 m, covering an area of 2.24 hectares in the centre of the site, and Trench 42, 66 x 40 m, covering an area of 0.26 ha towards the northern limit. The machine stripping removed on average 0.30 m of topsoil and, in places, a smaller amount of reddish–brown sandy silt subsoil. This did not leave a uniform surface but revealed an involved geological sequence which in places masked the archaeology.

The Bank

The majority of the stripped area comprised river gravel deposits made up of subangular flint pebbles. Across this expanse of gravel ran a band of light yellow sand, up to 75 m wide and running east–west, representing a former river channel.

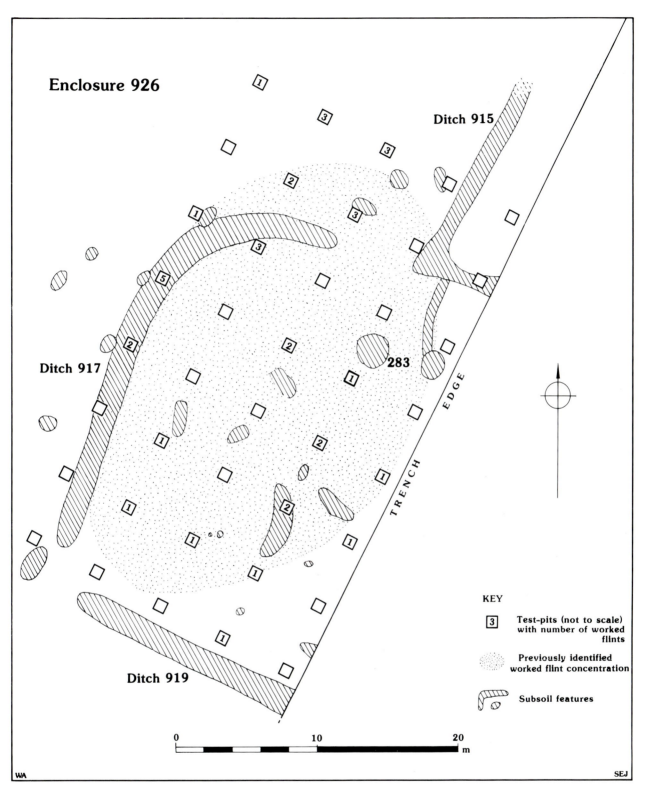

Figure 6   Bray: test-pits over enclosure 926

Superimposed on these deposits was the low bank noted during the evaluation; this ran north-east–south-west across the site, and on exposure was 60 m wide. Because of the interpretation of this feature as entirely natural, based on the absence of features found within it during the evaluation, it was left largely intact after the topsoil had been removed, although it later became clear that the uppermost layer of the bank, layer

591, had been largely removed during topsoil stripping where it lay on the lower slopes of the bank. The interpretation of the bank as natural, however, was found to be incorrect when the south-western length of the bank was removed during gravel extraction late in the excavation; an archaeological feature was found within the bank deposits. On closer examination, following further machine trenching and a hand excavated

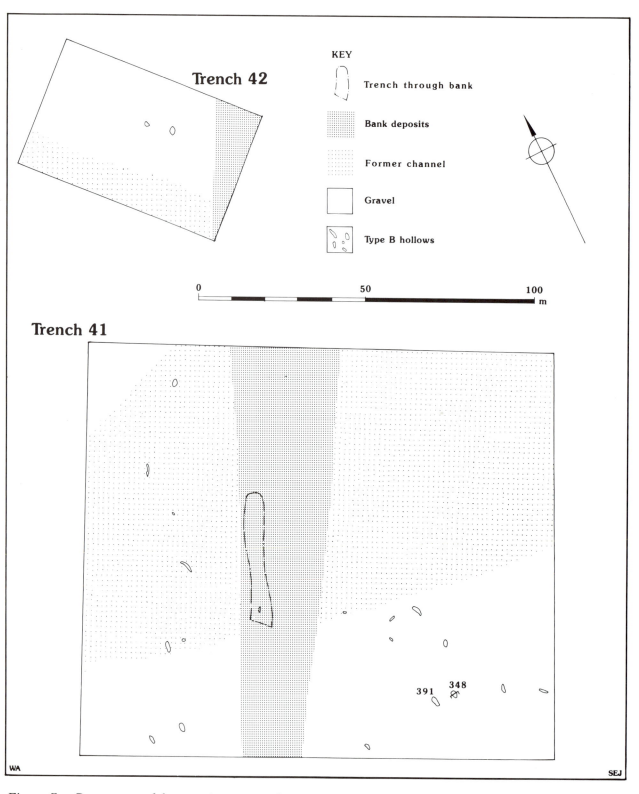

Figure 7   Bray: natural features in excavated areas

1-metre box through it, the bank appeared to be formed of four deposits. The lowest deposit was a very dark greyish-brown alluvial silt (184) which varied greatly in depth but which had a maximum thickness of 0.50 m. A single flint chip and four pieces (31 g) of burnt flint were found in this layer in the hand excavated box. Above this was a brown silty loam (699), 0.14 m thick.

Fifteen pieces (279 g) of burnt flint were found in this deposit. A number of features appeared to be cut from the surface of 699; these included the Middle Bronze Age ditch, 819, feature 326, and the post-holes of round-house 491. Above layer 699 was a dark yellowish-brown silt (591), 0.30 m thick, which contained much burnt flint as well as small amounts of worked flint.

Plate 2   Bray: gravel extraction in progress at the southern end of the site

Pottery ranging in date from later Neolithic to Romano-British was found within it. This was overlain by the modern topsoil (183).

The effect of the non-excavation of the bank was to all but mask a strip 30 m wide on the top of the bank running north-east–south-west through the centre of the site (Figs 7 and 8). Several machine trenches were later excavated to investigate the density of features across the centre of the site but because of the limitations of time it did not prove practical to completely remove the upper deposit.

In order to elucidate the nature of the bank a soil thin-section was prepared from the boundary between layers 699 and 591. Analysis (Acott, archive) suggested that 699 and 591 were not, in reality, different deposits, but that 591 had been homogenised by post-depositional disturbance, of which the top of layer 699 was simply the lower limit. Acott also found no evidence that either 699 or 591 included alluvium. The lower bank layer, 184, was not thin-sectioned.

The nature of the bank must remain unresolved, although as alluvial processes appear to be ruled out for the upper part at least, and it includes artefactual material, it seems that it may itself be an artefact rather than a natural feature. The identification, subsequent to excavation, of post-depositional disturbance in 591 throws doubt on the field observation that features were cut from the top of 699; all that can be said now is that they were cut from no lower than the base of the post-depositional disturbance.

The date and process of formation of this feature cannot be established with certainty, but it seems that it may have been a human construction rather than a natural feature. As it did not delimit the Bronze Age settlement, and indeed had Middle Bronze Age features cut into it from a fairly high level, it must be assumed to be of Early Bronze Age or earlier date. The possibility that it began as a natural feature, which was subsequently enlarged by human actions, cannot be entirely dismissed.

Archaeological Features

After the removal of the overburden 250 archaeological features were identified and planned (Fig. 8). The frequency of features was greatest towards the southern end of Trench 41 and in Trench 42. The revealed features generally corresponded well to the plotted cropmarks (Fig. 4) though several cropmarks were not represented by surviving archaeological features.

After planning, a portion of every feature was excavated. In the case of pits and post-holes the excavated portion was never less than 50% of the whole, while all ditch terminals were excavated, as was at least one section along its length. As the palaeo-environmental potential was considered to be high, 114 1.5 litre bulk samples were taken from all suitable contexts. After excavation the identified features were grouped into six categories: post-holes, pits, hollows (types A and B), linear features, and others. Type A hollows were irregular in shape and profile, with a minimum surface area greater than 0.60 m, while type B hollows were distinguished by having one side much steeper than the other. Apart from the bank only negative features were found. Almost certainly the ditches present were

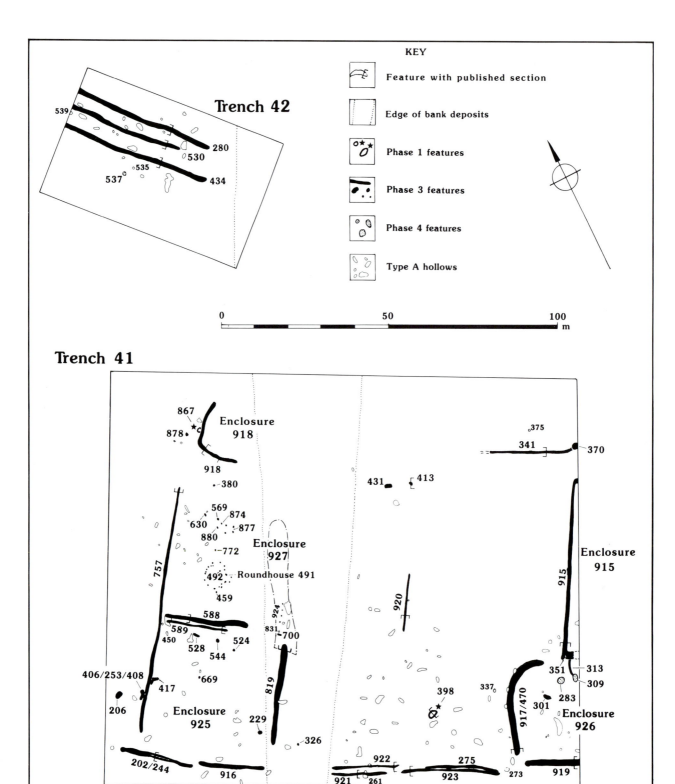

Figure 8   Bray: plan of excavated area

originally accompanied by banks, but no physical evidence of these survived.

Phasing

After the analysis of the artefacts, and in particular the pottery, it was possible to distinguish five phases of activity on the site. Three of these are represented by features; two by objects alone.

On completion of the post-excavation analysis 200 features or feature groups, such as structures, were identified. It was possible to date 58 of these securely, on artefactual and stratigraphic grounds. Eleven features could be identified as having been the result of either animal or modern disturbance. The remainder were attributed to the Middle Bronze Age phase, for whilst they were intrinsically undatable, their nature and distribution were such that they could be confidently assigned to the phase.

All radiocarbon dates given below are in years cal BC presented at 2 sigma, and calibrated using the University of Washington Quaternary Isotope Laboratory Calibration Program rev. 2.0 (1987) based on calibration curves as specified for each date. The radiocarbon dates from the site are summarised in Table 1.

Phase 1: Mesolithic
A small, but significant, Mesolithic component was identified in the flint assemblage. Cores (Fig. 16, 1), blades and bladelets (Fig. 16, 8 and 9), a piercing tool, and serrated pieces of Mesolithic–earlier Neolithic type were recognised. The flint was found both in the overburden and as residual material in later features. The fresh condition of the pieces was such that it is probable that they had not been transported far before deposition.

The presence of these artefacts in isolation is indicative of either a single or repeated use of the area rather than a long-term occupation, but no material occurred in primary contexts.

Phase 2: earlier Neolithic
The main evidence for earlier Neolithic activity on the site is the presence of at least 18 sherds (133 g) of pottery dated by form to the 4th millennium BC. In addition worked flint of an Early Neolithic nature was also found.

Two features (Figs 8 and 9), a pit (867), and a hollow of type A (398), situated 110 m apart in Trench 41, were dated to this period on artefactual grounds. The remains of identifiable pottery vessels of this date were recovered from both the pit (Fig. 18, P1) and the hollow (Fig. 18, P2), as well as blades and bladelets of Mesolithic–earlier

Neolithic date. Neolithic sherds were also found redeposited in the Bronze Age ditch 917.

Phase 3: later Neolithic/Early Bronze Age
As with the Mesolithic activity the evidence for this phase is based entirely on artefactual evidence, in this instance on pottery. Fifteen sherds (36 g) of pottery were identified as of this date, including two sherds of Peterborough Ware (Fig. 18, P5 and P6), and one very small sherd probably of the same tradition. These were all found redeposited in later features (*Cleal, below*).

Phase 4: Middle Bronze Age
The majority of the features excavated, including field ditches, structures, and other negative features, may be assigned broadly to the Middle Bronze Age, and appear to represent use of the site on a substantial scale over a long period.

Structures
The 'round-house', 491 (Figs 8 and 10), was actually oval in shape, measuring 7.70 x 6.80 m, and was defined by 15 post-holes. These were generally circular in plan with an average diameter of 0.28 m and an average depth of 0.24 m. Eleven of the post-holes, on average 1.40 m apart, formed the circumference of the structure whilst four others formed a south-east facing porch (at 126°). This was 1.10 m wide at its external entrance and opened up to 2.20 m wide where, defined by two double post-holes, it joined the main structure. The post-holes were cut through the lower bank material and were filled with dark greyish sandy loam with charcoal inclusions. No post-pipes were visible, which may suggest that the structure was dismantled rather than having decayed or been burnt *in situ*. Eleven pieces (37 g) of fired clay were found in component post-holes and in features in close proximity to the round-house, along with a general scatter of the material around the farmstead. These are likely to have been derived from the round-house, or neighbouring structures. Pottery, worked flint, burnt flint, and animal bone were recovered from the post-hole fills.

To the east of the porch inside the round-house a hearth, 492, was excavated. This was ovoid in shape, measuring 0.39 x 0.29 m, and was filled with a black sandy loam containing much burnt material; only one artefact, a flint flake was recovered from it.

A layer of material, 667 (Fig. 10), darker in colour than the surrounding lower bank material, was spread around the northern part of the round-house, the post-holes showing as cut through it. This was thought to represent an *in situ* occupation deposit. To investigate

Table 1: radiocarbon dates from Bray

Lab. No.	Context	Material	Date BP	Cal BC (1 σ)	Cal BC (2 σ)
UB–3513	basal fills ditch 589	animal bone	3204±138	1671–1323	1872–1129
UB–3514	716, 360: upper fills ditch 530, triple ditch system	animal bone	2612±193	981–422	1260–261

Calibration using the University of Washington Quaternary Isotope Laboratory Calibration Program 1987, Rev. 2.0 (Method A (intercepts) only, based on the calibration curve of Pearson and Stuiver (1986))

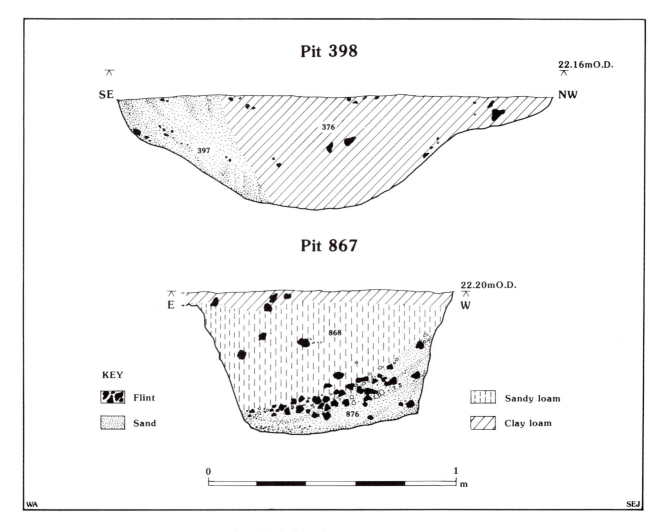

Pit 398

22.16mO.D.

SE   NW

376

397

Pit 867

22.20mO.D.

E   W

868

876

KEY

Flint

Sand

Sandy loam

Clay loam

0   1
                                     m

WA   SEJ

Figure 9   Bray: sections across earlier Neolithic pits

this fifty 1-metre squares, covering an area measuring 10 x 5 m, were excavated through the layer. These were carefully trowelled down to the underlying bank material, with artefacts recorded per square.

A total of 59 sherds (137 g) of pottery was found in this exercise, of which 32 were in Middle Bronze Age fabrics. The remainder was of indeterminate prehistoric date with the exception of a single sherd of Romano-British pottery considered as intrusive. When the distribution of this pottery was plotted (Fig. 10) only five sherds were found within the structure whilst 47 were found outside and immediately to the north of the porch, with another six sherds outside and to the rear of the structure.

The distribution of the worked flint and burnt flint displayed the same pattern (Fig. 10). Twenty-four pieces and 82 pieces respectively (676 g) were found. The worked pieces including cores, core trimming flakes, and residual blades. Of these only two worked pieces and four (16 g) burnt pieces were found within the structure whilst the remainder were found to the north of the structure. The distribution of the artefacts suggests that domestic activity and/or refuse disposal was concentrated in the area to the north of the porch.

Ten metres to the north-east of the round-house a four-post structure, 877, was excavated (Fig. 8). This was almost square, measuring 2.40 x 2.20 m. The four post-holes from which it was formed were generally circular, on average having a diameter of 0.29 m and a depth of 0.17 m, and were filled with dark greyish sandy loam with charcoal flecking. Within the fills 33 sherds (126 g) of Middle Bronze Age pottery, six pieces of worked flint, nine pieces (77 g) of burnt flint, and six pieces of animal bone were found. In addition 36 (42 g) pieces of fired clay were found in the component post-holes, perhaps derived from the associated, or a neighbouring, structure. This four-post structure was interpreted as a granary.

A number of pits, hollows, and post-holes were also excavated in the area around the round-house and four-post structure, but only a few contained artefacts. An increase in the density of burnt flint, particularly small pieces, was noted around the structures (*Barnes and Cleal, below*). No animal bone was found in any of these features though some was found in the structural post-holes. No other domestic objects were found in the features, the only one recovered in the vicinity being a ferruginous sandstone rubber found in the north-

Plate 3   Bray: round-house 491 viewed from the west with layer 667 under excavation

eastern terminal of ditch 757 to the west of the round-house (*Montague, below*).

This area of settlement was within a loosely-defined enclosure, 927, although, as will be described, the use of round-house 491 may not have been coeval with the ditches. Enclosure 927 was bounded to the south-west by ditch 588 and to the north-west by ditch 757, a shared boundary with field 925 (Figs 8 and 12). The ditches were filled with a series of sandy loams from which Middle Bronze Age pottery, worked flint, burnt flint, and animal bone were recovered. The area to the south-east was bounded by a fence, running north-east–south-west, composed of at least four post-holes which were found in a machine trench excavated through the bank deposits. The post-holes, generally circular with an average diameter of 0.20 m and depth of 0.19 m, were very evenly spaced, 2.07 m apart. This may well have extended beyond the area examined through the bank deposits. No evidence of any form of boundary was observed to the north-east.

Enclosure 925 was defined by five interrupted ditches (Figs 8 and 11). Ditch 589 defined the north-eastern edge, ditch 757 the north-western, 202 and 916 the south-western, and 819 the south-eastern. These were filled with a series of sandy loams from which considerable quantities of Middle Bronze Age pottery, worked flint, burnt flint, and animal bone were recovered. The field was square, measuring 40 x 40 m (1600 m^2). The recutting of ditch 202 and the possible recutting of ditch 819 attested to the maintenance of the field boundaries. The contemporaneity of enclosure 925 and enclosure 927 is suggested by the common use of ditch 757 as the north-western boundary.

Plate 4   Bray: remains of the pots in the base of 326

A single feature (326), apparently containing substantial parts of two pottery vessels (Fig. 19, P9, P10, and P11; Plate 4), was found just to the south-east of the southern corner of enclosure 925 (Fig. 8). No cremated

14

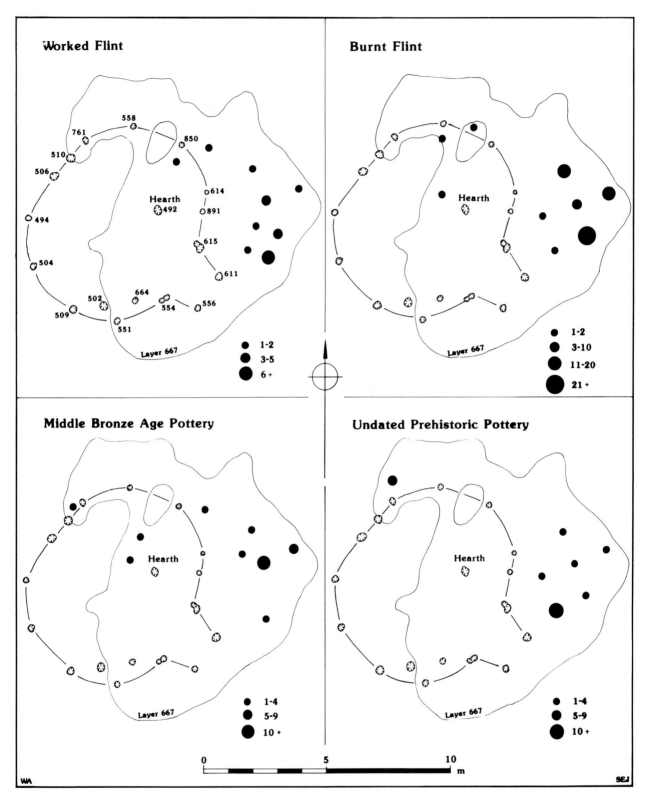

Figure 10   Bray: distribution of finds, quantified by number, in relation to round-house 491

bone was noted, and it is possible that this represents the burial of these vessels for storage or a similar function.

There is evidence for a further three enclosures within Trench 41. Enclosure 926 was defined to the south-west by ditch 919, to the north-west by ditch 917, both of which had been recut at least once, and to the

north-east by ditch 915, which in turn may have helped to define an enclosure of its own (Figs 8, 11 and 12). The component ditches of enclosure 926 were filled with a series of sandy loams from which Middle Bronze Age pottery, worked flint, burnt flint, animal bone, and a piece of human bone were recovered. The excavation of enclosure ditch 915, also filled with a sandy loam, again

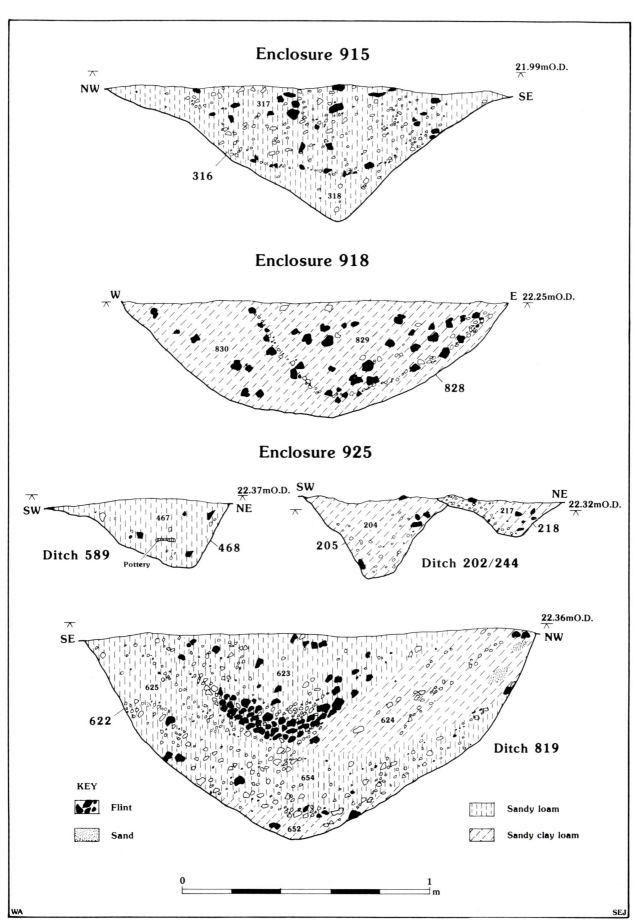

Figure 11   Bray: sections across enclosure ditches

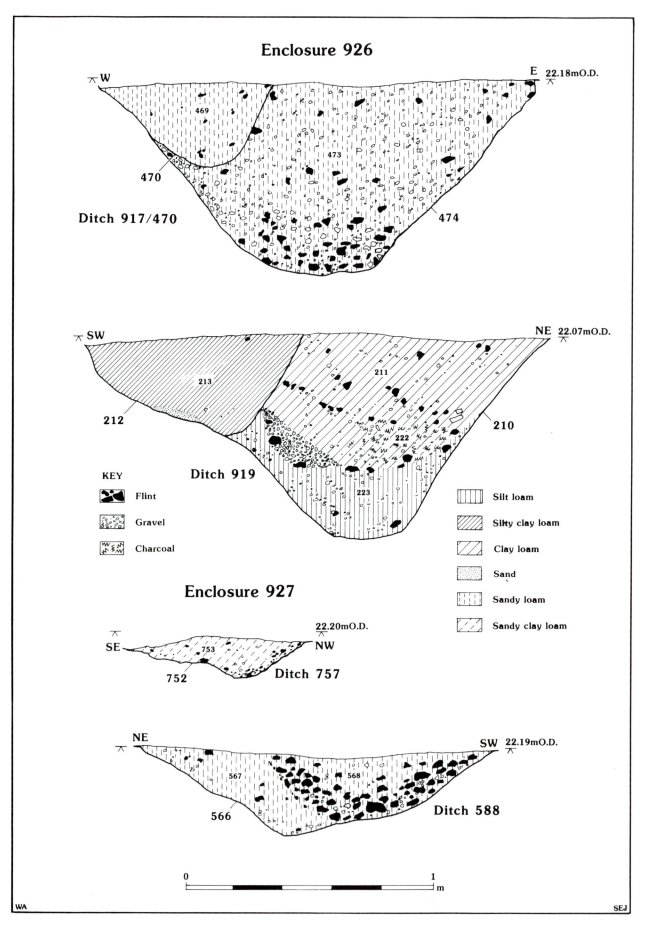

Enclosure 926

W E 22.18mO.D.

469

470

Ditch 917/470

473

474

SW NE 22.07mO.D.

213

212

211

210

KEY

Flint

Gravel

Charcoal

Ditch 919

222

223

Silt loam

Silty clay loam

Clay loam

Sand

Sandy loam

Sandy clay loam

Enclosure 927

SE NW 22.20mO.D.

753

752 **Ditch 757**

NE SW 22.19mO.D.

567 568

566 **Ditch 588**

0 1
m

WA SEJ

Figure 12 *Bray: sections across enclosure ditches*

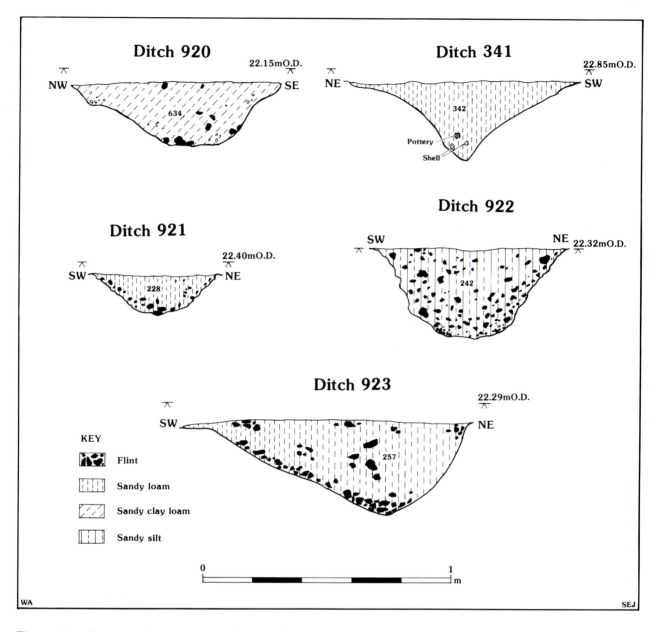

Figure 13   Bray: sections across enclosure ditches

produced pottery, worked flint, a single piece of burnt flint, and animal bone.

No coherent structural evidence was found within either of these enclosures. All that was found were two isolated post-holes and two pieces of fired clay (1 g) within enclosure 926, and a large post-hole, from which eight pieces of animal bone were recovered, in the base of the southern corner of ditch 915. Neither of the enclosures was entirely contained within the trench, indeed only a 5–metre strip of enclosure 915 was examined, and the bulk of the remains, in all probability including structures, must have lain to the south-east in an area which had already been quarried for gravel, and any remains lost unrecorded. Less survived of the third enclosure, 918, in the northern corner of Trench 41 (Fig. 8), than any of the others uncovered. Only two sides of the enclosure were excavated, as an L–shaped length of ditch; more may have existed but been masked by the bank material to the south-east. The ditch was

filled with a sandy loam in which five sherds of Middle Bronze Age pottery were found as well as worked flint and a single piece of burnt flint. No internal features were identified.

Four ditches, 275 and 921–3, ran south-east–north-west linking the southern boundaries of field 925 and enclosure 926, thus isolating the centre of the site and possibly forming a trackway. Ditch 920 was perpendicular to these and some 40 m to the north, bisecting the enclosed area. Ditch 341 represented the northern extreme of the field system; this had the same south-east–north-west alignment as the southern ditches. It is likely that other boundaries were obscured by the remaining bank material.

Triple ditch system

Trench 42 was positioned to investigate three parallel ditches identified on aerial photographs (Fig. 3) and later recorded during the evaluation. The three ditches,

Plate 5   Bray: the triple ditch system (280, 434, and 530) in Trench 42, viewed from the north-west

280, 434, and 530, ran parallel and equidistant, 4 m apart, a maximum of 45 m south-east into the trench (Fig. 8; Plate 5), terminating at the base of the alluvial bank. All three were filled with sandy loams (Fig. 14) which produced Bronze Age pottery, animal bone, and worked and burnt flint. Two objects of particular interest were found in ditch 280: a large awl or pointed gouge (Fig. 23) made from a cattle-sized long-bone and a fragment of sarsen saddle quern (Fig. 17).

In the area of the ditches a number of hollows and at least two hearths (Fig. 8, features 535 and 539) were found. These, with the large amount of pottery, the sarsen saddle quern, and particularly the animal bone, imply that there was domestic activity in the locality. There is no indication from the finds that the three ditches were other than contemporaneous, and it would seem that, on the grounds of their proximity to apparently domestic activity, they may have formed part of a settlement boundary. It may not be coincidence that the triple ditches terminate close to the bank, and this can perhaps be taken as an indication that the bank was already in existence when the ditches were dug, or that the construction of both ditches and bank was contemporaneous.

Cremation

A cremation burial, 375, was found 5 m to the north of field boundary ditch 341 (Fig. 8). It comprised 63.3 g of cremated adult human bone associated with 10 small sherds (5 g) of indeterminate prehistoric pottery in a circular cut measuring 0.55 m in diameter and 0.19 m deep. It is ascribed to the period by the loose association with field boundary ditch 341.

Hollows

A total of 147 hollows was excavated; these, apart from the area around the eastern corner of Trench 41, were spread evenly over the site (Figs 7 and 8) with no apparent clustering. During the excavation it was noted that although the hollows were mostly amorphous there was a single distinctive type: these had one edge near vertical whilst the opposite edge was shallow. During post-excavation analysis these distinct hollows were defined as type B hollows (Fig. 15). Both types generally contained sandy clay loam fills. These were often much darker in colour in the centre of the feature than around the outside; this is interpreted as a result of differential waterlogging.

Of the 125 excavated type A hollows, 48 produced finds, comprising a total of 141 sherds (1846 g) of mostly Middle Bronze Age pottery, 180 pieces of worked flint, 70 pieces (625 g) of burnt flint, and 27 pieces of animal bone. Of the 22 identified type B hollows, 12 produced finds, comprising one sherd (1 g) of prehistoric pottery, 12 pieces of worked flint, five pieces (68 g) of burnt flint, and, from a single feature, 21 pieces of animal bone. This gives a slightly greater mean artefact count for type A over type B (A:3.3, N=125; B:1.8, N=22), but given the small number of type B features this cannot be considered significant.

The interpretation of these two types of feature is that type B hollows are natural, whereas type A are likely to represent human or associated activity, such as shallow quarry scoops, working hollows, or areas where animals had been tethered. Some type B hollows are almost certainly tree-throw holes, but no features were observed which were entirely diagnostic of this type of

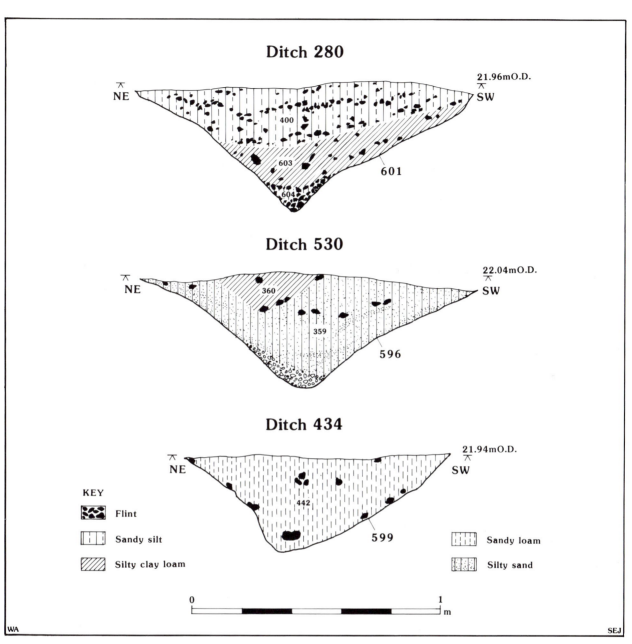

Ditch 280

NE

SW

21.96mO.D.

400

603

601

604

Ditch 530

NE

SW

22.04mO.D.

360

359

596

Ditch 434

NE

SW

21.94mO.D.

442

599

KEY

Flint

Sandy silt

Silty clay loam

Sandy loam

Silty sand

0   1
                                     m

WA   SEJ

Figure 14   Bray: sections across the triple ditches

hole, and it is also likely that other non-anthropogenic processes are represented.

Phase 5: Late Iron Age/Romano-British

A total of 77 sherds (693 g) of pottery dated to the Late Iron Age and early Romano-British period were found during the excavation. Of these, 62 (624 g) were recovered from pit 283 in the southern corner of the site (Fig. 8). This was a circular feature measuring 2 m in diameter, with a bell shaped profile 1.50 m deep. It was filled with eight silty loam deposits with varying gravel components from which, apart from the pottery, 43 pieces of worked flint, seven pieces (409 g) of burnt flint, and eight animal bones were recovered. The artefacts were recovered from throughout the fill sequence. The nature of the feature implied that it was originally either a storage pit or well.

Two other features were dated to the period on artefactual grounds. Hollow type A, 309, 3 m to the east of pit 283, contained four sherds (31 g) of Late Iron Age/Romano-British pottery whilst hearth 537 in Trench 42 contained a single sherd (1 g) of contemporaneous pottery. The largest concentration of fired clay, 20 pieces (124 g), was found in the vicinity of the hearth and was believed to be derived from it. Both features also contained small amounts of residual prehistoric pottery whilst the hollow contained a single piece of animal bone and the hearth a single piece of worked flint. Apart from the pottery recovered from these three features ten other sherds were found either as pieces considered as intrusive in features securely dated to earlier periods or in topsoil contexts.

The distribution of the Late Iron Age/early Romano-British evidence suggests that there was possibly an

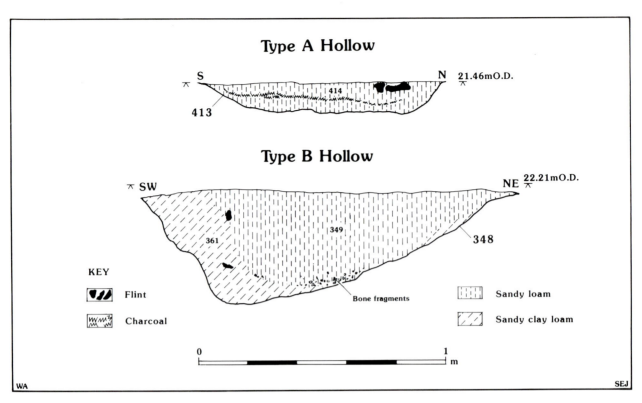

Figure 15   Bray: sections across type A and type B hollows

area of settlement to the south of Trench 41, of which features 283 and 309 were peripheral components.

7 Watching Brief

In the areas around Trenches 41 and 42 a watching brief was maintained during topsoil stripping prior to gravel extraction. Apart from two isolated, undated, hollows to the south of Trench 41, no archaeological deposits were encountered.

8 Finds

Flint, by R. Montague

A total of 1197 worked flints, weighing 13,038 g, was recovered. During the evaluation, 196 pieces (2514 g) were collected, and 1001 pieces (10,524 g) were collected during the excavations. The material has been treated as a single collection for this analysis.

Table 2 Bray: overall composition of worked flint assemblage

Context	1	2	3	4	5	6	7	Total	Burnt	Broken
Round-house 491	–	2	–	8	26	1	1	38	3	15
Four–poster 877	–	–	–	2	4	–	–	6	–	3
Enclosure 925	1	14	1	10	103	5	8	142	2	40
Other ditches	–	24	6	19	151	19	12	231	12	90
Pits	1	–	2	38	109	7	3	160	6	68
Unassigned post-holes	–	2	2	7	26	11	–	48	7	23
Hollows A	–	12	7	24	110	18	3	174	14	59
Hollows B	–	2	–	–	6	4	–	12	2	6
Other contexts	1	27	5	–	250	26	16	325	5	127
Layer 699	–	–	–	–	10	–	1	11	–	3
Other layers	–	9	3	3	28	4	3	50	3	20
Total	3	92	26	111	823	95	47	1197	54	454

1 = irregular waste; 2 = cores; 3 = core trimming flakes; 4 = chips; 5 = flakes; 6 = blades/bladelets; 7 = retouched

Table 3 Bray: flint cores

Context	1	2	3	4	5	6	Total
Round-house 491	–	–	–	1	–	1	2
Enclosure 925	–	1	2	9	–	2	14
Other ditches	3	1	4	14	–	2	24
Unassigned post-holes	–	–	1	–	–	1	2
Hollows A	2	1	2	5	1	1	12
Hollows B	–	–	1	1	–	–	2
Other contexts	7	–	4	16	–	–	27
Other layers	–	1	4	4	–	–	9
Total	12	4	18	50	1	7	92

1 = blade core; 2 = tested nodules, etc; 3 = single platform flake cores; 4 = multi-platform flake cores; 5 = keeled, non-discoidal flake core; 6 = unclassifiable/fragmentary

Worked flint was present in 54 out of a total of 112 samples. The overall composition of the assemblage is presented in Table 2. Chips were defined according to Newcomer and Karlin (1987; maximum surface area under 10 mm^2). These were retrieved from environmental samples which were sorted to a sieve size of 5.6 mm. Sieving was not employed during excavation, and this has undoubtedly led to the under-representation of chips in this collection. No concentrations of chips, which might indicate knapping areas, were noted.

The majority of the flint is of Middle Bronze Age affinity, but there are examples of material of Palaeolithic, Mesolithic, and Neolithic aspect.

Raw materials
The site lay on Kempton Park Gravels, and it seems that these were the source of virtually all the flint recovered. Where present, cortex is thin and worn, with a general rolled appearance typical of gravel flint. One nodule of 'Bull Head' flint is present (Dewey and Bromehead 1915, 18–19, described as 'green-coated flints'; Shepherd 1972, 114). This has been tested as a core with a couple of flake removals before being rejected. 'Bull-head' flint occurs at the base of the Reading Beds, the nearest outcrop of which is 1.5 km from the site (Dewey and Bromehead 1915, 2), and is also likely to occur in a derived context in the Thames river gravels.

The condition of the struck flint varies from fresh to rolled and abraded, with some plough-damage on material from the topsoil. The degree of patination varies quite markedly, and patches of iron-staining are present on some pieces. Thermal fractures are frequent.

Pre-Bronze Age material
Within the collection is a minority component which does not correspond to the general characteristics of Bronze Age flint industries, summarised by Ford et al. (1984) and which, on technological and typological grounds pre-dates the main Middle Bronze Age occupation of the site.

Included within the minority component is a large, heavy flake with a wide platform of probable Palaeolithic date. The flake is very rolled, patinated, and stained, with abraded arrises.

Of the cores, 13.0% are blade or bladelet cores (Fig. 16, 1 and 2). One core tablet is present (Fig. 16, 6). The regularity and form of the removals suggests that it is a pre-Bronze Age artefact. A total of 7.9% of the overall collection is made up of blades and bladelets. These are generally characterised by thin butts and diffuse bulbs, some with deliberate abrasion of the platform edges. The presence of blades and bladelets suggests a Mesolithic/earlier Neolithic presence (Pitts 1978, 185–8) with at least one bladelet core (Fig. 16, 1) certainly of Mesolithic type. Two cores had been used as hammerstones (Fig. 16, 3).

A broken backed bladelet (Table 4) (Fig. 16, 8), a burin, and an obliquely truncated bladelet (Fig. 16, 9) are further suggestive of a Mesolithic presence. An oblique arrowhead (Fig 16, 10) of Clark's (1934) type E, is the only diagnostic later Neolithic piece. Four serrated pieces (three blades and a flake), also occur (Fig. 16, 11); three of the four have silica gloss along the serrated edge. One unretouched blade also bears edge-gloss. Serrated pieces are a common component of Mesolithic (Pitts and Jacobi 1979, 173) and earlier Neolithic flint industries (Healey and Robertson-Mackay 1983, 16-17) alike.

There was no apparent concentration of earlier material in any one part of the site. Hollow 398 and pit 867 were the only features to contain pottery exclusively of Neolithic date and produced two and five bladelike pieces respectively.

Many features which contained Middle Bronze Age pottery also produced flint which can be ascribed a pre-Middle Bronze Age date on technological and typological grounds. Unassigned post-hole 380, and hollows 619 and 852 produced predominately blades and bladelike flakes, with thin butts and some platform abrasion; a serrated blade with edge gloss was present in the fill of hollow 619, and a blade with edge gloss in the fill of post-hole 380. The condition of these flints is very fresh, suggesting limited post-depositional transportation.

Mesolithic findspots are common in the vicinity of Bray (Wymer 1977, 4–5, 9) so the presence of Mesolithic elements on the site is unsurprising. Earlier Neolithic activity has also been recorded in the area — the shafts and pits at Cannon Hill (Bradley et al. 1981) 1.25 km to

Table 4 Bray: retouched forms

Contexts	1	2	3	4	5	6	7	8	9	10	Total
Round-house 491	–	–	–	–	–	–	1	–	–	–	1
Enclosure 925	–	–	4	1	1	1	–	–	1	–	8
Other ditches	–	1	2	1	2	3	–	–	2	1	12
Pits	–	–	2	–	–	–	–	–	1	–	3
Hollows A	–	–	2	–	1	–	–	–	–	–	3
Other contexts	–	–	11	1	–	1	–	1	2	–	16
Layer 699	–	–	1	–	–	–	–	–	–	–	1
Other layers	1	–	–	–	–	–	–	–	2	–	3
Total	1	1	22	3	4	5	1	1	8	1	47

1 = microlith; 2 = oblique arrowhead; 3 = scrapers; 4 = borers; 5 = serrated pieces; 6 = denticulates; 7 = burin; 8 = truncated piece; 9 = miscellaneous; 10 = hammerstone

the west; at Eton Wick (Ford 1986) 4 km to the east; and at the Staines causewayed enclosure (Robertson-Mackay 1987) 16 km to the south-east. The quantities recovered from Bray are too small for much further discussion to be meaningful.

The Middle Bronze Age assemblage
The technology and typology of the bulk of the collection are largely consistent with a Middle Bronze Age origin. However, problems with securely identifying residual earlier pieces in the collection, and its limited size (1197 pieces from an excavated area of 1.92 ha) have meant that only generalised conclusions can be drawn from the Bray collection. In consequence, it was felt that metrical analysis of the flint would not be meaningful.

There is evidence for the use of hard hammers in the Bronze Age material. A thermally fractured flint nodule had been used as a hammerstone and, in addition, two hammerstones had later been used as cores. Two flakes from core/hammers were also present. The striking platforms of many of the cores (Fig. 16, 5), and of some flakes also, frequently show incipient cones of percussion. These miss-hits indicate the use of a hard hammer and may be characteristic of the progressive loss of control over the material that is typical of Bronze Age industries (Ford *et al.* 1984). The majority of the cores are multi-platform flake cores (Table 3; Fig. 16, 4 and 5). Little preparation of the cores is evident, and they were generally unintensively worked. A few core trimming flakes are present (Fig. 16, 7). The flakes are characteristically broad, thick-butted and often with prominent bulbs of percussion. Faceted platforms occur very rarely, whereas hinge fractures are frequent. The collection has a general appearance of casualness in its manufacture.

Retouched forms (Table 4) include scrapers, borers, denticulates, and miscellaneous retouched pieces. This narrow range of implement types is entirely typical of Bronze Age lithic assemblages. Thirty-eight retouched pieces are present, with scrapers the dominant tool type at 57.9%. The scrapers are often, but not always, fashioned on thick flakes with steep edges. The removals are usually large and crude (Fig. 16, 14). The only apparently Bronze Age artefact to bear gloss is a scraper

on a core fragment (Fig. 16, 13). Here the gloss occurs on raised parts of the ventral surface (formed by the flake removal blow following a thermal fracture), and along the unretouched edge which has a very steep angle. It seems likely therefore that this gloss was formed by unintentional abrasion rather than deliberate use. Denticulates make up 13.2% of the tool types in the Bronze Age collection, and are also characterised by large crude removals. As with the scrapers, little selection is shown in the choice of blank — these include core fragments (Fig. 16, 17), cortical flakes (Fig. 16, 18), and thermally fractured pieces (Fig. 16, 19). Borers are also represented (Fig. 16, 15 and 16).

The bulk of the Bronze Age flint came from the fills of the ditches, which would have formed the largest 'artefact trap' on the site. Type A hollows also produced quantities of Bronze Age material (along with residual earlier material). As with the earlier flint, no particular concentrations were discernible in any one area (*see* Table 2). It is, however, difficult to make more than generalised statements about the distribution of the flint on the site as most small features were half sectioned but only some 10% of the ditches was excavated.

The Middle Bronze Age flint from Bray has few local excavated parallels but is comparable with typical Middle Bronze Age assemblages such as R4, Micheldever Wood, Hampshire (Fasham and Ross 1978), Fengate, Cambridgeshire (Pryor 1980), Black Patch, Sussex (Drewett 1982), Rowden and Cowleaze, Dorset (Harding 1991), and sites on the Marlborough Downs (Harding 1992).

Illustrated flint
Entries are ordered as follows: Category. Condition. Descriptive and/or other comment (if any). Context. Context description. All pieces are on gravel-type flint, presumably local.

1. Bladelet core. Very heavily patinated, frequent patches of iron-staining; plough-damaged. U/S B. Unstratified find from topsoil.
2. Blade core. Slightly glossed. 496. Ditch fill, cut 495, ditch 917.
3. Core/hammer. Rolled nodule. Patinated, blotches of iron-staining. 360. Ditch fill, cut 596, ditch 530.

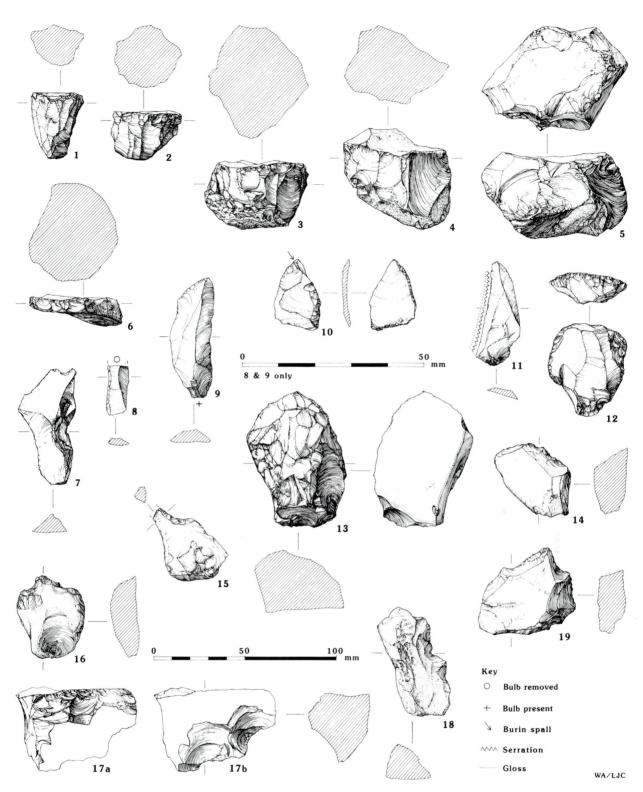

Figure 16   Bray: worked flint

4. Core. Rolled and abraded nodule. Fairly fresh condition. A few miss-hits present. 472. Ditch fill, cut 481, ditch 588.

5. Core. Rolled and abraded nodule. Fairly fresh condition. Numerous miss-hits. 583. Ditch fill, cut 481, ditch 588.

6. Core tablet. Abraded nodule. Fairly fresh condition. 467. Ditch fill, cut 468, ditch 589, part of field 925.

7. Core trimming flake. Fresh condition. 879. Pit fill, pit 878.

8. Backed bladelet. Patinated. Broken at proximal end. 734. Context belongs to group 667, near round-house 491.

9. Obliquely truncated blade. Patinated. Truncated at distal end. 293.

10. Oblique arrowhead. Patinated, slightly glossed. Burin-like removal at tip — possible impact fracture. Clark's (1934) type E. 359. Ditch fill, cut 596, ditch 530.

11. Serrated flake. Patinated with abraded arrises; gloss along serrated edge. 496. Ditch fill, cut 495, ditch 917.

12. Scraper. Edges and arrises slightly abraded. 343. Ditch fill, cut 345, ditch 915.

13. Scraper on core fragment. Fresh condition. Gloss of unknown origin on ventral surface and edge. 751. Ditch fill, cut 750, ditch 819, a part of field 925.

14. Scraper. Slight patination. Several miss-hits. 409. Fill of type A hollow 408.

15. Borer. Fairly fresh condition. Tip broken. 472. Ditch fill, cut 471, ditch 588.

16. Borer with scraper edge. Patinated. 281. Ditch fill, cut 600, ditch 280.

17. Denticulate on core fragment. Two phases of use indicated by patination on flake removal scars of core. 277. Ditch fill, cut 276, ditch 923.

18. Denticulate. Patinated. 360. Ditch fill, cut 596, ditch 530.

19. Denticulate. Large patches of iron staining. 467. Ditch fill, cut 468, ditch 589, part of field 925.

Burnt Flint, by I. Barnes and R.M.J. Cleal

A total of 689 pieces of burnt flint with a combined weight of 8897 g was recovered. The individual pieces varied in size between less than a gram and 1564 g.

The distribution of burnt flint was plotted by total weight, count, and mean weight (the last for contexts with more than five pieces only), by ditch section (as ditch sections and ditches were largely comparable in size, though volume of soil was not calculated). The count by weight is shown in Figure 24 and indicates three main areas of concentration, with a lesser scatter of burnt flint over much of the rest of site. The largest single concentration, in count and weight, was in the eastern terminals of ditches 588 and 589, and in these the mean weight of pieces was, respectively, 7.1 g and 17.8 g, indicating that the concentration was made up largely of small pieces. Other concentrations occurred in the middle sections cut through the triple ditches, and in the ditches demarcating enclosure 926. In the triple ditches the mean weight indicated small to medium size pieces (26 g in section 596 (ditch 530), 46 g in the evaluation trench section through ditch 280, and 10.3 g in the evaluation trench section through ditch 530). Around enclosure 926, however, the size of pieces seems to have been larger, with a mean weight in section 210 (ditch 919) of 66.7 g; counts were low in the western ditch 917/740, but the pieces were large, with a single piece in the northern terminal of 917/740 weighing 174 g and two in section 495 weighing 196 g.

On a more subjective basis there appears to be a concentration of fairly small pieces of burnt flint, of mean weight 1–10 g, around the round-house and four-poster.

The slight difference in size between different areas of the site might indicate differences in activity. The size of burnt flint would seem likely to be affected by length of time the flint is exposed to the heat, and by temperature, with extremes of both perhaps leading to greater fragmentation. Post-heating treatment is another factor which must be considered, as burnt flint would have been required in very large quantities for the production of flint-tempered pottery, and it is possible that some of the flint had undergone the early stages of temper preparation.

Burnt flint is a common occurrence on sites of Middle Bronze Age date (Buckley 1990), and there is at least one instance of a 'burnt mound' of flint occurring in a settlement site, at South Lodge, Dorset (Bradley and Barrett 1991, 161).

Stone, by R. Montague

Eight pieces of non-flint stone were recovered, one (weighing 3479 g) during the evaluation and seven (725 g) during the excavations. Four quartzite pebbles, one piece of coarse grained ferruginous Sandstone of unknown origin, and three pieces of sarsen were identified; their contexts of recovery are given in Table Mf1.

Two of the quartzite pebbles were burnt and broken, while the third and fourth show no signs of wear, burning, or iron-staining. Quartzite pebbles occur in some of the Thames river gravels (Dewey and Bromehead 1915, 77), so their presence is unremarkable. The coarse grained ferruginous sandstone is a possible rubber fragment with maximum dimensions of 65 x 45 x 30 mm. The original surface of the rubber remains only on one face, and this has smooth wear on a flat surface.

Two of the three fragments of sarsen are unmodified while the third fragment is from a saddle quern recovered from a fill of ditch 280 (Fig. 17). It is 190 mm wide, with 140 mm remaining of an unknown length, and 100 mm thick. The top, broken surface is flat and smoothed, and bears peckmarks aligned parallel to the length of the quern. The two unmodified fragments were probably derived from querns but it is not possible to confirm this. All three fragments are iron-stained. Sarsen boulders, although most characterisitic of the Chalk, are known to occur in the Woolwich, Reading,

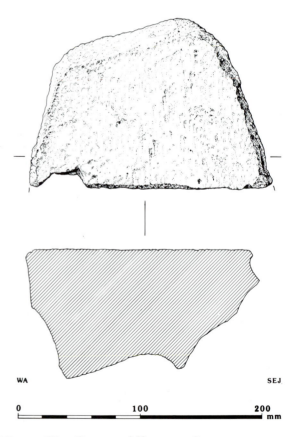

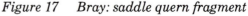

Figure 17   Bray: saddle quern fragment

and Barton Beds, the nearest of which (Reading Beds) occurs within 5 km of Bray (Dewey and Bromehead 1915, 58). They have been noted mainly from gravel pits, lying below the gravels (*ibid.*), so it cannot be assumed that they would have been locally exposed during the Bronze Age, but while the possibility of localised outcrops remains for the sarsen a more distant source cannot be invoked with confidence. There is also Chalk in the local area, as the Upper Chalk has a surface outcrop of about 15 km^2 just to the west of Bray (*op. cit.*, 7, fig. 1), but sarsens have not been recorded in this area. Further afield, sarsens are recorded within 20 km both to the north, in Buckinghamshire and Oxfordshire, and to the south, in north-eastern Hampshire/western Surrey (Bowen and Smith 1977, fig. 1–2), so a distant source, such as the well-attested northern Wiltshire concentrations, need not be the source in this case.

Pottery, by R.M.J. Cleal

A total of 1134 sherds (11,154 g) was recovered during the excavations. An additional 98 sherds (623 g) were recovered from the evaluation. Of the latter, 64 were recovered from the topsoil and have not been included in this report, since topsoil finds were not collected during the excavation because the topsoil had been mechanically stripped. The stratified material (34 sherds) from the evaluation is included in tables and totals. Sherds recovered during post-excavation sieving of samples are given separately in Table Mf3, but are not included in the overall totals given above, or in Table Mf2, although the single Neolithic rim sherd recovered by sieving is included in the discussion. The majority of the pottery in the collection is of Middle Bronze Age date, but some earlier Neolithic, Early Bronze Age, and later pottery is also present.

The sherds were assigned to fabrics using the standard Wessex Archaeology procedure (Morris 1992a), and were counted and weighed by fabric. Fabrics were assigned to periods mainly on the basis of the occurrence of diagnostic sherds, although in a minority of cases (eg fabric F4), the general appearance of the fabric was considered so characteristic of a period that it was assigned to one in the absence of diagnostic sherds.

Fabrics were defined principally by the occurrence and frequency of inclusion types and are referred to by alpha-numeric codes which comprise the initial letter of the major inclusion type and a number differentiating each fabric within the group of fabrics sharing the same major inclusion type. During the identification of fabrics sherds were examined under a binocular microscope at x20 magnification; once the fabrics were established, however, most sherds were assigned by eye. Fabric descriptions are given in Table 5.

Earlier Neolithic

Eighteen sherds are assignable to the earlier Neolithic, but this may be an underestimate because of the difficulty in distinguishing plain earlier Neolithic body sherds from those of the Middle Bronze Age. A single small rim sherd in fabric F6 (not illustrated) recovered

Table 5 Bray: abbreviated pottery fabric descriptions

Earlier Neolithic
F6   Hard; sparse, ill-sorted flint (<7%, <7 mm) and sparse quartz sand (<5%, <0.5 mm, most <25 mm). Diagnostic sherds are earlier Neolithic.
F9   Soft, sandy; sparse, ill-sorted flint (<7%, <8 mm) and common to abundant well-sorted quartz sand (25–40%, <0.5 mm, most <0.25 mm). Diagnostic sherds are earlier Neolithic.

Peterborough Ware
F10   Soft; sparse ill-sorted flint (<5%, <10 mm), rare to sparse quartz sand and mica (<3%, too small to measure at X magnification). Diagnostic sherds are Peterborough Ware.
F11   Hard; sparse well-sorted flint (<7%, <3 mm), rare angular quartz (<2%, <7 mm) and sparse quartz sand (<5%, <0.5 mm). Diagnostic sherds are Peterborough Ware.

Later Neolithic/Early Bronze Age
F7   Soft; rare to sparse ill-sorted flint (<3%, <4 mm), rare to sparse well-sorted grog (<5%, <1 mm), and rare to sparse well-sorted quartz sand (<3%, <0.25 mm). No diagnostic sherds, but appearance of fabric suggests later Neolithic or Early Bronze Age date.
G1   Soft sandy; moderate well-sorted grog (10–15%, <2 mm, most <0.5 mm), sparse ill-sorted quartz sand (<7%, <1.5 mm, most <0.5 mm), and rare to sparse well-sorted flint (3%, <1 mm). No diagnostic sherds, but one small body sherd almost certainly from fingernail decorated Beaker.

Middle Bronze Age
F1   Hard; moderate to common well-sorted flint (10–25%, <3 mm, most <1 mm).
F2   Hard; sparse to moderate well-sorted flint (<15%, <2 mm, most <0.5 mm).
F3   Hard; sparse to common ill-sorted flint (<25%, <7 mm, most <5 mm), rare to sparse quartz sand (<3%, <0.5 mm), and rare iron oxides (<3%, <0.5 mm).
F4   Hard; common ill-sorted flint (c.20%, <13 mm, most <5 mm).
F5   Soft; rare well-sorted flint (<2%, <1 mm, most <0.5 mm) and sparse well-sorted quartz sand (<0.5 mm).
F12   Hard; very common to abundant well-sorted flint (25–40%, <1.5 mm, most <1 mm), rare to sparse quartz sand (<3%, <0.5 mm), and rare to sparse well-sorted rounded to subrounded voids (<3%, <2 mm); voids likely to represent leached-out calcareous inclusions (possibly Chalk or Limestone).
F90   Code used for small flint-gritted sherds not assignable to fabric but which, from general appearance, are likely to belong to one of Middle Bronze Age fabrics.

Indeterminate prehistoric fabrics
F8   Soft sandy; sparse well-sorted flint (<5%, <2 mm, most <1 mm), rare to sparse, well-sorted

F99 Code used for sherds in which flint is major or only inclusion type visible, and which, although clearly prehistoric, are not assignable to period.

G2 Soft; sparse well-sorted grog (<5%, <2 mm, most <1 mm), rare to sparse well-sorted quartz sand (<5%, <0.5 mm), and sparse well-sorted flint (<5%, <2 mm, most <1 mm).

G99 As F99, except that grog is the major or only visible inclusion.

Q1 Soft sandy; common to very common well-sorted quartz sand (25–30%, <1 mm, most <0.5 mm). The general appearance of the fabric suggests that it could be of 1st millennium BC date.

Q2 Hard sandy; common to very common well-sorted quartz sand (20–25%, <1.5 mm, most <0.5 mm), and rare flint (<3%, <2 mm). The fabric is much harder than Q1, and is likely to be of 1st millennium BC date.

Q99 As F99 and G99, except that the major or only inclusion visible is quartz sand.

Late Iron Age and Romano-British fabrics
I101 Hard sandy; sparse well-sorted iron oxides (<7%, <2 mm, most <1 mm), and sparse well-sorted quartz sand (<7%, <0.5 mm, most <0.25 mm). One diagnostic sherd is Late Iron Age or early Roman.

Q101 Hard sandy; sparse to moderate well-sorted quartz sand (<15%, <0.5 mm) and rare mica and iron oxides, both too small to be measureable at x20 magnification. Vessels are wheelmade, early Roman.

Q102 Code used for Romano-British grey sandy wares. Sources unknown.

Q103 Code used for oxidised Romano-British wares. Sources unknown.

Q199 Code used for small fragments with quartz sand as the major or only inclusion type. Unlikely to be prehistoric.

Post-medieval fabrics
E740 Wessex Archaeology Established Fabric Code for undiagnositc fine white wares (including 'blue and white').

Undatable fabrics
Q900 Small fragments with some quartz sand, of completely indeterminable date.

V900 Soft sandy; sparse ill-sorted linear voids representing burnt-out organic inclusions (<7%, <10 mm in length), sparse well-sorted quartz sand (<7%, <0.75 mm, most 0.25 mm). No diagnostic sherds. On basis of general appearance fabric could be of Iron Age or Anglo-Saxon date.

during sieving of environmental samples, is likely to represent another vessel.

Two fabrics were identified, F6 and F9. Both were tempered with flint, but the frequency of quartz sand was much higher in F9. It is unlikely that any body sherds of F9 were mistaken for Middle Bronze Age sherds, because of the paucity of sand in the latter, but

this is not the case with F6 which, like the Bronze Age fabrics, contained little sand.

The presence of an earlier Neolithic component in the collection was only clear because of the obviously Neolithic featured sherds P1 and P3 (Fig. 18). The ill-sorting and uneven distribution of the flint in F6 could be paralleled in, particularly, fabric F3 (Middle Bronze Age), but one slight indicator which has been observed here, and generally, is that earlier Neolithic flint temper is often not as well crushed as most Middle Bronze Age flint temper. The latter often exhibits an almost rounded appearance, which seems only to be achievable when well-calcined flint lumps are crushed.

No complete profile is available for any of the minimum of four vessels represented (Fig. 18, P1–P4), nor for the vessel recovered from the sieving of environmental samples, although sufficient survives of P3 to suggest that it is unlikely to belong to a carinated vessel. The rim forms represented are Rolled-over, Externally Enlarged, and Expanded (types B, C, and D in Smith 1965, fig. 11). None of the sherds appear to be decorated; there is a slight indentation on the rim of P1, but it is not clearly intentional. The lack of decoration does not imply, however, that these vessels did not originally form part of a Decorated Style assemblage (Whittle 1977), as such assemblages do not necessarily contain a high proportion of decorated vessels, the 50% at Windmill Hill probably representing the maximum (*op. cit.*, 85). The Bray vessels would not be out of place in the assemblage from the Staines causewayed enclosure, 16 km to the south-east, in which only approximately 4% of the vessels are decorated (Robertson-Mackay 1987, 88), nor in that from Eton Wick, only 4 km to the east (Ford 1986; and author's notes). The Bray pottery is not comparable to the nearest earlier Neolithic assemblage, which is that from Cannon Hill, Bray, as that consists largely of carinated bowls (Bradley *et al.* 1981). There are no radiocarbon dates from Staines, and the date from Cannon Hill is of dubious validity as there was Mesolithic material in the same context, but in general terms the Bray pottery is likely to be contemporary with the use of the major causewayed enclosures of central southern Britain (ie, mainly 4th millennium BC).

The Neolithic pottery was recovered from three features (ditch 917, hollow 398, and pit 867), one of which (917) is certainly of Middle Bronze Age date. The two other features contain no pottery of later date, and may therefore be Neolithic. These features are widely dispersed (Fig. 8), and it cannot be assumed that they represent a single episode of use.

Later Neolithic and Early Bronze Age
Fifteen sherds almost certainly belong to this period, although there are very few diagnostic sherds. This includes two sherds certainly of Peterborough Ware (Fig. 18, P5–P6), both decorated with twisted cord impressions, and one possibly of this tradition. The two certain Peterborough Ware sherds are flint-tempered, the fabrics (F10 and F11) varying only in the frequency of quartz sand; the possible Peterborough Ware sherd is so small as to be unassignable to fabric, but does contain flint. The other two fabrics, G1 and F7, are both soft and contain grog; they would not be out of place in a coarse Beaker assemblage, and the combination of

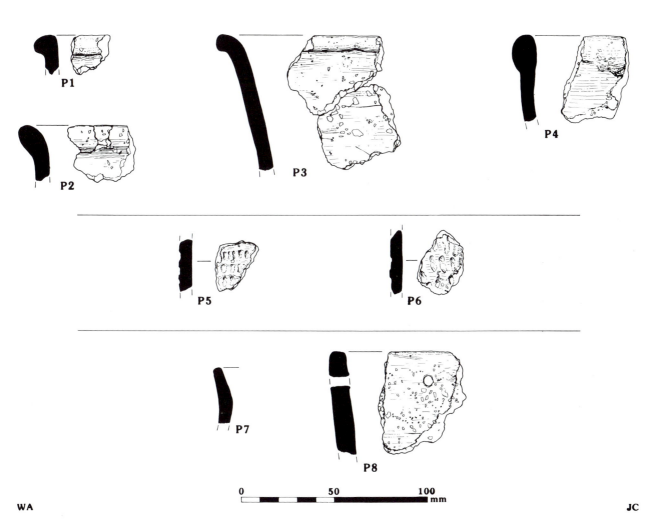

Figure 18   Bray: prehistoric pottery

flint and grog would be particularly characteristic of that tradition. A single, small, featured sherd (not illustrated) in fabric G1, from context 233 (ditch 202), carries a single horizontal non-plastic fingernail impression and is almost certainly from a Beaker.

The two certain Peterborough Ware sherds appear to represent separate vessels which could belong to either the Ebbsfleet or Mortlake substyles. The small sherd tentatively assigned to this tradition (not illustrated) appears to have very small nicks, probably executed with the fingernail, probably arranged in a curvilinear pattern. It is likely to be Fengate Ware, as both the technique and motif would be typical of that substyle. The dating of Peterborough Ware is still uncertain but it is likely to span the earlier to later Neolithic. At Staines 17 sherds, representing a minimum of 11 Ebbsfleet Ware vessels, were recovered only from the secondary ditch fills, indicating that the style probably came into use there towards the end of the earlier Neolithic (Whittle 1987).

Both Ebbsfleet/Mortlake Ware sherds were recovered from features in the western part of the site. One sherd (Fig. 18, P6) was from a post-hole (559) just outside the porch of the round-house 491, while the other, P5, was in a feature with no other artefacts (hollow 407). The possible Fengate Ware was from feature 370, in the

north-eastern part of the site. The possible Beaker sherds are scattered over the site in later features.

Middle Bronze Age
A total of 962 sherds may be assigned to this period, but it is likely that some fragmentary material, assigned to fabric code F99 and therefore not included in this total, is also of this date. A minimum number of 19 vessels was estimated, on the basis of rim form and fabric. Almost all the material can be assigned to the Middle Bronze Age Deverel–Rimbury tradition, but a small element within the assemblage may be of slightly later date; the arguments for this are presented below.

Six fabrics were defined, all of which are flint-tempered (Table 5). All but one include diagnostic sherds; the exception, fabric F4, is so similar in general appearance to the other Middle Bronze Age fabrics that it was also assigned to this period. The fabrics were not well-defined and some difficulty was encountered in dealing with the coarser element of the assemblage, as frequency and size of inclusions can vary considerably even within one vessel. The fabrics may, however, be grouped into at least finer and coarser elements. Fabrics F1 and F2 show a high degree of temper preparation, with well-controlled and small inclusion size, and some vessels have well-finished surfaces. Fabric F3 is a

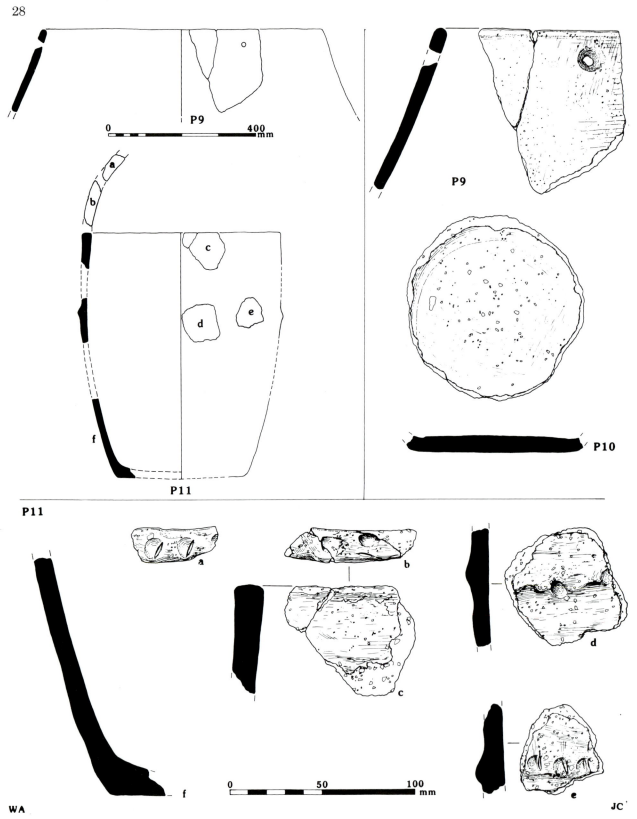

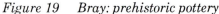

Figure 19   Bray: prehistoric pottery

loosely-defined fabric which allows for the fairly wide range of inclusion size, frequency, and distribution exhibited by some vessels. This would appear to represent the coarser element of the assemblage, with fabric F4 representing the extreme of that end of the range. Fabric F5, on the other hand, which is probably only represented by one vessel (Fig. 20, P14), is extremely fine in comparison with the rest of the assemblage.

Fabric F12, the only Middle Bronze Age fabric to contain sizeable inclusions other than flint and sand, falls between the two ends of the range; the other inclusion present in this fabric is represented only by voids, which may have been left by leached-out Limestone, probably Chalk in view of the geology of the area.

No complete vessel profiles survive, although at least one is visually reconstructable with some confidence

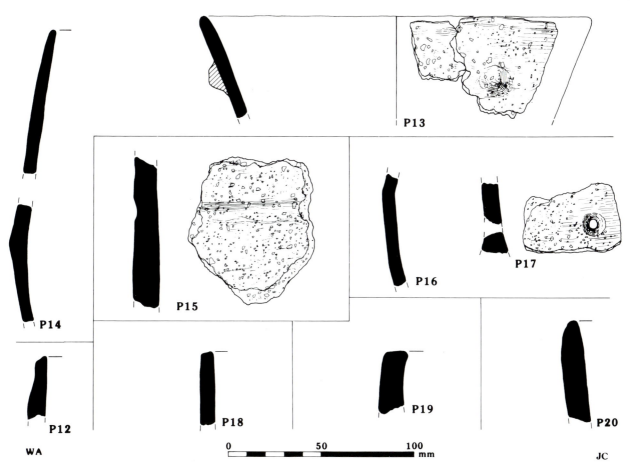

Figure 20   Bray: prehistoric pottery

(P11). However, the following forms appear to be present in the assemblage:

Bucket-shaped: (ie, slightly wider at the rim than the base, to nearly cylindrical) — P8, P11, P27, and possibly P28. It is likely that most of the rim sherds belong to this type of vessel, although too little survives of most vessels for the profile to be reconstructed.

Globular Urns: P9, P23, and P26;

Biconical: (NB *not* Biconical Urns) — P14 and P21 (although the lie of the rim in P14 is not certain and it is possible that the form is more open than shown;

Truncated conical: (ie, markedly more splayed than bucket-shaped forms) — P13;

Convex-bodied: (possible Barrel Urn?) — possibly P25 and P32

Among the unreconstructable body sherds, seven, probably representing no more than four vessels (P16, P34) show a change of angle at the shoulder; in most cases the carination is moderately sharp. A single small carinated sherd (not illustrated) was also recovered from the evaluation. It was considered important to establish whether there was any possibility that these might represent later Bronze Age bowl or jar forms. The single small sherd from the evaluation was originally con-

sidered to be from a bowl, partly on the basis of a very well finished interior surface which it seemed might have been intended to be visible, but the small size of the sherd and the subsequent identification of larger carinated vessels renders this identification dubious. The angled sherds were not concentrated in any one area of the site, and in only one case did an angled sherd certainly come from the upper fill of a feature (a single sherd from ditch 919 was in the upper fill) and therefore possibly have been deposited late in the use of the site. There is no circumstantial evidence, therefore, to assign these sherds to a later phase than the majority of the material. The angular sherds in fabrics F1 and F2 in particular could be interpreted as belonging to Globular Urns with angular profiles, such as some of those from Kimpton, Hampshire (Dacre and Ellison 1981, fig. 16), although it must be noted that such angular forms are not common. Most conclusively, P14 is well-associated with a radiocarbon date (UB–3513, Table 1), which places it within the middle centuries of the 2nd millennium BC.

Out of the total of 962 Middle Bronze Age sherds only 26, probably representing no more than 10 vessels, are decorated. A very limited repertoire of decoration is exhibited: a single finger-groove (Fig. 20, P15), both plain and fingernail-decorated horizontal cordons (Figs 19, 21 and 22, P11, P25, P33), unperforated and perforated lugs (Figs 20–22, P13, P22, P26, P31), perforation (Fig. 18, P8), and fingernail impression on the rim top (Fig. 19, P11). The presence of shallow finger-groove

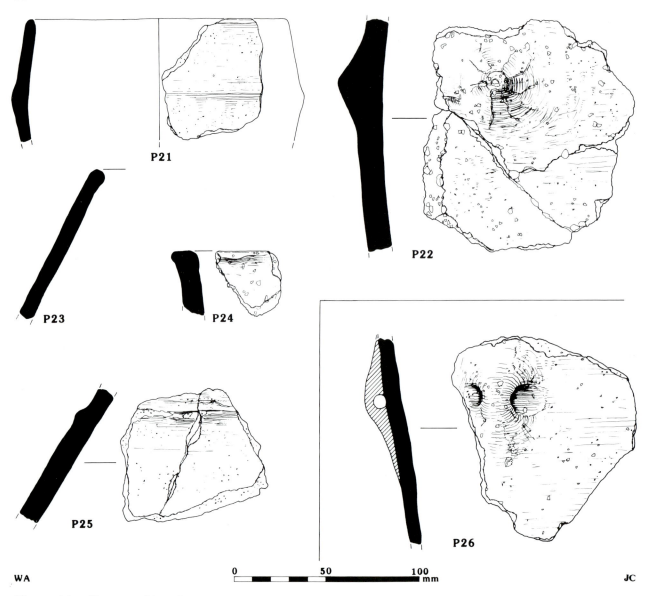

P21

P22

P23

P24

P25

P26

WA

0   50   100 mm

JC

Figure 21   Bray: prehistoric pottery

(P15) (sometimes referred to as a 'girth groove' because of its usual position running around the body of the pot) should be noted, as this is a feature more characteristic of Dorset and neighbouring areas (eg, at Knighton Heath, Petersen 1981, 112; and Simon's Ground, White 1982) than of the Thames Valley.

The majority of the pottery may be assigned to the Deverel–Rimbury tradition of the Middle Bronze Age. It includes at least two of the typical elements of that tradition: bucket-shaped vessels and Globular Urns, although the assemblage is not directly comparable to the classic Deverel–Rimbury assemblages from central Wessex. There is in addition, however, a minority element, including some of the angular sherds already discussed, which does not fall readily into this tradition, even with allowances made for the distance of the site from the classic Deverel–Rimbury sites of Wessex.

The dominant element in the Deverel–Rimbury component of the assemblage is of moderately coarse to coarse bucket-shaped vessels with limited decoration, represented by illustrated vessels P8, P11, P15, P19, P20, P22, P24, P27, P29, P30/31, and possibly P28.

These vessels may vary considerably in size and often carry very limited decoration, in particular cordons, both plain and decorated, and lugs. Bucket-shaped vessels occur both in the classic Deverel–Rimbury assemblages of central Wessex, such as Thorny Down, Wiltshire (Stone 1941, fig. 5, 5), Down Farm, Dorset (Barrett 1991, eg, fig. 8.6, 6; fig. 8.7 10, 46, 47, 59), and elsewhere in Dorset (Calkin 1964, figs 12 and 23), and in the Thames Valley, as at Ashford Common, Sunbury, Middlesex, and Acton (Barrett 1974, figs 1, 2 and 4). Both pre-firing perforations and lugs, as well as fingernail-decorated cordons, occur at Sunbury (*op. cit.*, fig. 2 nos 19, 22, and 26) and lugs, pre-firing perforation and cordons are features of the assemblage from Acton (*op. cit.*, fig. 4).

The Globular Urn component of the Bray assemblage comprises P9, P23, and P26. Although very little survives of each vessel it is clear that there is no decoration on at least the upper body of P9, and P23 may also be plain; P26 carries only a horizontally perforated lug, presumably one of two or more originally present. The straight profile of P26 is paralleled by the single Globular Urn from Yiewsley (*op. cit.*, 121, fig. 5, 2), which also carries a horizontally perforated lug. Globular Urns are a less common feature of sites in the Lower Thames Valley (*op. cit.*, 121) than they are elsewhere, although it has been suggested that this may be a reflection of the bias in the record due to the predominance of cemetery evidence in the region (Needham 1987, 110–11). Some are now known from Muckhatch Farm, Surrey, in a domestic context, and in a probably domestic group from Osterley (*op. cit.*, 111).

Barrel Urns do not appear to be represented in the Lower Thames Valley, and the assemblage from Bray has done nothing to alter this. A single large body sherd (Fig. 21, P25), however, appears to be derived from a large, convex-bodied vessel, this interpretation being based on the curvature shown by the cordon, which appears horizontal when held at the angle shown in Figure 21. The vessel seems unlikely to belong to a Globular Urn on the grounds of wall thickness and the presence of a cordon, although the fabric is one which occurs in the Globular Urns from the site. Even if the vessel is correctly interpreted as a convex-bodied form, it could not confidently be identified as a Barrel Urn in the absence of any corroborating detail such as an expanded rim; the convexity of the body also seems excessive for a Barrel Urn. The rim of P32 suggests a convex body, but the straight-sided sherd P33, which appears to belong to the same vessel, seems to contradict this; the slightly thickened rim would also be consistent with the vessel being a Barrel Urn, but, as with P25, the identification cannot be certain.

Only three vessels (P7, P14, and P21) are difficult to accommodate within the Deverel–Rimbury tradition. Two are biconical vessels, one in fabric F2 (P21) and one in the unusual fabric F5 (P14) which may only be represented by this one vessel. P21 was found in the same context (in ditch 530) as P22, a large sherd of a bucket-shaped vessel in good condition and therefore unlikely to be redeposited in that context. This fact, and the use of fabric F2 for P21, may be taken as an indication that although its form seems anomalous it may yet belong to the Deverel–Rimbury tradition. Its small size also suggests that, if it were found in a funerary context, it would be classed as an accessory vessel, a class in which there tends to be more variety than in the larger forms.

These arguments cannot, however, be extended to P14, which is anomalous not only in form but also in fabric. The fabric of this vessel, F5, contains more sand and less flint than any of the other Bronze Age fabrics from the site, and the flint is exceptionally finely crushed (Table 5). Sandy fabrics are extremely rare in Middle Bronze Age assemblages, not becoming common until the Late Bronze Age/Early Iron Age (eg, Petters Sports Field, Egham, O'Connell 1986, 61–2). The vessel represented by P14 also differs from the majority of the Bray assemblage in its pale brown surface colour, which contrasts with the generally dark greys, browns, and black of many of the vessels. The form, however, cannot be paralleled closely among the Late Bronze Age assemblages of the Thames Valley. Although angularity is a feature of some of these assemblages the deep upper body of P14, the absence of any degree of concavity in the upper body profile, and the lack of an out-turned rim distinguishes it from the majority of vessels at, for

instance, Aldermaston (Bradley *et al.* 1980, figs 11–18) or Runnymede Bridge (Longley 1980, figs 43–5; Longley 1991, figs 76–105).

Only one vessel can confidently be suggested as later than the majority of the assemblage. The single rim sherd P7 appears to belong to a form with an upright or slightly everted simple rim above a rounded or straight upper body, the angle between the body and rim being well-defined. This form, unlike that of P14, does have parallels in the assemblage from Aldermaston, where such rims occur on vessel types 1, 2, 8, and 9 (Bradley *et al.* 1980, fig. 11) and at Runnymede (Longley 1991, vessels P35, P51, P131, P178, and others). These forms include jars (Aldermaston types 8 and 9) and bowls (Aldermaston types 1 and 2). The small size of the rim of P7, and the fact that the angle of lie of the rim is not certain, prevent this vessel being assigned to one class of vessel rather than the other.

Ditch 589, from which P14 was recovered, has produced a date which calibrates to within the 2nd millennium BC (UB–3513; Table 1). The fill of ditch 589 appeared homogeneous, and the dated material (animal bone) was from the basal fill. Although the range is large, this is an acceptable date for a Deverel–Rimbury assemblage, and is not markedly earlier than, for instance, those from the enclosure at Down Farm, Woodcutts, Dorset (BM–1852N1–N4: 3120±50 BP, 3270±50 BP, 3100±50 BP, 3150±50 BP; BM–2980±50 BP; BM–1853N: 2980±50 BP; BM–1854R: 3030±110 BP; Bowman 1991, 5; Green *et al.* 1991, 200) which were derived from the upper fills of the enclosure ditch at that site. The radiocarbon date for ditch 530, the feature which contained P21, however, falls mainly within the 1st millennium cal BC (UB–3514; 1260–261 BC) and is later than would be expected for a Deverel–Rimbury assemblage.

Later Prehistoric

A small number of sherds are in fabrics which may be of 1st millennium BC date (fabrics Q1, Q2, F8). No featured sherds are present and it is not possible to do other than record the presence of the featureless material (Table Mf2). A single rim sherd in fabric I101 is probably from a Late Iron Age cordoned bowl. This is the only indication from the site of any activity during the Late Iron Age.

Romano-British

A small quantity of Romano-British pottery was recovered, mainly from pit 283 (Table Mf2). The vessels represented are all coarsewares of unknown source. Diagnostic forms include a single platter, and one Butt Beaker with rilling, both dating to the 1st century AD.

Summary and conclusions

Although the ceramics from Bray are dominated by the Middle Bronze Age assemblage the importance of the earlier Neolithic pottery should not be overlooked, as evidence of earlier Neolithic activity other than in causewayed enclosures is always rare and often discovered by chance. The condition of at least P3 from the Middle Bronze Age ditch 917 suggests that the Neolithic sherds probably came from features subsequently disturbed, and this is consistent with finds from elsewhere, where

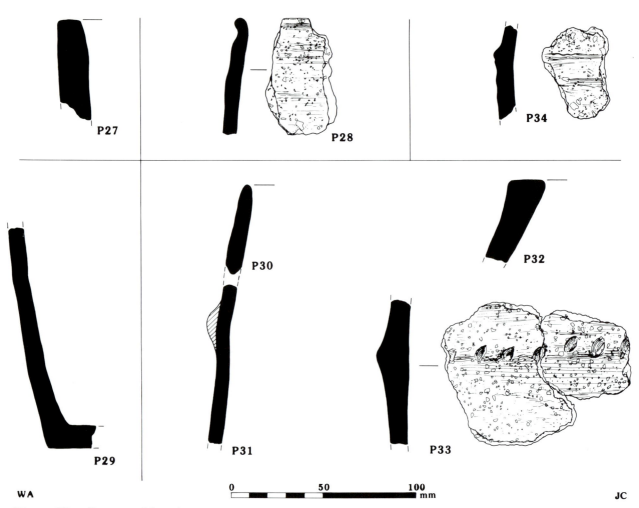

Figure 22   Bray: prehistoric pottery

WA

JC

earlier Neolithic pottery has survived mainly in pits: for example, in the Stonehenge area where almost no earlier Neolithic pottery was found during extensive surface collection but has been found in negative features (Richards 1990). Use of this part of the Thames Valley in the earlier Neolithic is also attested by excavated material from causewayed enclosures at Staines (Robertson-Mackay 1987) and Eton Wick (Ford 1986), and from Cannon Hill, Bray (shafts, possibly natural) (Bradley *et al.* 1981).

The value of the Middle Bronze Age pottery assemblage from Bray lies principally in its contribution to filling the Middle Bronze Age settlement 'gap' in the Middle to Lower Thames Valley. Cemetery sites with Deverel–Rimbury urns have long been known, although often discovered during gravel-quarrying. Signs of settlement, perhaps less obvious than burials in recognisable urns, may have been missed by the same operations, or may be sparse in reality. Only close monitoring of sites such as Bray will be able to establish their real frequency in areas as yet untouched by mineral extraction or building.

Although the evidence of settlement firmly associated with the Deverel–Rimbury pottery at Bray is not as extensive or as comprehensive as some of the Deverel–Rimbury sites of the southern chalk downlands, the fact that pottery of this period is associated

with a field system and other indications of settlement suggests that settlement was more widespread and intensive than the paucity of finds in the Middle Thames Valley to date has suggested.

Illustrated pottery
In the site archive sherds have both Pottery Record Numbers (PRN) and vessel numbers. PRNs were assigned individually to featured sherds, and grouped by fabric and context for featureless sherds. Vessel numbers, which were assigned in addition to PRNs, were used to distinguish those groups of sherds which were judged to belong to individual vessels, and could therefore occur in more than one context. In the archive the pottery is arranged by context.

Phase 2 : Earlier Neolithic

P1   Fabric F6/Neo. Ext. dark grey to brown, Int. grey-brown, core grey. 868, pit 867. (PRN 3282, vessel 22).

P2   Fabric F9/Neo. Ext. dark brown, Int. orange brown, core obscured. 376, cut 398 (hollow). (PRN 3106, vessel 8).

P3   Fabric F6/Neo. Ext. grey–brown, Int. dark grey, core obscured. 479, cut 478 (group: ditch 917). (PRN 3170, vessel 15).

P4   Fabric F9/Neo. Ext. orange–red, Int. pale brown, core obscured. 479, cut 478 (group: ditch 917). (PRN 3171, vessel 16).

Phase 3: Later Neolithic/Early Bronze Age

P5 Fabric F11/Pet. Ext. orange, Int. grey, core obscured. 407, cut 406 (hollow). (PRN 3114, vessel 10)

P6 Fabric F10/Pet. Ext. dark grey–brown, core and Int. orange. 557, post-hole 559, immediately outside round-house 491. (PRN 3202).

Phase 4: Middle Bronze Age

P7 Fabric F2/MBA. Ext. grey–brown, Int. dark grey, core grey. 503, cut 504 (post-hole of round-house 491). (PRN 3184, vessel 17).

P8 Fabric F3/MBA. Rim sherd with pre-firing perforation. Ext. pale brown, dark grey, core obscured, Int. dark grey. 379, cut 380. (PRN 3110, vessel 9).

P9 Fabric F2/MBA. Two conjoining rim sherds, one with post-firing drilled hole. Hole had been started from interior but abandoned. Completed perforation drilled from ext. Vessel also shown with probable rim diameter. Object no. 4001, 327, cut 326. (PRN 3085–86, vessel 3).

P10 Complete basal sherd, which has become detached below first coil; belongs to same vessel as P9. Wear varies very strikingly, with half ext. surface of base very worn and other half unworn. Object no. 4001, 327, cut 326. (PRN 3088, vessel 3).

P11 Fabric F3/MBA. Partially reconstructable urn with applied fingernail-impressed cordon. Top of rim also fingernail decorated. Ext. dark grey to pale brown, Int. dark grey to buff, core dark grey–brown. 327, cut 326. (PRN 3089–3094, vessel 4).

P12 Fabric F3/MBA. Ext. grey–brown, Int. dark grey, core black. 472, cut 471 (group: ditch 588). (PRN 3161, vessel 14).

P13 Sherd with unperforated applied lug. Fabric F3/MBA. Ext. black to pale orange, Int. black to orange–brown, core black. 467, cut 468 (group: ditch 589). (PRN 3139, vessel 11).

P14 Fabric F5/MBA. Ext. brown to dark grey, Int. and core grey to dark grey. Surfaces well-finished; no burnish visible, although possibly has worn off. 467, cut 468 (group: ditch 589). (PRN 3145, vessel 12). Five sherds of this fabric, including one rim sherd which joins with sherds from ditch 589, found in hollow 544 (545, PRN 3191–3194).

P15 Sherd with shallow groove. Fabric F3/MBA. Surfaces black to buff, core obscured. 216, cut 209 (group: ditch 202). (PRN 3021).

P16 Fabric F2/MBA. Ext. pale brown, Int. dark grey, core grey. 479, cut 478. (PRN 3175).

P17 Sherd from just above base, hole drilled after firing mainly from ext. Fabric F3/MBA. Ext. dark grey–brown, core and Int. black. 473, cut 474 (group: ditch 917). (PRN 3163).

P18 Fabric F1/MBA. Surfaces dark grey–brown, core pale brown. 317, cut 316 (group: ditch 915). (PRN 3080, vessel 2).

P19 Fabric F3/MBA. Ext. orange, Int. pale brown, core black. 257, cut 279 (group: ditch 923). (PRN 3039, vessel 1).

P20 Fabric F3/MBA. Ext. grey, Int. and core dark grey. 626, cut 627 (group: ditch 920). (PRN 3228, vessel 20).

P21 Fabric F2/MBA. Ext. grey to dark grey, Int. black, core dark grey. 716, cut 596 (group: ditch 530). (PRN 3237, vessel 21).

P22 Fabric F3/MBA. Ext. pale orange, Int. pale brown, core orange. 716, cut 596 (group: ditch 530). (PRN 3241).

P23 Fabric F1/MBA. Dark grey throughout. 360, cut 596 (group: ditch 530). (PRN 3103, vessel 7).

P24 Fabric F3/MBA. Ext. orange, core and Int. dark grey. 360, cut 596 (group: ditch 530). (PRN 3102, vessel 6).

P25 Fabric F2/MBA. Ext. red–brown, Ext. margin orange, core grey–brown, Int. red–brown, black. Cordon almost certainly worked-up rather than applied. 060, cut 59 (=20), evaluation; group: ditch 530 (no PRN).

P26 Fabric F1/MBA. Ext. pale orange, core and Int. orange. 140, cut 138 (evaluation; not reconciled with feature in excavations). (no PRN).

P27 Fabric F3/MBA. Ext. dark brown, Int. orange, core obscured. 342, cut 341. (PRN 3095, vessel 5).

P28 Fabric F3/MBA. Ext. and core dark grey, Int. dark grey to dark brown. 469, cut 470. (PRN 3156, vessel 13).

P29 Fabric F3/MBA. Ext. grey–brown, Int. orange to dark grey, core dark grey. 475, cut 528. (PRN 3167).

P30 Fabric F12/MBA. Ext. orange, pale orange, core obscured, Int. pale orange. 571, cut 621. (PRN 3211, vessel 19).

P31 Fabric F12/MBA. Ext. light grey to dark grey, Int. light brown, core obscured. Same vessel as P30. 571, cut 621. (PRN 3210, vessel 19).

P32 Fabric F3/MBA. Dark grey throughout. 571, cut 621. (PRN 3208, vessel 18).

P33 Fabric F3/MBA. Ext. black, orange, core black, Int. grey, buff. Probably same vessel as P32. (571, cut 621). (PRN 3207.)

P34 Fabric F3/MBA. Ext. dark brown, Int. brown to dark grey, core black. 631, cut 630. (PRN 3231).

Fired Clay, by Elaine L. Morris

Eighty pieces of fired clay were recovered from the excavation (Table Mf5). All except one were recovered from Middle Bronze Age contexts or were intrusive in natural features.

Four fabrics were differentiated using a x10 power binocular microscope. These were defined using Wessex Archaeology's pottery recording system (Morris 1992a), adapted for fired clay. Details are available in archive.

FC1 Dense, poorly-wedged, slightly sandy (5 fragments/weight 4 g)

FC2 Fine, dense, smooth, buff–pale orange (5/27 g)

FC3 Sandy (43/167 g)

FC4 Porous, smooth, fine, buff (27/32 g)

Several contexts contained fragments which display more than an irregular shape (Table Mf5). The range of forms consists of pieces with a single smoothed surface, thick pieces with a single smoothed surface, and those with evidence for wattle-and-daub structure. The latter occurs in only one context, in ditch 589. Smoothed pieces were recovered from post-hole 504 of round-house 491, ditches 202 and 919, and post-holes 816 and 858 of four-post structure 877. This suggests that structures, whether hearths or buildings requiring clay plastering or daubing, may have occurred in these areas, if the fragments were not derived from objects such as loom-weights. In addition, one smooth-sided piece of fired clay, which had been subjected to a high temperature and partially fused, was found in post-hole 814, north-east of round-house 491 (adjoining post-hole 772, Fig. 8); this shows one smoothed curved surface and the remains of what appears to be a perforation. The possi-bility that it was used in metalworking was considered, but it seems more likely to be part of a spindle whorl that has been fortuitously subjected to a fairly high temperature.

None of the fired clay fabrics is similar to the pre-historic pottery fabrics, all of which are tempered with flint or grog. There is no certain evidence to suggest that any of the pieces recovered were utilised to make objects such as spindle whorls or loomweights similar to those from Aldermaston Wharf (Bradley *et al.* 1980, 243–4), although there are three pieces present in the collection which have been tentatively identified as such (Table Mf5). The fabrics of the Aldermaston examples were not described in that report and cannot, therefore, be direct-ly compared with the Bray material. The absence of any tempering agent in the fabric of several thick pieces of fired clay with single smoothed surfaces at Bray suggests that some of these pieces may be the remains of loomweights (cf. Lowther 1939, 190–2, fig. 82), as this is typical of the fabric of loomweights, but there is no other indication that such objects are present.

Worked Bone Object, by Elaine L. Morris

A single worked bone object (Fig. 23) was found in ditch 280, part of the triple ditch. It is a large awl or pointed gouge made from a cattle-sized long-bone which was split longitudinally. The implement was well-polished at the use end and the tip had been broken in antiquity. During excavation, the artefact was damaged in several places.

Awls and gouges have been recovered from Middle Bronze Age sites such as Brean Down, Somerset (Foster 1990, 162, figs 113, 47–8, 50–1, 54 and 114, 58), Pound-bury (Greep 1987, fig. 80, 1–2), Middle Farm (Stacey and Walker in prep.), Down Farm (Legge 1991, 90–2) and South Lodge (Pitt Rivers 1898, plates 234, 237–8) in Dorset, and Itford Hill (Burstow and Holleyman 1957, fig. 29, 1–3) and Black Patch (Drewett 1982, fig. 34, 12), Sussex.

Human Bone, by Jacqueline I. McKinley

Fragments of cremated bone were noted (archive) but only a single cremation burial was recovered, from feature 375, 9 m north of Middle Bronze Age ditch 341. The feature was a small, shallow cut, containing the human bone in a very dark fill; there were no accom-panying grave-goods.

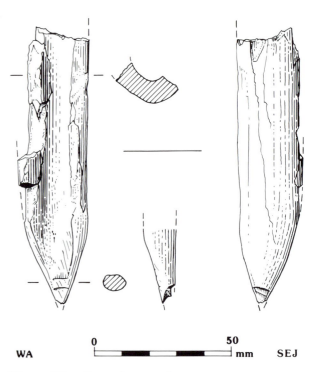

WA   0   50   mm   SEJ

Figure 23   Bray: bone awl

Cremation from feature 375

The cremated bone was badly plough-damaged. Small fragments of burnt bone recovered from 31 environ-mental samples were also examined.

The cremated bone was passed through three sieves, 10 mm, 5 mm, and 2 mm mesh size, to obtain percentage fragmentation by weight. The maximum fragment size for skull and long-bone was noted. Identifiable bone was separated out for further analysis in four skeletal categories of skull, axial, upper, and lower limb. Any variation in colour from the usual buff/white was re-corded.

Age was assessed from the degree of epiphyseal fusion (McMinn and Hutchings 1985); the general de-gree of cranial suture fusion. Details of identification may be found in the archive. Measurements were taken according to Gejvall (1981).

The total bone weight recovered was 103.6 g, of which 24.5% was identifiable. Maximum fragment sizes were skull, 20 mm and long-bone, 54 mm. The cremation was that of an adult.

The extreme white colouration of the bone indicates that it was well oxidised. The high level of disturbance to this cremation, resulting in the loss of an unknown quantity of bone, precludes any further discussion, other than that the presence of a single adult must be con-sidered a minimum.

Faunal Remains, by Janet Egerton and Clive Gamble

A total of 478 bone fragments came from the evaluation and excavation. Of these only 115 (24%) were identi-fiable. Table 6 gives species by percentage.

Given the very small sample size, it is difficult to know how valid is the apparent dominance of cattle

Table 6 Bray: animal bone

	No. of fragments	%
Cattle	65	56.5
Sheep/goat	43	37.4
Pig	7	6.1

(Table 6). On one hand its dominance fits with other local Bronze Age sites such as Anslows Cottages, Burghfield (Coy 1992) where cattle accounted for 15.6% and sheep/goat 8%; and Runnymede Bridge (Done 1980) with cattle 57% and sheep/goat 27%. On the other hand, examination of the anatomical parts makes the differential preservation of cattle long-bones a factor which may be skewing the results (Table Mf6). No horse, dog, or wild animals were represented.

All the material was highly fragmented, including many modern breaks and, with the exception of context 467, was heavily weathered allowing minimal recognition of butchery. There were a few burnt fragments.

The majority of the sample formed a low density scatter throughout the features on the site. The exception was context 467 which contained 75 fragments identified as 21 cattle, 9 ovicaprid, 1 pig, and 44 indeterminate. The identified specimens were dominated by head elements and included a young ovicaprid (1 year old) and a juvenile cow.

The assemblage can be interpreted as general domestic waste with no differential disposal of material from the different stages of butchery and food consumption. Young animals are present and while there are no neonates, the sample is too small to determine whether this was due to culling or natural deaths. Unlike the Bronze Age sites referred to above, it is not certain that cattle dominated, and the absence of other animals (ie, horse, dog, wild animals) would also seem to be atypical.

Plant Remains, by A.J. Clapham

Thirty-four samples were analysed for charred plant macro-remains (excluding charcoal): one sample from the earlier Neolithic phase (Phase 2), 27 of Middle Bronze Age date (Phase 4) and six of Late Iron Age/Romano-British date (Phase 5).

The samples were processed following standard Wessex Archaeology flotation procedures. Charred plant macro-remains were identified using a Wild M5 stereo-microscope, and critical identifications were carried out using a modern reference collection based at the Pitt-Rivers Room, in the Department of Archaeology, University of Cambridge. Nomenclature follows that of Stace (1991). The results are presented in Tables 7–12 and discussed below.

Earlier Neolithic
A single sample was analysed from type A hollow 398, which contained only fragments of unidentifiable cereal remains. This provides evidence of Neolithic cereal cultivation, presumably locally, but due to the paucity of preserved remains little further can be added.

Middle Bronze Age
Samples from nine post-holes of round-house 491 were analysed (Table 8). A reasonable amount of charred plant remains were identified, the most common, apart from indeterminate cereal grains and fragments, being that of flax (*Linum usitatissimum*), found in seven samples. Both emmer and spelt wheat (*Triticum dicoccum, T. spelta*) were represented: one grain of emmer wheat in post-hole 504, to the rear of the round-house, and five glume bases of emmer in the post-holes of the porch and entrance. No grains of spelt wheat were identified, although three samples from post-holes contained a total of three glume bases. Other post-holes included cereal grains of hulled barley (*Hordeum vulgare*) (3), indeterminate grains (2), barley (1), and rye (*Secale cereale*) (1). It was not possible to determine from the rachis fragment, nor from the hulled grain, whether the barley represented the six or two row variety.

Flax, the largest category recovered, was represented by 107 seeds and 465 fragments. From the south side of the entrance flax was found in three post-holes (551, 554, and 556), and from a further three on the north side of the entrance (614, 615, and 611). At the back of the round-house one post-hole (494) also contained flax. It is clear, therefore, that the flax seeds are concentrated around the entrance of the round-house.

Weed seeds were found in most of the samples and although a reasonable number of taxa were identified (14) there was not a large number of any taxon (Table 9). Single finds of buttercup (*Ranunculus acris / repens / bulbosus*), sheeps's sorrel (*Rumex acetosella*), violet (*Viola* sp.), scentless mayweed (*Tripleurospermum inodorum*), purging flax (*Linum catharticum*), and a possible example of a mineralised apple pip (*Malus sylvestris*) were recorded from the samples. Fat hen (*Chenopodium album*), black bindweed (*Fallopia convolvulus*), dogwood (*Cornus sanguinea*), hazel (*Corylus avellana*), cleavers (*Galium aparine*), large and small grasses, and indeterminate legume cotyledons were found in greater quantities but not large enough for a satisfactorily comprehensive interpretation.

It can be suggested that most of the weeds found in these samples are indicative of a ruderal or segetal habitat (ie, any disturbed ground including cultivated fields). The presence of scentless mayweed, cleavers, black bindweed, and fat hen may suggest that there was arable land in the vicinity. The presence of both hazel and dogwood suggest that woodland or scrubby areas may also have been present in the environs.

The plant remains from the hearth (492) within the round-house, to the east of the entrance, consisted mainly of charcoal and only a single emmer glume base was identified. It might be expected of a hearth that accidents while cooking would lead to carbonised remains being preserved within it, but this does not seem to be the case here.

Layer 667 has been interpreted as being an occupation layer associated with the round-house (491). Only one barley grain and 14 fragments of unidentifiable cereal grain were recovered.

Table 7 Bray: charred cereal remains from Middle Bronze Age and Late Iron Age/Romano-British contexts

	MBA	LIA/RB
Emmer wheat		
Triticum cf *dicoccum* grain	7	–
T. dicoccum spikelet fork	9	–
T. dicoccum glume base	15	1
T. dicoccum rachis fragment	2	1
Spelt wheat		
T. cf *spelta* grain	5	–
T. spelta spikelet fork	2	–
T. spelta glume base	5	28
Club wheat		
T. aestivo-compactum grain	–	1
Indeterminate wheat		
Triticum indet. grain	29	1
Triticum indet. spikelet fork	55	6
Triticum indet. glume base	161	99
Barley		
Hordeum vulgare hulled grain	15	2
Hordeum indet. grain	55	–
Hordeum rachis fragments	5	8
Wheat/barley		
Triticum/Hordeum sp. grain	86	–
Rye		
Secale cereale grain	7	–
Flax		
Linum usitatissimum	107 + 465f	–
Miscellaneous cereal remains		
Indet. rachis fragments	11	3
Embryo and sprouts, indet.	11	6
Cerealia indet.	4878f	111
Avena sp.	2	–
Avena awn fragment	1	1
Culm node	8	–

f = fragments

Table 8 Bray: charred wild plants from Middle Bronze Age and Late Iron Age/Romano-British contexts

	MBA	LIA/RB
Ranunculus acris/repens/ bulbosus	1	–
Corylus avellana	898f	–
Chenopodium album	20+189f	–
Atriplex sp.	5f	–
Chenopodiacae indet.	6+1f	1f
Stellaria media	1	–
Persicaria cf *laxiflora*	1	–
Polygonum aviculare	5+3f	–
Fallopia convolvulus	12+33f	–
Rumex acetosella	2	–
Rumex sp.	3	2
Polygonaceae indet.	1	–
Viola cf *odorata*	2	–
Rorippa sylvestris	1	–
Brassica sp.	1	–
Brassicaceae indet.	1	–
Aphanes arvensis	1	–
Prunus sp. cf *instititia*	7f	–
Prunus thorn	1	–
Mineralised *Malus sylvestris*	1	–
Vicia hirsuta	2	–
Vicia indet.	104	1f
Medicago sp.	4+1f	–
Trifolium sp	1	–
Legume cotyledon.	59+1f	–
Legume hilum	1	–
Legume/*Brassica* embryo	1	–
Cornus sanguinea	2f	–
Linum catharticum	1	–
Solanum cf *nigrum*	1	–
Plantago lanceolata	4	–
Galium aparine	5+6f	–
Valerianella dentata	1	–
Tripleurospermum inodorum	2	1f
Compositae sypsela	1	–
Compositae indet.	1f	1
cf *Lolium* sp.	–	3
Small Poaceae	16+1f	–
Large Poaceae	12+1f	6f
Grass stem	4+1f	–
Chara oogonia	2	–
Flower base	1	–
Stem	6	–
Shoots	–	5
Root	8	–
Parenchymatous tissue	2f	–
Moss stem	–	1
Other	20	3

One of the post-holes (818) of the four–post structure 877, 10 m north-east of the round-house, was analysed for plant remains and was found to contain relatively little evidence of cereals (1 wheat glume base, 2 rye grains, 1 wheat embryo, and 24 fragments of indeterminate cereal grain), and a fragment of hazel. From the arrangement of the post-holes this structure has been interpreted as a granary or storage building.

The sample taken from the eastern terminal of ditch 589 (single fill of cut 468) contained a considerable amount of charcoal as well as charred plant remains. Emmer was represented by a number of items: a single tail grain, 7 spikelet forks, 9 glume bases, and 2 rachis fragments. Two spelt glume bases were also present. Other wheat finds were identifiable only to genus: these include grains, spikelet forks, and a large number of glume bases (Table 10). Hulled barley, oats, and rye grains were found and barley was associated with rachis fragments and the oats with an awn fragment. Other miscellaneous cereal remains such as embryos, sprouts, and culm nodes were noted, including 397 fragments of indeterminate cereal grains. Weed seeds include tasteless water pepper (*Persicaria* cf. *laxiflora*), black bindweed, sheep's sorrel, creeping yellow-cress (*Rorippa sylvestris*), *Brassica* sp., a *Prunus* sp. thorn, indeterminate legume, medick (*Medicago* sp.), and cleavers. Fat hen, possible bullace (*Prunus domestica* spp. *insititia*), ribwort plantain (*Plantago lanceolata*), and large and small Poaceae were found in larger amounts (Table 11). This sample could well represent the remains of crop processing, where the crop has been cleaned as far as glume and weed seed removal and then, for some reason after burning, the waste fraction had been deposited in the ditch (589). Most of the weed species found in the sample can be found as arable weeds; rye could also have been a weed of the main crop. Although there is a mixture of crop types in the sample, the crop is most likely to have been emmer wheat, with the other potential crop species being present as contaminants.

The sample from feature 326, outside the southern corner of enclosure 925, contained a large amount of small pieces of charcoal as well as wheat (a grain, a spikelet fork, and glume bases), barley (2 grains), and a large number (86) of indeterminate cereal grain fragments. The weed seeds consisted of a single find of black bindweed and one of black nightshade (*Solanum nigrum*).

Cremation 375, to the north of field boundary ditch 341, produced a considerable amount of charcoal, some of which was slaggy in appearance, suggesting that it had been heated to a high temperature. Apart from the charcoal only one piece of indeterminate parenchymatous tissue was present.

Two samples were taken from the single fill of recut 244 of the east–west ditch 202. Both samples contained very few plant remains (Tables 10 and 11) although there was rye in cut 218. The only difference between the two samples was the presence of undifferentiated wheat (spikelet fork and glume base) from cut 232.

The plant remains from the uppermost fill of ditch 280 (cut 600), of the triple ditch system, consisted of crop remains such as emmer (2 grains and a spikelet fork), spelt (2 grains), indeterminate wheat (8 grains as well as a spikelet fork and glume bases), and barley (8 hulled, 12 indeterminate, and a rachis fragment). The rachis fragment could not help determine whether the barley was two or six row. Cereal remains that were not possible to identify to species were present in quantities. Weed seeds include fat hen, knotgrass (*Polygonum aviculare*), black bindweed, docks (*Rumex* sp.), possible sweet violet (*Viola odorata*), parsley-piert (*Aphanes arvensis*), vetch (*Vicia* sp.), medick, cornsalad (*Valerianella dentata*), a scentless mayweed, and small and large Poaceae. All of these species were found in low concentrations except for the vetch (98) and indeterminate legume cotyledons (39) which are most likely to be of the vetch type. Further identification of the vetch was not possible due to the lack of a hilum on any of the intact seeds. All of the species of weed found in this sample are capable of growing in an arable situation. The presence of parsley-piert may indicate that the crop

was sown in winter and grown on sandy soil, as this weed has a tendency to germinate at cold temperatures. Cornsalad is also a good indicator of arable fields, but it must be stressed that because only a small number of finds are involved (in most cases, only single examples) it is only possible to surmise that arable was present in this case. The presence of relatively large quantities of the vetch may also be taken as indicative of an arable origin, and it is also likely that this sample represents some stage of crop processing, probably a stage after threshing and winnowing but before final sieving.

Small quantities of remains were found in six other features sampled. These are summarised in Tables 10–12. A large number of hazel nutshell fragments was found in hollows 630 and 852 and in pit 569 (Tables 9 and 11) which may be taken as an indication that these hollows could be collapsed storage pits. Another piece of evidence that may lend support to this interpretation is from feature 413, situated in the apparently blank area between enclosure 927 and ditch 915. This sample contained over 1000 fragments of indeterminate cereal grain, along with three emmer wheat grains, and a spikelet fork. Spelt wheat was also recorded (3 grains and 2 spikelet forks). A number of grains, spikelet forks, glume bases, and rachis fragments of indeterminate wheat species were also present. Some of the grains (84) were so badly distorted that it was not possible to determine whether they were wheat or barley. Weed seeds include fat hen, orache (*Atriplex* sp.), knotgrass, black bindweed, hairy tare (*Vicia hirsuta*), and cleavers. These weeds can be found in most disturbed habitats and are most likely to represent plants growing with the crop. The interpretation that can be suggested for this sample is one of storage of a semi-cleaned crop.

Late Iron Age/Romano-British

Pit 283, from which four of the eight silty loam deposits were sampled and analysed, was probably a storage pit rather than a well. The presence of glume bases and associated weed seeds may suggest the presence of the final stages of grain cleaning, which may have been stored, perhaps as a source of tinder. Another possibility is that the remains represent the remainder of the stored crop which has been charred to sterilise the pit, resulting in the presence of a burnt layer at the bottom.

Type A hollow 309, 3 m east of pit 283, produced evidence for emmer (a glume base and rachis fragment) and spelt wheat (glume bases), and oats (an awn). Indeterminate wheat finds include a single grain, glume bases (48, nine of which were upper portions) and rachis fragments. Fragments (61) of unidentifiable cereal grain were also found. Weed seeds were generally absent from the sample and only a single find of a fragment of fat hen and large grass caryopsis fragments were identified. From the plant remains it can be suggested that this hollow is a collapsed storage pit.

Hearth 537 produced grains of compact wheat (*Triticum aestivo-compactum* s.l.) and indeterminate cereal.

Discussion

The charred plant remains from Bray show that crops were grown in the vicinity of the site during the Bronze Age. Emmer and spelt wheat as well as barley were

Table 9 Bray: samples associated with round-house 491 and four-post structure 877

	6058	6059	6076	6077	6064	6066	6067	6071	6074	6055	6093	6106
Sample no.												
Context no.	493	503	612	613	550	552	553	555	610	480	730	871
Context type	Post-hole	Post-hole	Post-hole	Post-hole	Post-hole	Post-hole	Post-hole	Post-hole	Post-hole	Hearth	Layer	PH of four-post structure
Feature no.	494	504	615	614	551	558	554	556	611	492	667	818
Sample volume (litres)	9	14	15	3	6	5	8.5	7	14	7	15	10
Flot volume (ml)	11	24	50	8	20	10	10.5	20	30	40	7	11
Wheat												
Triticum cf dicoccum grain	–	1	–	–	–	–	–	–	–	–	–	–
T.dicoccum glume base	–	–	1	–	–	–	1	1	3	1	–	–
T. spelta glume base	1	1	–	–	–	–	1	–	–	–	–	–
Triticum indet. grain	1	2	2	–	–	–	–	–	1	–	–	–
Triticum indet. spikelet fork	–	–	1	–	2	–	–	–	–	–	–	–
Triticum indet. glume base	4	3	13	1	2	1	5	–	3	–	–	1
Barley												
Hordeum vulgare hulled grain	1	–	–	–	2	–	–	–	–	–	–	–
Hordeum indet. grain	–	–	–	–	–	–	2	–	–	–	1	1
Hordeum rachis fragments	1	–	–	–	–	–	–	–	–	–	–	–
Wheat/barley												
Triticum/Hordeum sp. grain	1	1	–	–	–	–	–	–	–	–	–	–
Rye												
Secale cereale grain	–	1	–	–	–	–	–	–	–	–	–	2
Flax												
Linum usitatissimum	1	–	40+157f	3+20f	28+119f	–	26+139f	1+8f	1+21f	–	–	–
Misc. cereal remains												
Cerealia indet.	58f	27f	67f	48f	31f	17f	36f	17f	29f	–	14f	24f
Embryo indet.	–	–	–	–	–	–	–	–	–	–	–	1
Culm node	–	–	–	–	–	–	1f	–	–	–	–	–
Wild plants												
Ranunculus a/r/b	–	–	–	–	–	–	1	–	–	–	–	–
Corylus avellana	1f	–	–	–	1f	–	–	–	–	–	–	1f

Context	493	503	612	613	550	552	553	555	610	480	730	871
Chenopodium album	2+4f	4f	5+2f	–	–	–	1f	1f	–	–	–	–
Chenopodiacae indet.	–	–	1f	–	–	–	6	–	–	–	–	–
Fallopia convolvulus	–	–	4f	–	–	–	2+1f	–	–	–	–	–
Rumex acetosella	–	–	–	–	–	–	–	–	1	–	–	–
Polygonaceae indet.	–	–	–	–	1	–	–	–	–	–	–	–
Viola cf *odorata*	–	–	–	–	–	1	–	–	–	–	–	–
Malus sylvestris mineralised	–	–	–	–	–	–	–	–	1	–	–	–
Legume cotyledon	–	1f	1	–	–	–	–	–	1	–	–	–
Legume/Brassica embryo	–	–	–	–	–	–	1	–	–	–	–	–
Cornus sanguinea	–	–	–	–	–	–	1f	–	1f	–	–	–
Linum catharticum	–	–	–	–	–	–	–	–	1	–	–	–
Plantago lanceolata	–	–	–	–	–	–	–	–	–	–	–	–
Galium aparine	2f	1f	1f	–	1	–	–	1	–	–	–	–
Tripleurospermum inodorum	–	–	1	–	–	–	–	–	–	–	–	–
Compositae cypsela	1	–	–	–	–	–	–	–	–	–	–	–
Compositae indet.	–	1f	–	–	–	–	–	–	–	–	–	–
Small Poaceae	1	1	1f	–	1	–	1	–	–	–	–	–
Large Poaceae	–	1f	1	–	–	–	–	–	–	–	–	–
Stem	–	–	2	–	–	–	–	–	–	–	–	–
Unidentified	1	–	2	–	2	–	1	–	1	–	–	–

f = fragment

40

Table 10 Bray: charred cultivated plant remains from the Middle Bronze Age ditches and hollows

	6006	6019	6054	6007	6010	6045	6117	6075	6100	6002	6116
Sample no.	6006	6019	6054	6007	6010	6045	6117	6075	6100	6002	6116
Context no.	217	281	467	211	231	376	414	631	851	200	393
Context type	Ditch	Ditch	Ditch	Ditch	Ditch	Hollow	Hollow	Hollow	Hollow	Hollow	Hollow
Cut no.	218	600	468	210	232	398	413	630	852	199	391
Feature	244	280	589	919	244						
Sample volume (litres)	10	10	10	10	10	10	10	10	10	10	4
Flot volume (ml)	10	20	74	8	231	13	35	10	24	9	4.5
Emmer wheat											
Triticum cf dicoccum grain	–	2	–	–	–	–	2	–	1	–	–
T. cf dicoccum tail grain	–	–	1	–	–	–	1	–	–	–	–
T. dicoccum spikelet fork	–	1	7	–	–	–	1	–	–	–	–
T. dicoccum glume base	–	–	9	–	–	–	–	–	2	–	–
T. dicoccum rachis fragment	–	–	1	–	–	–	–	–	–	–	–
T. dicoccum basal rachis fragment	–	–	1	–	–	–	–	–	–	–	–
Spelt wheat											
T. cf spelta grain	–	2	–	–	–	–	3	–	–	–	–
T. spelta spikelet fork	–	–	–	–	–	–	2	–	–	–	–
T. spelta glume base	–	–	2	–	–	–	–	–	–	–	–
Indeterminate wheat											
Triticum indet. grain	–	8	3	1	–	–	7	–	–	–	1
Triticum indet. spikelet fork	–	1	42	–	1	–	6	–	–	–	–
Triticum indet. glume base	–	9	84	–	1	–	11	–	–	–	–
Barley											
Hordeum vulgare hulled grain	–	5+3f	1	2	–	–	–	–	–	–	–
H. vulgare tail grain	–	–	1	–	–	–	–	–	–	–	–
Hordeum indet. grain	1	18+2f	18	–	1	–	8+2f	–	–	–	–
Hordeum rachis fragments	–	1	3	–	–	–	–	–	–	–	–
Wheat/barley											
Triticum / Hordeum sp. grain	–	–	–	–	–	–	84	–	–	–	–

Context	217	281	467	211	231	376	414	631	851	200	393
Rye											
Secale cereale grain	1	–	3	–	–	–	–	–	–	–	–
Miscellaneous cereal remains											
Indeterminate rachis fragments	–	–	–	–	–	–	11	–	–	–	–
Indeterminate embryo	–	1	4	–	–	–	3	–	–	–	–
Sprout	–	1	1	–	–	–	–	–	–	–	–
Cerealia indet.	12f	3+147f	397f	31f	36f	11f	1000+f	7f	2+84f	–	5f
Avena sp.	–	–	2	–	–	–	–	–	–	–	–
Avena awn fragment	–	–	1	–	–	–	–	–	–	–	–
Culm node	–	–	1	–	–	–	4	–	–	–	–

f = fragment

Table 11 Bray: charred wild plant remains from the Middle Bronze Age ditches and hollows

Sample no.	6006	6019	6054	6007	6010	6045	6117	6075	6100	6002	6116
Context no.	217	281	467	211	231	376	414	631	851	200	393
Context type	Ditch	Ditch	Ditch	Ditch	Ditch	Hollow	Hollow	Hollow	Hollow	Hollow	Hollow
Cut no.	218	600	468	210	232	398	413	630	852	199	391
Feature	244	280	589	919	244	–	–	–	–	–	–
Sample volume (litres)	10	10	10	10	10	10	10	10	10	10	4
Flot volume (ml)	10	20	74	8	231	13	35	10	24	9	4.5
Corylus avellana	–	–	–	–	2f	–	5f	345f	138f	–	–
Chenopodium album	–	1	3+19f	–	–	–	8+113f	–	–	–	–
Atriplex sp.	–	–	–	–	–	–	5f	–	–	–	–
Stellaria media	–	–	–	1	1	–	–	–	–	–	–
Persicaria cf laxiflora	–	–	1	–	–	–	–	–	–	–	–
Polygonum aviculare	–	3	–	–	–	–	2+3f	–	–	–	–
Fallopia convolvulus	–	3+6f	1f	–	–	–	6+24f	–	–	–	–
Rumex acetosella	–	–	1	–	–	–	–	–	–	–	–

42

Context no.	217	281	467	211	231	376	414	631	851	200	393
Rumex sp.	–	3	–	–	–	–	–	–	–	–	–
Viola cf *odorata*	–	1	–	–	–	–	–	–	–	–	–
Rorippa sylvestris	–	–	1	–	–	–	–	–	–	–	–
Brassica sp.	–	–	1	–	–	–	–	–	–	–	–
Aphanes arvensis	–	1	–	–	–	–	–	–	–	–	–
Prunus domestica cf *instititia*	–	–	7f	–	–	–	–	–	–	–	–
Prunus thorn	–	–	1	–	–	–	–	–	–	–	–
Vicia hirsuta	–	–	–	–	–	–	2	–	–	–	–
Vicia indet.	–	98	–	–	–	–	6	–	–	–	–
Medicago sp.	–	3	1+1f	–	–	–	–	–	–	–	–
Trifolium sp.	–	1	–	–	–	–	–	–	–	–	–
Legume cotyledon	–	39	1	1f	–	–	17	–	–	–	–
Legume hilum	–	–	1	–	–	–	–	–	–	–	–
Plantago lanceolata	–	–	4	–	–	–	–	–	–	–	–
Galium aparine	–	1+2f	1	–	–	–	1	–	–	–	–
Valerianella dentata	–	1	–	–	–	–	–	–	–	–	–
Tripleurospermum inodorum	–	1	–	–	–	–	–	–	–	–	–
Small Poaceae	–	7	6	–	–	–	–	–	–	–	–
Large Poaceae	–	2	8	–	–	–	–	–	–	–	–
Grass stem	–	3	1	–	–	–	–	–	–	–	–
Chara oogonia	–	2	–	–	–	–	–	–	–	–	–
Stem	–	–	1	–	1	–	1	1	–	–	–
Root	–	7	1	–	–	–	–	–	–	–	–
Parenchymatous tissue	–	–	1f	–	–	–	–	–	–	–	–
Indeterminate	–	10	2	–	–	1	–	–	–	–	–

grown, as evidenced by the presence of cereal grains and of chaff, such as spikelet forks, glumes, and rachis fragments. Because of the relatively small number of cereal grains present it is not possible to say which of the three crops was the dominant cultivated cereal, or whether there was any change in preference for any crop through time.

The greatest amount of any economic plant found on this site was that of flax, the majority of which was found in the post-holes around the entrance of round-house 491. It is not possible to determine whether the crop was grown for fibre or for seed (the seed is edible and produces a useful oil when the seeds are crushed). As the site is so close to the river it is possible that the flax was grown for its fibre, as water is desirable for the processing of the flax stems to release the fibre (retting). It is more likely, however, that the crop was grown for both purposes. As the finds are from post-holes of the round-house it could be suggested that the seeds were either being stored as a source of food and oil or as seed for the next year's crop.

Other food sources that were found on site include hazelnuts. These were discovered in the hollows, which could have been collapsed storage pits. Although use of hazelnuts is well-attested during the Neolithic, two of the features (630 and 852) contain Middle Bronze Age pottery, and the remaining feature (569) lies within one of the main concentrations of Middle Bronze Age finds. The presence of such large quantities of hazel nutshell fragments indicates that the occupants of the site were actively involved in gathering wild food resources and therefore exploiting the habitats surrounding the site. Hazel can be found growing at woodland edges or in scrub, and can be coppiced and the wood used; in this context it can be assumed that the nuts were collected from local scrub. Other indicators of woodland edge, scrub, or hedge are found in the presence of fragments of fruitstones of dogwood and possible bullace stones. Bullace is edible, and therefore could have been gathered as a wild food, although the fragments were found in a ditch sample (from ditch 598), along with an unidentified *Prunus* sp. thorn and a large amount of charcoal. These may be more suggestive of a hedge boundary above a ditch than of woodland, but, without identification of the charcoal, it is not possible to say which is correct.

The weed seeds found in general are indicative of disturbed habitats; this category includes all segetals and ruderals. It can be seen from Table 8 that some of the weeds are classic arable weeds, for example, black bindweed, knotgrass, fat hen, scentless mayweed, black nightshade, cleavers, parsley-piert, cornsalad, and hairy tare. In most of the samples these weeds and others are associated with crop remains such as glume bases, spikelet forks, and, in some cases, cereal grain. Although the numbers of weed seeds and cereal remains were low, this suggests that the crops were grown locally and were processed on the site.

The single find of purging flax may suggest that base-rich (calcareous/non acidic) grassland was present in the area but, although it is characteristic of this habitat, it is in no way confined to the base-rich soils and can be found in sandy habitats (Clapham *et al.* 1989).

Other evidence for grassland in the surrounding vicinity is also very sparse, with only possible ryegrass being identified, along with buttercup, ribwort plantain, and large and small undifferentiated grasses, to indicate the presence of this habitat. These species, of course, can also be found in disturbed habitats.

The two finds of sweet violet from the Middle Bronze Age may indicate the presence of base-rich soils. The modern day habitats in which this species is usually present are semi-enclosed areas such as scrub and hedgebanks; it can also be found in woodlands.

The only evidence of wetland in the immediate area of the site are finds of tasteless water-pepper and stonewort; these were found in ditch samples, which suggests that they may have contained water.

Emmer and spelt wheat can be sown either in winter or autumn. If sown in autumn the crop has a longer growing season, increasing the yield. Harvesting would be earlier and in more reliable weather, reducing the chance of spoilage in the ear. Sprouting or rotting grain in the ear would occur with spring sown cereals and later harvesting in deteriorating weather. The weed seeds cannot help clarify the situation as most of those found at Bray can germinate in either spring or winter.

Flax, on the other hand, is a spring sown crop. It requires a slightly acid soil although the seed varieties are more adaptable. Well drained loams, especially silt loams, clay loams, and silty clays are best, sandy soils are generally avoided. It is a very exhausting crop requiring at least seven years between sowings on the same land and it should never be sown after a fallow period as the soil may contain many pests of flax. It is usually sown after a leguminous crop such as field beans.

Flax has weak roots which tend to grow close to the surface and therefore careful preparation of the ground is required. The soil needs to be tilled to a depth of at least 15 cm to allow full root development. Today the ground is prepared in the winter to allow frost action to break up the soil. The seed is usually sown in the first week of April. Weeding is a necessity as it is unable to compete successfully. This is of course labour intensive and backbreaking work.

Harvesting of flax varies, depending on whether it is for fibre or seed. In modern practice, fibre crops are harvested when the stem changes from green to yellow (about a month after the first flowers appear). The crop is harvested by pulling. After the weeds and soil from the roots have been removed, the stems are left to dry for one or two days before being gathered and made into stooks to dry completely; this can take up to 14 days. After drying the stems are rippled to remove the capsules, although archaeological evidence suggests that this was not always the case (Pals and Dierendonck 1988). One traditional way of removing the seed capsules is to lay the straw on a smooth floor and beat them with a wooden mallet. The extraction of the fibres by retting is the next stage. Harvesting of flax grown for seed (linseed) takes place later than that of fibre flax, although it is still harvested by uprooting, and capsule removal is by combing (rippling).

Table 12 Bray: charred plant remains from other Middle Bronze Age contexts

Sample No.	6035	6044	6069	6085	6096
Context No.	327	374	570	540	785
Context description	shallow circular feature	cremation burial	pit	hearth	post-hole
Feature No.	326	375	569	539	820
Sample volume (litres)	15	15	10	11	1
Flot volume (ml)	3	30	30	10	1
Indeterminate wheat					
Triticum indet. grain	1f	–	–	–	–
Triticum indet. spikelt fork	1	–	–	–	–
Triticum indet. glume base	3	–	1	–	–
Barley					
Hordeum indet. grain	2f	–	–	–	1
Flax					
Linum usitatissimum	–	–	–	1	–
Miscellaneous cereal remains					
Cerealia indet.	86f	–	25f	1f	–
Culm node	–	–	1	–	–
Wild plants					
Corylus avellana	–	–	405f	–	–
Chenopodium album	–	–	1+45f	–	–
Fallopia convolvulus	1+1f	–	–	–	–
Brassicaceae indet.	–	–	1	–	–
Solanum cf *nigrum*	1	–	–	–	–
Grass stem	1f	–	–	–	–
Flower base	–	–	1	–	–
Parenchymatous tissue	–	1f	–	–	–

Comparison with other sites in the area

Because of the paucity of evidence for settlement in the Middle Bronze Age in the Middle Thames Valley there is virtually no contemporaneous material with which to compare the Bray assemblage. There are, however, a number of sites with plant remains dating to the Late Bronze Age, such as Aldermaston and Knight's Farm, Burghfield, and Bray shows both differences from and similarities to these.

At Aldermaston Wharf, Arthur (in Bradley *et al.* 1980) identified charred plant remains from 25 pits, 17 of which contained grain. Unlike Bray, no rachis internodes or glume bases were identified, suggesting that crop processing did not take place there. This may well have been the case, but this interpretation could be due to biased sampling, as samples were taken only from the pits.

The wheat at Aldermaston consisted entirely of emmer; no spelt was identified. Barley was also found, the percentage of wheat and barley being 13% and 87% respectively. The barley was of both naked and hulled types, with 76% of the former and 24% of the latter variety. Only hulled barley was found at Bray along with both spelt and emmer wheat. Other economic plants identified at Aldermaston include oats and flax, although flax was not found in such quantities as at Bray.

Weed species found at Aldermaston were of a similar nature to those found at Bray, apart from finds of *Veronica hederifolia* (ivy leaved speedwell) and *Jasione montana* (sheep's bit). The presence of sheep's bit is slightly unusual but, as it prefers acid soils, is perhaps more evidence for the degradation of the soils surrounding the site, which is shown by the presence of *Calluna* (heather) in pollen form at the site (Ware 1980). There is no evidence for soil degradation at Bray.

Knight's Farm is also on the Kennet gravels and because of its low-lying position, waterlogged samples were used for the plant macrofossil analyses. Samples were taken from features that were interpreted as pond fills. The plant remains from these fills (Robinson 1980) do not imply the presence of cultivated fields in the vicinity of the ponds, although pollen analysis (Clark 1980) does suggest that pasture may have been present in the area. There is little evidence for the exploitation of this type of habitat at Bray apart from the finds of unidentifiable grass remains, which could also have been present in association with the crop remains.

The Late Bronze Age site at Runnymede lies *c.* 13 km from Bray (Needham 1991). The plant remains from this site were extracted from waterlogged contexts on the Thames waterfront. Charred plant remains occurred with the majority of waterlogged ones (Greig 1991).

Greig identified representatives of spring germinating annuals and those often found on light sandy soil. Possible cornfield weeds from the Late Bronze Age include poppy, parsley-piert, and black bindweed, all as waterlogged remains. Charred remains of cornfield weeds included hairy tare, black bindweed, cleavers, and scentless mayweed. All these species were found at Bray. Seven grains of rye and no rachis internodes were identified from Bray; this suggests that the plant was present as a cornfield weed and not as a crop. This conclusion is supported by Greig's interpretation of the rye remains at Runnymede. It must be stressed that, although the rye is only present as a weed, it is still an early record in Britain. The oats, both at Bray and Runnymede, can be interpreted as cornfield weeds.

Spelt and emmer were also identified at Runnymede in a ratio of c. 3:1. The small quantities of finds of each species of wheat found at Bray does not allow the determination of which was dominant. As at Bray, barley was found in small quantities at Runnymede, as were waterlogged flax seeds and capsule fragments. At Bray only charred seeds were identified. The presence of glume bases and other cereal chaff led Greig to the conclusion that cereal processing occurred on the site at Runnymede, as at Bray.

In the waterlogged Runnymede samples, representatives of different habitats were preserved such as arable, grassland, scrub, woodland, wetland, and aquatic. Possible charred representatives of these habitats were found at Bray but only in small quantities, despite the proximity of the site to the Thames. No wetland or aquatic indicators were present at Bray apart from a small number of finds of tasteless water-pepper and stonewort in the ditch samples.

Overall, the site at Bray differs from those at Aldermaston Wharf and Knight's Farm. At Aldermaston Wharf storage of ready-cleaned crop was largely in evidence and at Knights Farm pasture was probably present while at Bray there is no evidence for pasturage but for the cultivation and processing of cereals as well as the storage of two types of wheat (emmer and spelt) and the cultivation of a third economic plant; flax. These activities make Bray more similar to Runneymede than other previously mentioned sites. Soil degradation was also evidenced at Aldermaston Wharf by the presence of Calluna pollen. Evidence of soil degradation was not present at Bray.

Possible representatives of woodland/scrub/hedgebank/grassland, disturbed, and arable habitats were recognised in the Bray samples and were most likely to have been exploited by the inhabitants of the site. Wild foods such as hazel and possible bullace were additions to the Middle Bronze Age diet at Bray. The cereals grown at Bray could have been sown in the autumn or spring, but the flax was definitely sown in spring.

7 Discussion, by R.M.J. Cleal

Bray — the Settlements

The earlier phases of activity at Bray appear to have been insubstantial, and must, in view of the paucity of

earlier material in secure contexts, remain ill-defined. Only two features (867 and 398) may be attributed with any confidence to use of the site during the earlier Neolithic, and these are more than 100 m apart. The pottery found in the Middle Bronze Age ditch 917, however, would seem likely to have been derived from a feature destroyed by that ditch, which is only 25 m from feature 398. It may, therefore, indicate that there was more activity in the south-eastern part of the excavated area than is suggested by the single excavated feature.

The later Neolithic/Early Bronze Age sherds are widely scattered, and occur in ditches 202/244, 589, 915, and 917/470, as well as in features 253, 370, and 559. Hollows 253 and 370 were cut by Middle Bronze Age features, and it would be tempting to interpret these as contemporaneous with the pottery, but there are no grounds for this. Hollow 370 contains a large sherd of indisputably Bronze Age fabric, and 253 contains similar material (Table Mf2).

The Middle Bronze Age settlement does not appear, superficially at least, to be a complex one. It is obvious that at least one domestic settlement is present, based around the round-house 491 and four–post structure 877, and the remainder of the area appears to include both fields and other areas of possible settlement. Regardless of the general paucity of stratigraphic relationships between elements of this picture, it is still possible to suggest that the real situation is more complex than this. The enclosures in the excavated areas cannot be seen as a unitary phenomenon and it can be seen, in fact, that there are hints of change through time in several elements of the site.

There is evidence that there may have been some pre-enclosure activity on the site during the Middle Bronze Age, as there are a small number of features which are cut by Middle Bronze Age ditches, two of which contain Middle Bronze Age pottery. These are pit 370, which is cut by ditch 341, and hollow 253, itself cut by ditch 757. However, because it is impossible to establish a sequence for the construction of the enclosures, it is not possible to state that there were no enclosures in the area at the time these features were dug, only that ditches 757 and 341 were not in existence.

Although it is not possible to establish a sequence it is clear that there are different elements to the system of enclosures which are unlikely to have been in contemporaneous use. In particular, the layout and physical form of the ditches suggests that they are unlikely to all have been constructed at the same time. For example, the ditches running along the western edge of the excavated area (ie, 202/244, 916, 921, 922, 275, 923) could possibly be interpreted as demarcating a droveway for at least some of their length (eg, 921, 922) but this does not seem as convincing an explanation as that they represent replacement and recutting of a single boundary. There is evidence of recutting in at least 202/244, and 275 and 923 seem too close together for the space between to have functioned as a droveway.

This boundary seems to belong to a layout of enclosures which includes ditch 757, ditch 920, and possibly ditch 915, running on a north-east–south-west alignment, and ditches 589, 341, and the shorter arm of ditch 915, running north-west–south-east. These are shallow, simple features, with no certain evidence for recutting.

Two ditches which share these alignments, but which differ in character, are ditch 588 and ditch 819. The former lies approximately 0.5 m north-east of ditch 589, and is therefore unlikely to have been in use at the same time. The feature may have been recut, though the evidence is slight. Although ditch 819 shares the same alignment as this system, it is markedly different in character to the other ditches as it was a deep, broad feature, with a maximum depth of c. 0.7 m and a width of 1.8 m. It also showed a substantial recut in its upper fill. Because both ditches 588 and 819 so clearly fit into the field system described above it seems reasonable to interpret them as a secondary feature of it, with 588 replacing ditch 589, and ditch 819 replacing and completely obliterating a previous ditch on that alignment. This does not explain, however, the lack of a replacement ditch or recutting of ditch 757, which therefore leaves the north-western side of the putative late stage of the field system unbounded.

Enclosure 926 would also seem to fit within this system, yet perhaps not as a primary feature of it. Ditch 917, a substantial feature with dimensions similar to 819 (0.7 m deep and 1.7 m wide), is also recut, at least along some of its length (ditch 470). This is also true of ditch 919, with a depth of 0.8 m, a width of c. 1.6 m, and a possible recut along part of its length. It seems that this enclosure was placed to utilise part of ditch 915 as its boundary, and this strengthens the impression that this enclosure may be a secondary feature of the system.

The remaining enclosure, or part enclosure, bounded by ditch 918, does not seem to share the same alignment as the other ditches in Trench 41, and it is impossible to place this in temporal relation to them, standing as it does in isolation. It is a smaller feature than ditches 917 and 819, but, like them, may have been recut. It was sectioned in four places but produced only five sherds (weighing 7 g) of Middle Bronze Age pottery. A curious feature of 918 is that it appears to avoid pit 867, which contains nothing later than earlier Neolithic pottery, and it must be supposed that the latter was recognised as a feature when ditch 918 was dug.

Unless the bank is aligned on it, the triple ditch system similarly stands in isolation, and although it is clear that there was Middle Bronze Age activity in the vicinity, the radiocarbon date of 1260–261 BC (UB–3514; Table 1) throws doubt on whether the occupation debris and the ditches were contemporaneous.

The nature of the settlement associated with these enclosures is difficult to identify. Analysis of the excavated material, however, does allow some tentative conclusions to be drawn. The most obvious evidence of occupation recovered from the excavation is clearly the round-house 491, which lies within enclosure 927, and is close to the four–post structure 877. It is tempting to see this as a single family farmstead, lying within its own enclosure. There are indications, however, that this was not the case.

The ditches of enclosure 927 show a remarkable paucity of finds, compared with other Middle Bronze Age enclosures, as do features within the enclosure which might be thought to be associated with the occupation of the house. Finds from these were plotted, but so few features contained finds that the plots are not reproduced here. Most of the features lying between the house and ditch 757 to its north produced no finds of any kind, the majority of finds from this area coming from the features of the house and four-post structure, or from features, such as 380, which were so far north-east on the open side of the enclosure that they may not belong to it at all.

Direct comparison with other sites is difficult because of differences in presentation, but the ditch around the Middle Bronze Age enclosure at Down Farm, Cranborne Chase, for example, produced many hundreds of sherds; even with allowance made for the limited nature of the excavation at Bray and differences in ditch dimensions, this seems to be on an entirely different scale to the amount of material recovered from one section through 757 and three through 588; three of these sections produced less than 10 g of pottery each (Fig. 24). A possible explanation for this is that the ditches lack occupation material because by the time the occupation occurred they were already full.

Similarly, the carbonised plant remains also hint that the house may not have been in contemporary use with the ditches, as the flax remains which are such a feature of the round-house are absent from the ditches. Although spatial differentiation of tasks could be invoked as an explanation for this, it seems unlikely that at a site where flax was cultivated and probably processed in the vicinity no seeds at all found their way into the ditches. A simpler explanation is that they are absent from the ditches because the ditches were not open at the time.

The question of whether the ditches existed, or were full when the house was in use, or, in other words, whether the house pre- or post-dates the enclosure, appears to be resolved by the pottery. Only one sherd, P7 (Fig. 18), could be suggested as Late rather than Middle Bronze Age, and this was from a post-hole of the round-house. One alternative interpretation of the house and associated features would be that the south-western boundary of enclosure 927 was formed not of 588, which, it has been argued, might be late, but by ditch 589, which contains much more material than its neighbour. This would therefore place the round-house with the earlier stages of the field system.

There are, however, two arguments against this interpretation. Firstly, that it does not accommodate the probably late sherd in the round-house, which could post-date most of the Middle Bronze Age pottery from the site, and would, in any case, be too late to be contemporary with ditch 589, the contents of which are securely dated to the Middle Bronze Age by the date 1872–1129 BC Table 1). More tellingly, it is unlikely that the material in ditch 589 derives from a settlement in enclosure 927, as some of the material in it was quite clearly derived from the enclosure to its south, 925. Within this enclosure, feature 544 contained a rim sherd which joins P14, the vessel which was found in the terminal of ditch 589 (see Cleal, above and Table Mf2). There is some other evidence of settlement in this enclosure, including a large fragment of the lower part of a Middle Bronze Age vessel from hollow 528 (P29). The terminal of 589 also shows concentrations of animal bone and burnt flint (Fig. 24).

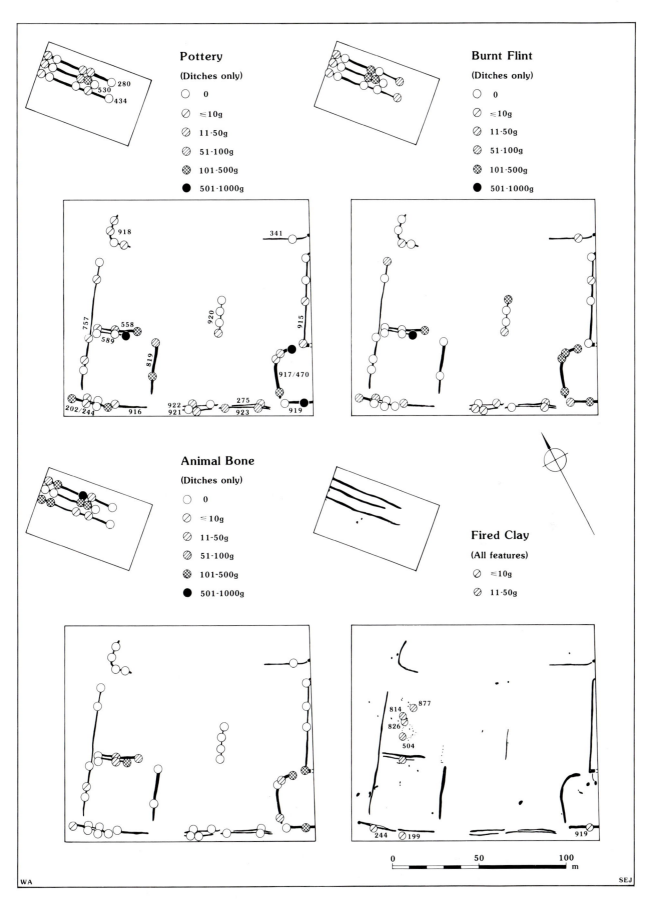

Figure 24   Bray: distribution of finds

The preferred interpretation of this western part of the excavated area is, therefore, that a field system was laid out, perhaps in the middle quarters of the 2nd millennium BC, in which the fields were marked by shallow, small ditches on north-west–south-east and north-east–south-west axes. Some very small scale Middle Bronze Age occupation had already occurred in the area, and the subsequent occupation associated with these fields was mainly in the north-eastern part of enclosure 925. Subsequently two boundaries of the field were replaced. The occupation centred around the round-house 491 may have taken place late in the Middle Bronze Age, extending into the Late Bronze Age, and was possibly unenclosed (the continuation of fence line 924 being uncertain, and the ditches probably largely full). It may not have gone out of use and been dismantled until a time when post-Deverel–Rimbury pottery forms were in use. The abandonment of this settlement may have been part of a settlement shift, as Late Bronze Age to Early Iron Age material is known to have been found in the Hoveringham Gravel Pit, less than 1 km to the south-east.

Apart from the perhaps successive occupation areas in the western part of trench 41, the finds distributions (Fig 24) suggest at least two other focii of settlement during the Middle Bronze Age: within enclosure 926, and around the triple ditches in trench 42, and in particular associated with the central ditch 530. It is not possible, using the ceramic evidence, to establish a sequence to the occupation of these areas, or to suggest their temporal relationship to the two areas of occupation in the western part of the site. The occupation around the triple ditches includes a sherd of Globular Urn (P23) and this is probably also the case with the occupation associated with enclosure 925. Vessel P26, which was recovered from a ditch fill during the evaluation, is interpreted as a slack-sided form of Globular Urn, and almost certainly came from ditch 757 where it forms the south-western side of enclosure 925.

The position of the evaluation feature could not be exactly reconciled with the ditch excavated in 1991, and the evaluation trench was not recorded during the excavation, but the best fit, matching up other excavated features which occurred also in the evaluation, is a length of ditch 757 towards the northern corner of enclosure 925, and it seems likely that a small surveying discrepancy between the two episodes of excavation is at fault. This location for P26 is entirely consistent with the other evidence for settlement in the north-western part of the enclosure. In the case of enclosure 926, although there are no Globular Urn sherds from the enclosure, its character is completely consistent with the material from the triple ditches and from enclosure 925.

Although it is clear that there was some time-depth to the occupation within the Middle Bronze Age, and that it is impossible to certainly establish a sequence for it, it is worth reiterating that the majority of the occupation was during the Middle Bronze Age.

With the exception of the round-house, which may be late in the site's history, there is a marked lack of easily identified structures. This may be due in part to the difficulty of identifying small features in the subsoil, but it may reflect a real absence of substantial earthfast structures. The general paucity of fired clay may also be due to a lack of structures covered with wattle-and-daub. Only one piece identified as probably from such a structure was recovered, from ditch 589, which presumably is to be associated with the putative occupation of enclosure 925.

Bray — the Landscape

Pre-Bronze Age

The pre-Middle Bronze Age activity at Bray can be seen to be part of a wider pattern of utilisation of this stretch of the Thames Valley both in the Mesolithic and Neolithic. Neolithic causewayed enclosures have been excavated at Staines and Eton Wick, and lengths of interrupted ditches which almost certainly represent another, are visible on aerial photographs on the opposite bank of the Thames at Dorney Reach (Fig. 3; Carstairs 1986, fig. 2, site D). Later Neolithic/Early Bronze Age material also occurs as a dense scatter of worked flint running along a ridge of gravel parallel to the river and 600 m long south-east from the Dorney Reach causewayed enclosure. During both the earlier and later Neolithic groups of finds and isolated objects from the river and the floodplain attest to use of the area (Holgate 1988, 103–5). In the immediate vicinity of Bray finds from the Hoveringham Gravel Pit included a possible Neolithic inhumation found close to an antler comb; sherds of Neolithic plain bowl pottery were also recovered (*op. cit.* 1988, 278; SMR SU97NW 378–80). A sherd of Grooved Ware was also found in this gravel pit (SMR SU97 NW 376).

Bronze Age

The Middle Bronze Age settlement at Bray, although unusual in the Middle Thames Valley in that it has survived and been subject to excavation, does not stand in splendid isolation. The landscape of which it was an element and the society in which its occupants played their parts is hinted at by surviving features of that landscape, by evidence from the excavation, and by comparison with contemporaneous settlements within and outside the region.

The immediate area around Bray has produced some Middle Bronze Age finds, although generally without firm contexts, as the finds have been made during gravel extraction or dredging of the River Thames, the former principally at the Hoveringham's Gravel Pit site (Bray Marina), 0.8 km to the south-east, and the latter mainly around Monkey Island, 0.5 km to the east (Fig. 3). At Monkey Island the find of a basal-looped spearhead is one of many of this type in the Thames Valley, particularly in the Middle Thames, leading Rowlands to suggest that this area functioned as a production centre, producing spearheads which appear to have been widely traded to the continent (Rowlands 1976, 63). These spearheads are considered to belong to the 'Taunton Phase' of approximately 1400–1200 BC (*op. cit.* 1976, 59; Burgess 1980, 131–59). The calibrated date range for ditch 589, calibrated at 1 sigma to 1671–1323 BC (Table 1) lies at least partly within this period, although it suggests that the origins of the Middle Bronze Age settlement may lie in the earlier rather than later Middle Bronze Age.

Two reviews of Bronze Age settlement in the Thames Valley within the last 15 years have summarised the state of knowledge to the 1980s, and for the Middle Bronze Age at least, the picture does not seem to have changed radically in the succeeding years. This picture is one of a far greater concentration of Deverel–Rimbury finds in the Middle and Lower Thames than in the Upper, mainly from Berkshire eastwards, and particularly on the river gravels (Barrett and Bradley 1980a, 251). These finds are overwhelmingly of cemeteries, particularly dense in the area of west London, with finds at Acton, Sunbury, Yiewsley, Kingston-on-Thames, and Walton-on-Thames, but there are some finds of occupation material which hint at the settlements which must have existed in the area, such as at Staines, where a small group appears to be occupation material (Needham 1987, 133), Phase 2 at Petters Sportsfield, Egham (O'Connell 1986, 8–9), and the enclosed occupation site at Muckhatch Farm, Thorpe, where a roughly circular enclosure was probably associated with circular structures, pits, and linear ditches (Needham 1987, 111; Johnson 1975, 19–23). On the Buckinghamshire side of the river, work in recent years in the Dorney area (Carstairs 1986) has drawn attention to the extensive field systems and other features on the Buckinghamshire side of the river, some of which may have their inception in the Bronze Age.

The closest parallels for the Bray settlement, however, remain the well known Deverel–Rimbury settlements on the Wessex Chalk, and although the effect of the different topography and soils must be acknowledged, comparison between the two areas remains a valuable exercise because it is clear that in terms of material culture the settlements along the Thames are part of the same network of contacts as those to the south and west. Although it may be tempting, in view of the lack of metalwork from Bray and the absence of artefacts likely to have been imported to the area, to view the site as a small, impoverished, isolated farmstead, with little or no contact outside the local area; the ceramics at least demonstrate that this is not the case, and the picture gained from the distribution of metalwork in the Middle Bronze Age, and even to some extent in the Early Bronze Age, suggests that the Thames Valley was not peripheral or isolated at any time in the 2nd millennium BC.

The ceramic assemblage from the ditches, both in its fabric and forms, clearly belongs within the Deverel–Rimbury tradition. There are differences between this material and the classic assemblages of Bucket, Barrel, and Globular Urns of central and southern Wessex, as there are between that material and the assemblages from the Middle Bronze Age sites of the Marlborough Downs in northern Wessex, but these are in the nature of variations on a theme, not alternative traditions. It seems clear that the makers of the Bray pottery, probably working on or close to the site itself, were aware of the basic forms and vessel types current over large areas of southern central Britain.

The evidence from a number of Wessex sites, and from Bray, is summarised in Table 13, and this highlights some aspects of the site at Bray which are typical, and some which appear atypical of this period. Comparison by quantification is impossible in this, as the sites differ widely in type, and have been excavated to differing degrees and under very different conditions. Overall, however, it suggests that Bray is rather more typical than atypical of sites of this period.

It is clear, for instance, that Bray is not alone in showing very little evidence for textile production in the form of spindle whorls and loomweights. This may be in part due to the small areas excavated on some sites (eg, Dean Bottom, Wiltshire), but this is unlikely to be the explanation at Thorny Down, where the excavation was extensive and the importance of such evidence fully appreciated (Stone 1941, 114). Loomweight fragments were present at Down Farm, but were not quantified; their occurrence is described as: 'in common with other sites on the Wessex chalk, the Down Farm enclosure contained very few loomweights' (Green et al. 1991, 203) which emphasises the general dearth of this form of artefact on sites of this type. Similarly, the utilisation of mainly local sources of stone seems to reflect a general pattern.

The presence of saddle querns on Middle–Late Bronze Age occupation sites is common (eg, Cox 1991, 95; Drewett 1982, 378, 390–1). In particular, at Dean Bottom on the Marlborough Downs, approximately 70 km to the west of Bray, sarsen trimming flakes from quern production were recovered from the Middle Bronze Age enclosed settlement (Gingell 1992, 30); and at Burderop Down, a later Bronze Age settlement also on the Marlborough Downs, sarsen and Limestone saddle querns were recovered (ibid., 177–80). The destination of the sarsen querns produced at Dean Bottom is unknown, but it is unlikely to have included Bray, as a more local source is probable here. Of general interest is the presence of nine fragments of querns of uncertain type and differing stone types recovered at the Late Bronze Age settlement at Aldermaston (Bradley et al. 1980, 245) and the single gabbro saddle quern from Late Bronze Age occupation at Knight's Farm (ibid., 275).

The lack of metalwork and metalworking debris at Bray is more problematic, and is difficult to explain in terms of excavation strategy or problems of retrieval. The area excavated at Bray was not insubstantial, and the sieving undertaken for environmental samples would also have recovered fragmentary metal. Of the sites listed in Table 13 only Down Farm, Cranborne Chase, and Rockley Down, on the Marlborough Downs, lack metal and, in the case of the latter, the limited nature of the excavation may well explain this. Excavation scale and technique is unlikely to account for the absence of metal from Down Farm, but in that case there was a Taunton phase spiral ring recovered only 145 m away, in ploughsoil. It is perhaps tempting to draw an analogy between this and Bray, with its Middle Bronze Age metal finds in the Thames: a metal-free settlement in close proximity to metalwork in non-settlement contexts.

The faunal assemblages from the sites listed in Table 13 are not directly comparable with the Bray assemblage, as the latter is so unsatisfactory in size and condition, but Bray seems to fit the general pattern in having little horse, pig, or wild animal. There is also, perhaps rather surprisingly, a general paucity of worked bone implements, and in this too Bray seems to fit the pattern.

Table 13 features of Deverel–Rimbury settlements

Site	No. sherds	Metalwork	Metalworking	Stone	Textile equipment	Animal bone	Worked bone
Weir Bank Stud Farm, Bray	962 MBA	–	–	Sarsen saddle quern + frag.	2 ?loomweight frags; 1 ?spindle-whorl frag.	Sample size very small (478; only 115 ident.); cattle do not seem to be dominant; no horse, dog, or wild animal	1 awl or gouge
Thorny Down, nr Salisbury, Wiltshire[1]	'Not plentiful'	Bracelet frags; double-looped spearhead	–	2 complete Sandstone querns (saddle) + frags and probable rubbers	Frags of 2 loom-weights; no spindle-whorls	'Remarkably scarce'; no wild animals	1 needle or bodkin
Bishops Cannings Down, Marlborough Downs, Wiltshire[2]	1493 (inc. minority earlier; main assemblage early MBA	Rapier blade; rivet; knife; ?pin shank; ?ferrule or binding awl	Riser or sprue-cup of mould; 2 casting droplets	Grindstones; whetstones; rubbers; burnishers (nb, not quantified); mainly Greensand, some Sandstone	–	9000+ frags; cattle outnumber sheep/goat, high prop. of calves; pig, horse, wild species poorly represented	Comb, needle, gouge; 2 points/awls; 1 piece drilled tooth (?decorative); modified antler tine
Dean Bottom, Marlborough Downs[2]	3600 (564 analysed)	Cast ring; flat-sectioned ring; 2 uniden. cast frags; bracelet; wire frag.; 'spatula'; blade frag.	?rod; ?sheet bronze frag.	Sarsen working industry, apparently producing saddle querns	–	c. 13,000 in MBA contexts; sheep/goat outnumber cattle but higher prop. of calves; pig, horse, dog, wild animals poorly represented	5 awls/points; modified antler
Rockley Down, Marlborough Downs[2]	1384 (inc. some later pottery)	–	–	–	–	Sheep/goat out-number cattle, but in ditch deposits cattle dominate	–
Down Farm, Cranborne Chase, Dorset[3]	106 from interior features; 1837 from ditch	–	–	c. 100 rock frags, c. 78% sarsen (local); minority utilised, mainly as rubbers/whetstones	'Very few'	Cattle most common, then sheep/goat; may be partly post-depositional causes	3 points; some pieces abandoned in process of ?pin making; modified antler
South Lodge, Cranborne Chase[4]	1537 from Pitt-Rivers' excav.	2 razors; awl; bracelet; bundle of wire; side-looped spearhead	Probable clay mould frag.	2 Sandstone saddle quern frags	Not reported	Not reported	2 awls; 1 pointed and perforated piece

[1] Stone 1941; [2] Gingell 1992; [3] Green et al. 1991; [4] Bradley and Barrett 1991

Plant remains have not been included in Table 13, although they have been recovered from some of the sites. Dean Bottom, for example, produced a deposit of clean, processed grain, mostly barley (Carruthers 1992, 143), and Down Farm produced very few grains of wheat and barley (Jones 1991, 49–50). Jones notes, in relation to Down Farm, that the sparseness of the dataset for Down Farm is 'itself a feature of the data; a feature which is shared by data-sets from a number of pre-Iron Age sites, and which is in striking contrast to the regularly prolific nature of carbonised assemblages from sites such as Ashville, Danebury, and Gussage All Saints' (*ibid.*).

At Bray Clapham has found sufficient data to suggest that the deposit from ditch 589 represents the remains of crop processing, the crop probably being emmer wheat. Because of the limited nature of the evidence from other sites it seems impossible to determine at present whether the paucity of data is due to the limited nature of arable cultivation in the Middle Bronze Age, to the nature of the processes carried out within the sites examined leading to little opportunity for carbonisation and therefore survival, or deficiencies in excavation strategy and recovery. The Bray evidence suggests that the last two rather than the first may be the major contributors. It is unfortunate that one of the most interesting features of the Bray carbonised plant assemblage, the evidence for flax cultivation and processing, cannot be unequivocally placed within the main Middle Bronze Age use of the site on archaeological grounds. However, the slightly later dating suggested for the house does accord with the presence of flax, as there seems to be increasing evidence for flax cultivation in the Late Bronze Age. The Late Bronze Age settlement at Aldermaston produced flax from one sample, but larger amounts have more recently been recovered from a settlement of similar date at Reading Business Park (Area 3100), where a series of waterlogged pits have been interpreted as flax retting pits (Moore 1992, 41; Campbell 1992, 108). Cultivation of flax in the Early–Middle Bronze Age is known from East Anglia, where a pit at West Row Fen, Mildenhall, Suffolk, has similarly been interpreted as for flax retting (Martin and Murphy 1988), but there seem to be no instances certainly earlier than the Late Bronze Age in the Thames Valley.

Comparison with the the Wessex sites also throws into high relief the nature of the settlement at Bray, highlighting the fact that if the house and four–poster are accepted as of later date, the remaining settlement lacks recognisable structures and consists mainly of artefactual evidence, ditches, and insubstantial and amorphous features, with the possibility, discussed above, that there may even have been a short occupation preceding the digging of the field ditches. This is not the picture which is generally invoked of settlement in the Middle Bronze Age, typically consisting of farmstead settlements looking not unlike their Iron Age successors, only lacking the iron, and is not the picture presented by the Wessex sites. But it should not perhaps be as surprising at it seems. Even in Wessex it has become clear that the apparently simple Wessex enclosed sites are not as uncomplicated as they seem, and that, in particular, they may conceal a long history

of change and development. At South Lodge, in Cranborne Chase, enclosure took place late in the site's history, following periods during which lynchet formation had taken place and the existence of an earlier open phase of settlement is postulated preceding the enclosure (Bradley and Barrett 1991, 144–83). Post-holes of a structure within the enclosure have produced dates of 3240±120 BP and 3110±110 BP (BM–1921R and 1922R) which give calibrated ranges of 1872–1260 and 1630–1050 BC (University of Washington Calibration program, Rev 2.0, Method A). Similarly, at Down Farm, it seems that a pre-enclosure phase is likely (Green *et al.* 1991, 186).

Nor should the nature of the settlement at Bray occasion surprise when seen in relation to what has preceded it. The development of a 'parceled-up' landscape in the Middle Bronze Age is certainly a striking development of the mid 2nd millennium BC, but it might perhaps be expected that a site which may date to a period early in this process, such as Bray, would show, if we are not to invoke major and traumatic social upheaval, some of the features of settlement already established. During the later Neolithic and Early Bronze Age occupation sites are notable, apart from their general paucity, for insubstantial features, a restricted artefactual assemblage and a lack of recognisable structures. In Wessex early, insubstantial, phases of settlement associated with the early stages of field systems appear to have been superseded by the enclosures easily recognised and now regarded as 'typical' of the Wessex Chalk. It is possible that in some areas this development did not take place, and, where it did not, Middle Bronze Age settlement will undoubtedly prove more difficult to recognise. It is possible that the Middle Thames gravels are such an area, which would offer an explanation for why, given the recovery of funerary urns, so little settlement has been recorded: a few dozen or even hundred sherds and bones are less likely to have been recovered in past gravel extraction than recognisable vessels.

This view of Middle Bronze Age settlement in the area is perhaps supported by the increasing occurrence, on later sites, of small Deverel–Rimbury elements in the ceramic assemblages; a comprehensive review of these might increase our view of the Middle Bronze Age settlement of the area, but is outside the scope of this report.

Bray is, then, a notable addition to our knowledge both of the Middle Thames Valley in the Middle Bronze Age and in more general terms. In the Middle Thames it assists in filling a settlement 'gap' which it was clear, on the basis of both the many finds of metalwork of this date in the Thames and the existence of cemeteries, was more apparent than real. In more general terms it demonstrates that a site which it would have been quite reasonable to have interpreted, after the initial evaluation, as a small Middle Bronze Age farmstead, has produced evidence of a long history of changing use and occupation which stretches from the early phases of the Neolithic to the later stages of the Bronze Age. Its wider implications are that Middle Bronze Age settlement in this Middle Thames zone may not be as easily recognisable as elsewhere.

2. An Analysis of Worked Flint Artefact Concentrations from Maidenhead Thicket, Maidenhead

by W.A. Boismier

An analysis is presented of the flint artefacts recovered by a two stage evaluation undertaken at Maidenhead Thicket in 1990. Three concentrations of later Neolithic/earlier Bronze Age flint artefacts were revealed. Assemblage characteristics for the southern and central artefact clusters indicated that the two concentrations were the remains of limited activity quarry or extraction sites while those for the northern cluster suggested that it was probably the remains of a residential site. A spatial analysis identified a number of significant artefact class group associations and the broad locations of intrasite activity areas for the three concentrations. These are then related to the larger regional distribution of broadly contemporaneous flint concentrations and isolated findspots known for the area. The results of the analysis have documented that it is possible to obtain substantive archaeological information from archaeological evaluations beyond the simple presence/absence of artefactual materials and subsurface deposits and indicate that much more care and attention could be profitably devoted to the collection, analysis, and interpretation of evaluation datasets.

1 Introduction

In the spring of 1990 Wessex Archaeology was commissioned by English Heritage to undertake two stages of archaeological evaluation along the proposed route of the new A423(M) road in north-east Berkshire. The route through an area of woodland owned by the National Trust was known as Maidenhead Thicket. Maidenhead Thicket lies immediately to the west of Maidenhead, centred on grid reference SU 8527 8090 (Fig. 25) on the low Chalk plateau of east Berkshire. Upper Chalk overlain by thin deposits of Plateau Drift and sealed by argillic brown earth soils is the predominate lithology for the area (Jarvis *et al.* 1984). It lies in an area of gently undulating relief that slopes very slightly towards the south-east at a height of between 50 m and 60 m OD. The woodland is primarily deciduous with a thick thorn scrub understorey. An area of about 5.50 ha of Maidenhead Thicket, along a corridor *c.* 1.0 km in length, was examined by the evaluation.

The first stage of the evaluation was carried out in March 1990 and identified three concentrations of later prehistoric worked flint composed primarily of waste materials. The second stage was undertaken between August and September 1990 and involved both further assessment and intensive sampling. It was focused on recovering a larger sample of the artefact populations from the three identified concentrations and more closely delimiting their boundaries. This report describes the analysis of the flint assemblages recovered from both stages of the evaluation. It has three main aims: firstly, to present the technological details of the assemblages, their relative date, and the possible function of the three concentrations; secondly, to determine whether it is possible to define any intrasite spatial patterning for the three concentrations on the basis of the small dispersed test excavation units employed for data recovery; and thirdly, to place the three concentrations within their broader regional context.

2 Background

Prior to the evaluation known archaeological resources for Maidenhead Thicket were restricted to the occurrence of three earthwork features and a few isolated findspots of worked flint, Roman coins, and medieval pottery. Slit trenches of First and Second World War date were also known to occur within the area. A linear feature of probable Iron Age date, an undated enclosure adjacent to the A4–A423 roundabout, and a Late Iron Age enclosure known as Robin Hood's Arbour (Cotton 1961) comprise the three earthworks known to occur within Maidenhead Thicket. The linear earthwork and undated enclosure were intersected by the line of the road corridor and largely or entirely destroyed by construction activities associated with the building of the new road. Robin Hood's Arbour is situated 500 m to the west of the road corridor and was not adversely affected by construction activities.

The linear earthwork feature existed in the form of a bank and ditch running more or less west to east. It was first recorded in 1861, initially excavated in 1939, and subsequently re-excavated during 1982 in advance of the A423(T) road widening scheme (Bowden *et al.* 1982). The results of the 1992 excavation suggested that the bank, 6.0 m wide and ditch, 2.50 m wide and 1.20 m deep, were of Middle or Late Iron Age date, and that the feature probably functioned as a linear territorial marker rather than as part of an enclosure. Finds recovered by this excavation included Bronze Age, Iron Age, Roman, and medieval pottery and a worked flint assemblage of 270 pieces. This flint assemblage was interpreted by the excavators (*ibid.*, 28) as a rare example of an Iron Age flint industry.

The undated enclosure was in the form of a partial, low rectilinear feature formed by a low bank and ditch: its existence was first identified in 1985. Trial trenching

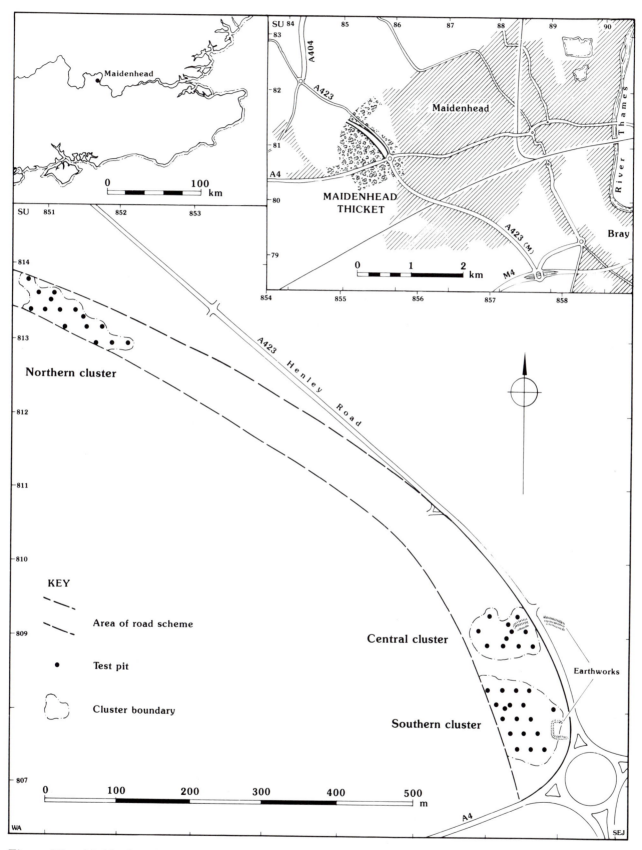

Figure 25   Maidenhead Thicket: location plan

of this feature, during both stages of the evaluation, did not recover any finds and was taken as an indication that the feature was of recent origin.

In the spring of 1990 English Heritage commissioned Wessex Archaeology to undertake an archaeological evaluation of the finalised line of the A423(M) trunk road through Maidenhead Thicket. Stage I of the evaluation was carried out in March 1990 over a period of three weeks and consisted of 38 manually excavated 1 m² test-pits and thirteen 1.5 m wide machine trenches of varying length distributed along the entire length of the road corridor (Newman *et al.* 1990). The evaluation recovered a number of worked flint artefacts of later prehistoric date and broadly identified three distinct clusters occurring at the northern and southern ends of the corridor and to the south-west of the linear feature. A 320 m length of the northern portion of the road corridor was also identified as being badly disturbed by First and Second World War slit trenches.

In response to these results a research design for a second stage was initially prepared by Berkshire County Council consisting of a systematic unaligned strategy employing small 0.30 m hand test-pits spaced at 10 m intervals as collection units. The design was considered by Wessex Archaeology to be inappropriate for the purposes of secondary fieldwork and an alternative design for Stage II was prepared and accepted by Berkshire County Council and English Heritage (Newman *et al.* 1991). This alternative design also consisted of a systematic unaligned strategy employing 38 1 m² test excavation units spaced at 20 m intervals across the areas of the three flint concentrations identified by the Stage I fieldwork. Its aim was to recover a larger sample of the artefact populations from the three concentrations to allow their date and function to be ascertained, and to more closely delimit their boundaries. Investigation of the enclosure adjacent to the roundabout by two intersecting trenches to determine its date and function was also identified by the design as an element of fieldwork. This enclosure proved to be ephemeral in nature and probably of recent origin; it is not considered further within this report. Stage II field-

work was carried out between August and September 1990. The design as implemented in the field largely fulfilled its stated objectives in relation to defining the distribution, nature, and characteristics of the artefact assemblage.

3 Assemblage Characteristics

The two stages of the evaluation produced a total of 1859 pieces of recognisably worked flint. Of these, 109 (5.86%) were recovered by Stage I and 1750 (94.14%) by Stage II. Table 14 lists the artefact class groups recovered by the two stages of fieldwork. The three identified concentrations or clusters of flint artefacts form the basis for the analysis presented below with the artefacts recovered by the two stages pooled and grouped by associated cluster to provide a larger sample of the artefact populations from these three 'sites'. Artefacts recovered from non-cluster areas were similarly grouped.

Condition

Patination ranges from a light film to a mottled bluish grey or greyish white, and was simply recorded as being either present or absent on individual artefacts. In total, 1408 pieces (75.74%) show signs of some degree of patination with 451 (24.26%) unpatinated.

Post-depositional edge damage and breakage occurs in varying degrees on all major classes of artefacts. Some 604 pieces (32.49%) exhibit evidence of post-depositional edge damage or breakage with the remaining 1335 (71.81%) largely undamaged. Most of this damage is attributable to excavation although a number of pieces possess attributes more characteristic of plough, rather than excavation, damage (Mallouf 1982) and indicate that at some time in the past the area was under arable. The small size and abraded condition of the Roman and prehistoric pottery suggest that this may have been during the later prehistoric and Roman periods.

Table 14 Maidenhead Thicket: artefacts recovered during the two stages of the evaluation

| | *Stage 1* | | | | | *Stage II* | | | | |
	1	*2*	*3*	*Total*	*%*	*1*	*2*	*3*	*Total*	*%*
Cores	1	–	–	1	0.91	19	2	–	22	1.20
Core renewal flake	1	–	–	1	0.91	1	–	–	1	0.06
Flakes	77	23	1	101	92.66	1291	295	40	1626	92.91
Blades	2	–	–	2	1.83	18	5	2	25	1.42
Undiagnostic	3	–	–	3	2.75	57	2	1	60	3.42
Nondescript shatter	1	–	–	1	0.91	10	–	–	10	0.57
Other	–	–	–	–		2	–	–	2	0.11
Utilised	–	–	–	–		2	–	–	2	0.11
Retouched	–	–	–	–		3	–	–	3	0.17
Total	85	23	1	109		1403	304	43	1750	

1 = complete; 2 = fragment; 3 = burnt (*also for Tables 15–19, 21, 22b*)

Table 15 Maidenhead Thicket: southern cluster assemblage composition

	1	2	3	Total	%
Cores	8	2	–	10	1.04
Core renewal flake	1	–	–	1	0.10
Flakes	721	171	16	908	94.58
Blades	9	2	1	12	1.25
Undiagnostic	15	2	1	18	1.87
Nondescript shatter	9	–	–	9	0.94
Tested/flawed nodule	1	–	–	1	0.10
Retouched	1	–	–	1	0.10
Total	765	177	18	960	

Raw Material

All pieces examined were flint and no other raw material was present. Cortical condition indicate that nodules occurring in the Upper Chalk were the primary source of raw material.

Assemblage Composition

Tables 14 to 18 present the major artefact classes of the assemblages recovered from the three concentrations and from the areas between them. Various categories of 'waste' account for 99.73% of the assemblages recovered, with the tool component accounting for less than one per cent (0.27%). Assemblage composition for the southern and central clusters is dominated by a much wider range of waste class groups than the northern cluster and reflect probable differences in site function. These are discussed in more detail below.

Cores

A total of 22 cores and core fragments was recovered by fieldwork from the three clusters. None were recovered from the areas between. They comprise 20 complete cores (90.91%) and two fragments. Eight cores and two core fragments were recovered from the southern cluster, eight from the central cluster, and four from the

Table 16 Maidenhead Thicket: central cluster assemblage composition

	1	2	3	Total	%
Cores	8	–	–	8	1.65
Core renewal flakes	1	–	–	1	0.20
Flakes	348	89	5	442	90.95
Blades	8	–	–	8	1.65
Undiagnostic	23	–	–	23	4.73
Nondescript shatter	2	–	–	2	0.41
Tested/flawed nodule	1	–	–	1	0.20
Utilised	1	–	–	1	0.20
Total	392	89	5	486	

Table 17 Maidenhead Thicket: northern cluster assemblage composition

	1	2	3	Total	%
Cores	4	–	–	4	1.05
Flakes	275	52	20	347	90.83
Blades	3	3	1	7	1.83
Undiagnostic	21	–	–	21	5.49
Utilised	1	–	–	1	0.26
Retouched	2	–	–	2	0.52
Total	306	55	21	382	

northern cluster. The cores are all simple, unprepared flake cores and comprise 11 single platform (50.0%), eight multi-platform (36.36%), one joint or keeled platform (4.54%), and two unclassifiable (9.04%) cores. Table 19 lists the core types by cluster.

Core renewal flakes
Two core renewal flakes were recovered. A core edge from the southern cluster and a core face from the central cluster.

Debitage
A total of 1830 artefacts classifiable as debitage (98.44% of the total number of pieces) was recovered by fieldwork. This broad category contains flakes and blades, undiagnostic struck pieces, nondescript shatter, and tested/flawed nodules. The southern cluster contains 948 pieces, the central cluster 476, and the northern cluster 375. Flakes account for 91.28% of the total debitage, blades 1.45%, and the remaining class groups 7.27%.

Flakes and blades
The flakes comprise 1368 complete pieces, 313 fragments, and 41 burnt pieces and fragments. Unretouched flakes make up between 90.0% and 94.5% of the assemblages from the three concentrations and 97.0% of those collected from areas between. Blades in this study are defined as flakes whose length is twice their width with those recovered being incidental by-products of core reduction strategies rather than deliberate blanks of predetermined shape. The blade component consists of 21 complete pieces, five fragments, and two burnt pieces. Blades account for less than 2% of the assemblages recovered from the three concentrations and around 3% of the material from non-cluster areas.

Table 18 Maidenhead Thicket: non-cluster assemblage composition

	1	2	Total	%
Flakes	24	6	30	93.75
Blades	1	–	1	3.12
Undiagnostic	1	–	1	3.12
Total	26	6	32	

Table 19 Maidenhead Thicket: cores recovered by cluster

| | Southern cluster | | | | Central cluster | | Northern cluster | |
	1	2	Total	%	1	%	1	%
Single	5	2	7	70.0	3	37.5	1	25.0
Multiple	2	–	2	20.0	3	37.5	3	75.0
Joint	–	–	–		1	12.5	–	
Unclassified	1	–	1	10.0	1	12.5	–	
Total	8	2	10		8		4	

Table 20 Maidenhead Thicket: primary, secondary, and tertiary pieces by cluster

| | Southern cluster | | Central cluster | | Northern cluster | | Non-cluster | |
	No.	%	No.	%	No.	%	No.	%
Primary	182	20.16	84	18.88	32	9.61	1	9.68
Secondary	390	43.19	201	45.16	135	40.54	12	38.71
Tertiary	331	36.65	160	49.85	166	49.85	16	51.61
Total	903		445		333		31	

Unburnt flakes and blades were divided into primary (dorsal surface wholly cortical), secondary (dorsal surface partially cortical), and tertiary (dorsal surface non-cortical) technological classes. Table 20 presents the subdivision of the assemblages into these technological classes for the identified artefact clusters and pieces recovered from non-cluster areas. In the sample as a whole, primary pieces account for 17.58% of the total number of unburnt pieces, secondary 43.11%, and tertiary 39.31%. At the assemblage level, primary pieces comprise 20.16% and 18.88% of the assemblages from the southern and central clusters and around 9.6% of the assemblages from the northern cluster and noncluster areas. Secondary pieces range from 40.54%–45.16% of the assemblages with the southern and central clusters possessing marginally greater proportions of secondary pieces. Secondary pieces account for 38.71% of the assemblage recovered from non-cluster areas. Tertiary pieces for the southern and central clusters are both around 36.9% of their assemblage totals with 49.85% and 51.61% of the assemblages from the northern cluster and non-cluster areas respectively, composed of tertiary pieces.

Other debitage classes

The composition of the remaining debitage classes is presented in Table 21. Undiagnostic struck pieces account for 82.89% of those recovered, nondescript shatter 14.47%, and tested/flawed nodules 2.63%. Undiagnostic pieces comprise 64.28% of the assemblage recovered from the southern cluster, 88.46% of that recovered from the central cluster, and 100.0% of the northern cluster.

A single piece of undiagnostic struck flint was also recovered from non-cluster areas. Non-descript shatter and tested/flawed nodules occur only in the southern and central clusters.

Tools

A total of five utilised and retouched tools was recovered from the three concentrations. No tools were found in the non-cluster areas. The assemblage from the southern cluster contained one borer, that from the central cluster a utilised piece, with the assemblage from the northern cluster producing a utilised piece, a notched flake, and a single example of a spurred piece.

Table 21 Maidenhead Thicket: miscellaneous debitage class groups by cluster

| | Southern cluster | | | | | Central cluster | | Northern cluster | |
	1	2	3	Total	%	1	%	1	%
Undiagnostic	15	2	1	18	64.28	23	88.46	21	100.0
Nondescript shatter	9	–	–	9	32.14	2	7.69	–	
Tested/flawed nodules	1	–	–	1	3.57	1	3.85	–	
Total	25	2	1	28		26		21	

Table 22 Maidenhead Thicket: flake shape and termination classes used to establish relative date

	Southern cluster		Central cluster		Northern cluster		Non-cluster	
	No.	%	No.	%	No.	%	No.	%
Blades/narrow flakes	46	6.17	27	7.63	22	7.86	2	9.09
Proportional flakes	321	43.09	158	44.63	126	45.0	10	45.45
Squat flakes	242	32.48	100	28.25	71	25.36	8	36.36
Irregular flakes	136	18.25	69	19.49	61	21.78	2	9.09
Total	745		354		280		22	

Table 22a: flake shape classes

Hinge	231	39.02	86	28.29	74	30.96	9	39.13
Step	37	6.25	17	5.59	21	8.79	–	
Normal	309	52.19	197	64.03	129	53.97	8	34.78
Other	15	2.53	4	1.31	15	6.28	6	26.09
Total	592		304		239		23	

Table 22b: flake termination classes

Blades/narrow blades = incidental blades and bladelike flakes
Proportional flakes = flakes with equal dimensions

4 Interpretation

Dates for the assemblages recovered from the three artefact concentrations and non-cluster areas have been established on the basis of broad technological characteristics related to flake shape and termination classes. While the criticisms levelled at the use of flake shape as an indicator of relative date (Ford *et al.* 1984; Ford 1987b) are acknowledged, full metrical analysis could not be attempted as it was not considered appropriate within the limitations of the project's aims. Only those pieces for which shape and termination classes could be unambiguously determined were used to establish relative date. Table 22 presents the subdivision of the assemblages into shape and termination classes. Patterns of proportional representation for the shape and termination classes in the assemblages indicated by the table are within the range of those documented as characteristic of the later Neolithic/ earlier Bronze Age (Richards 1978; Ford *et al.* 1984; Ford 1987b) and suggest that all three concentrations and associated material from non-cluster areas can be dated to this period. The spurred piece recovered from the northern cluster is a characteristic tool form of the later Neolithic/earlier Bronze Age and supports the relative date indicated for this concentration on broad technological characteristics.

The Iron Age date for the worked flint artefacts suggested by Bowden *et al.* (1982) recovered during their excavation of the linear earthwork intersecting the central cluster is not supported by the comparative study of other dated flint assemblages. Small numbers of worked flint were recovered from a number of contexts by the excavation (*ibid.*, 27) but they are most likely residual elements of a portion of the central cluster destroyed by the construction of the earthwork.

A number of differences and similarities in assemblage composition are apparent for the three concentrations of artefacts and can be interpreted in relation to their probable function. To determine whether the apparent patterning in assemblage composition was real and reflected functional characteristics or simply a product of different sample sizes, a series of t–tests for the differences between proportions (Blalock 1979, 232–4) was carried out between the various waste class groups. The number of tools recovered from all three concentrations was too low to produce any meaningful value for the test statistic and were excluded from the analysis. Table 23 presents the results of the tests for the waste class groups.

The southern and central clusters exhibit a high degree of correspondence in artefact class group composition and proportional representation. Minor differences were found to occur between them only in the proportion of undiagnostic struck pieces and simply reflect the differential recovery of this class group by fieldwork as opposed to any major functional differences between the two concentrations. The results of the remaining tests found no significant differences in the proportional representation of artefact class groups and indicate that the assemblages reflect a very similar, if not identical, function for the two concentrations.

Assemblage composition for the northern cluster is somewhat different with core renewal flakes, nondescript shatter, and tested/flawed nodules absent from the artefact inventory. Comparisons based on the difference of proportions test have been, as a result, limited to the remaining waste artefact class groups. Differences in

58

Table 23 Maidenhead Thicket: difference of proportions test results

	Southern and central clusters	Southern and northern clusters	Central and northern clusters
Cores	0.014	0.080	0.800
Flakes	0.692	4.220*	4.590*
Blades	1.220	1.200	0.200
Undiag.	3.180*	72.400*	0.630
Misc. debitage	0.170	–	

Table 23a: general assemblage characteristics

Primary	0.565	4.390*	3.560*
Secondary	0.690	1.000	1.320
Tertiary	0.254	4.260*	3.860*

Table 23b: technological classes

Starred values for t significant at 0.05 level

Cores = cores and core fragments
Misc. debitage = core renewal flakes, nondescript shatter pieces, tested/flawed nodules

general assemblage characteristics between the northern cluster and the other two concentrations were found to occur only in the proportions of flakes with the significant result of the test for undiagnostic struck pieces between the northern cluster and southern clusters largely attributable to the differential recovery of this class group. The remaining tests found no significant differences in the proportional representation of artefact class groups. These results simply indicate that flintworking was a major debris producing activity at all three concentrations with significant differences in the quantity of unretouched flakes occurring between the northern cluster and the other two concentrations.

The tests for the three technological classes were more informative concerning functional differences between the northern cluster and the southern and central clusters. Significant differences were found to occur in the proportions of primary and tertiary pieces and to reflect the inverse pattern of proportional representation occurring between the northern cluster and the other two concentrations. Primary pieces account for around 20.0% of the assemblages from the southern and central clusters, whereas in the northern cluster they make up only 9.61% of the assemblage. Tertiary pieces comprise 49.85% of the northern cluster's assemblage and around 36.0% of the assemblages recovered from the other two concentrations. Such differences, when taken in conjunction with the occurrence of core renewal flakes, nondescript shatter, and tested/flawed nodules, indicate major functional differences in assemblage

characteristics between the northern cluster and the southern and central clusters.

Most of the artefact class groups recovered from the southern and central clusters are flintworking by-products and include cores, core renewal flakes, flakes and incidental blades, undiagnostic struck pieces, nondescript shatter, and tested/flawed nodules. One tool was also recovered from each cluster.

The recovery of a relatively high percentage of primary pieces in conjunction with nondescript shatter and tested nodules discarded because of internal flaws attest that the acquisition, assessment of nodule quality, and the initial reduction and shaping of nodules into suitable cores were the primary activities performed on them. Such patterns in assemblage characteristics are largely diagnostic of limited activity quarry or extraction sites where the acquisition and initial reduction of lithic raw material occurred (Collins 1975; Driskell 1986; Ford 1987b) and firmly support the interpretation of the southern and central cluster as some form of specialised quarry or extraction site.

The removal of core preforms from the clusters for further reduction elsewhere is consistent with this interpretation and accounts for the lack of differences in the proportion of cores between these two concentrations and the northern cluster.

While most of the artefact class groups recovered from the northern cluster are also flintworking byproducts, a number of differences are apparent in assemblage characteristics that indicate a different function for this cluster when compared to the other two concentrations. Core renewal flakes, nondescript shatter, and tested/flawed nodules are absent from the artefact inventory with tertiary pieces accounting for almost 50.0% of the unretouched flakes and blades recovered from it. Three tools, comprising two retouched forms and one utilised piece, were also recovered from the concentration. Technological class group proportional representation, in conjunction with tool occurrence and the absence or under representation of debris class groups related to primary flintworking, attest that core reduction related to the production of suitable blanks for tool manufacture and tool utilisation were the major activities carried out here. Such patterns in assemblage characteristics are more indicative of domestic or residential sites where the manufacture, maintenance, and use of tools occurred (Driskell 1986; Ford 1987b; Zvelebil et al. 1987; Richards 1990) and suggest that this concentration probably functioned as some form of residential site.

An alternative interpretation is that the northern cluster functioned as some type of indeterminate limited activity site where a narrower range of activities were performed which generated flaking debris similar to that recovered from residential sites. Available data is unable clearly to resolve these conflicting interpretations and the northern cluster is preferentially interpreted as a probable residential site in the absence of any conflicting evidence. The recovery of three tools from the small number of test excavation units intersecting it tends to support its interpretation as some kind of residential site.

5 Spatial Patterning

The spatial analysis of the three artefact concentrations presented in this section is oriented towards the discovery of 'activity areas' or clusters of associated artefact class groups which co-occur spatially. Its purpose is to determine whether it is possible to define intrasite spatial patterning within the three artefact concentrations on the basis of the 1 m² test excavation units.

Methods

There are a number of quantitative techniques and statistical tests that can be applied to the analysis of artefact distributions (Carr 1984; Hietala 1984; Blankholm 1991). The process of pattern recognition employed in the analysis involved three main steps:

1. the delineation of a concentration's overall area employing contour mapping of artefact densities per test excavation unit volume;
2. the identification of associational patterns for artefact class groups on the basis of Kendall's tau statistic; and
3. the spatial delineation of intra-site activity areas utilising contour mapping of joint artefact densities per unit volume.

Contour mapping was chosen over more conventional representations of spatial patterning such as proportional circles on the basis of its general agreement or concordance (Carr 1987) with the spatial characteristics of artefact distributions. Artefact distributions can be considered for the purposes of pattern recognition as being more or less continuous across space with highly variable density characteristics, their patterning in terms of spatial configuration and population size representing a source of archaeological information concerning the organisation and utilisation of space by people in the past. In form these distributions are most closely approximated by the isopleth or contour map. This map type is based on the concept that the variable being mapped is continuous across its surface with the values for small dispersed sampling units assumed to be representative of the area immediately surrounding them. With its congruence to the general characteristics of artefact distributions and its assumption of unit representativeness, contour mapping provides a basic analytical tool for describing spatial structure or pattern within the artefact concentrations defined by fieldwork at Maidenhead Thicket.

Contour mapping per test excavation unit volume was undertaken employing floating averages (Cole and King 1970, 203). To reduce the effects of different test units depths on artefact recovery rates, artefact frequencies were converted into artefact densities per test unit volume. Artefact density per test excavation unit volume was estimated by:

$$d_{vol} = \frac{n}{v}$$

where n = artefact frequency per test excavation unit
v = excavation unit volume, ie length x width x depth

Floating averages is a pattern recognition technique for determining the general intensities of artefact distribution across space. Artefact density for each excavation unit is added to the density values for the units immediately surrounding it then divided by the number of units to produce an average artefact density value for the excavation unit. This procedure is summarised by:

$$d_{fa} = \frac{\sum d_{vol}}{N}$$

where d_{vol} = density per excavation unit volume
N = the number of excavation units

The density values obtained by this procedure were then plotted onto the corresponding excavation units on a 1:1000 map and contouring undertaken manually on the basis of the plotted values. This procedure was utilised both for estimating the overall extent of a concentration's area and for delimiting intrasite activity areas.

The identification of intrasite patterns of association occurring among the various artefact class groups was based on calculated values for Kendall's tau–b statistic (Kendall 1970; Blalock 1979) — a non-parametric rank correlation coefficient that measures the degree of agreement or association between two sets of ordinal rankings. The statistic makes no assumptions about the shape of the population from which the samples were drawn and is well suited for the recognition of associated patterns between artefact class groups where normality cannot be assumed (Hietala and Stevens 1977; Boismier 1981). Tau–b reduces the inflational effect of tied ranks on tau values produced by low artefact frequencies and is calculated by:

$$\tau_b = \frac{S}{\sqrt{\frac{1}{2}N(N-1) - Tx}\sqrt{\frac{1}{2}N(N-1) - Ty}}$$

where S = the sum of concordant and discordant pairs
Tx = ½ Σt(t-1), with t being the number of tied observations in each set of ties in artefact class x
Ty = ½ Σt(t-1), with t being the number of tied observations in each set of ties in artefact class y
N = the number of test excavation units in concentration i

Values for tau–b extend from +1.0 to –1.0 with a value of +1.0 indicating a perfect association between two artefact class groups and one of –1.0 perfect negative association or complete segregation of the two class groups in space. If the two class groups are completely unrelated tau–b will be zero.

For those values of tau–b which occur between +1.0 and –1.0 it is necessary to carry out a significance test to determine whether the observed value indicates the existance of a significant association between the two artefact class groups. When N is greater than 10, the significance of an observed value for tau–b can be determined by comparing it to a normal distribution possessing a standard deviation of:

$$\sigma_\tau b = \sqrt{\frac{2(2N+5)}{9N\,(N-1)}}$$

with the probability of any observed value of tau–b under a null hypothesis of no association given by:

$$z = \frac{\tau b}{\sigma_\tau}b$$

The alternative hypothesis in spatial situations being either association or segregation depending upon the particular value of tau–b that is tested. If the resultant probability is equal to or less than the chosen significance level, the null hypothesis of no association is rejected in favour of the alternative.

Results

Spatial extent
Figure 26 shows the estimated spatial extent and overall patterns of artefact density per unit volume for the three concentrations defined by fieldwork. What is immediately apparent is the differences between the concentrations in both their estimated area and artefact density. The southern cluster extends across an estimated area of 0.93 ha and possess a core area with a mean density of 2.34 artefacts per cubic centimetre of test unit volume. The central cluster covers an estimated area of 0.59 ha with a mean density of 1.54

artefacts within its core area. The northern cluster is much more elongated and irregular in outline with an estimated area of 0.72 ha and a core area density of 1.07 artefacts.

These differences in area and density appear to indicate differences in their function and length of utilisation or occupation. The testing of nodule quality and the initial reduction and shaping of nodules into suitable cores carried out at the southern and central clusters generated considerable quantities of flaking debris and nodule rejects that are reflected in the density of artefacts recovered from the test excavation units intersecting them. Differences in their area and density suggest differences in the length or intensity of utilisation with the southern cluster possibly in use longer or more intensely exploited. Available data is unable to resolve this question. The functional differences between the northern and the other two clusters identified by the artefact analysis is reflected in its density characteristics where the density of artefacts indicates a different intensity of flintworking activities.

Associational patterning and activity areas
Tables 24 to 26 present the tau–b values for the three concentrations with those significant at the 0.05 level starred. To meet the requirements of the statistic, class groups consisting of single examples were either excluded from the analysis or pooled with a closely related group to form more general artefact class groups reflecting a particular range of activities. Cores and core fragments in the southern cluster were also pooled together into a more general class.

The southern cluster
Tau–b values for the southern cluster are listed in matrix form in Table 24. Significant associations were

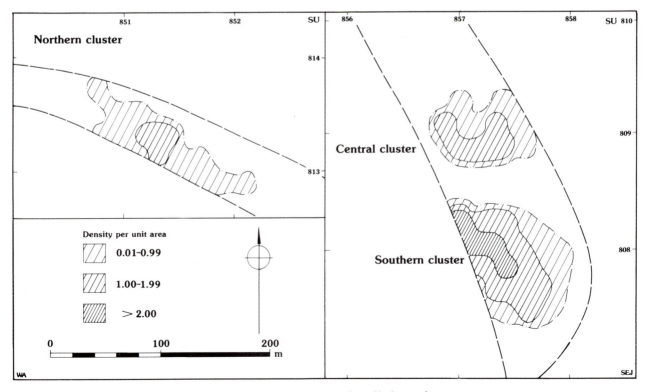

Figure 26   Maidenhead Thicket: density distributions for all three clusters

Table 24 Maidenhead Thicket: matrix of tau–b values for the southern cluster

	P	S	T	C	M	U
P	–					
S	.633*	–				
T	.660*	.678*	–			
C	.352*	.348*	.209	–		
M	.001	.084	.104	.429*	–	
U	.179	.245	.167	.334	.119	–

P = primary pieces; S = secondary pieces; T = tertiary pieces; C = cores and core fragments; U = undiagnostic struck pieces; M = miscellaneous debitage (nondescript shatter, tested/flawed nodules, core renewal flakes

* = values significant at the 0.05 level

Table 25 Maidenhead Thicket: matrix of tau–b values for the central cluster

	P	S	T	C	M	U
P	–					
S	.709*	–				
T	.645*	.915*	–			
C	.041	.363*	.296	–		
M	.222	.403*	.315	.395*	–	
U	.408*	.580*	.664*	.216	.080	–

For key see Table 24

found to occur between five of the six class groups in varying pairwise combinations thus indicating patterns of artefact association. The first is a general background pattern of association occurring between primary, secondary, and tertiary pieces and reflects their general co-occurrence in virtually all of the test excavation units intersecting the cluster. Figure 27a shows the joint density distribution of the three technological classes with two distinct concentrations occurring within the cluster's boundaries. The second pattern is a much more distinct pattern of association between cores, primary, and secondary pieces and the general miscellaneous debitage class group composed of nondescript shatter, tested/flawed nodules, and core renewal flakes. This second associational pattern reflects the general spatial co-occurrence of flaking debris which probably relates to primary flintworking activities. The joint density distribution of the four artefact class groups comprising this pattern is shown in Figure 27b where two distinct concentrations occur within the cluster's boundary and overlap with those identified for the first pattern.

The joint density distributions for the two associational patterns plotted together are shown in Figure 27c. The high degree of spatial correspondence between the concentrations identified for the two patterns of artefact class group association indicate that the concentrations are part of two activity areas intersected by the test excavation units. Both activity areas represent generalised locations where nodule quality was assessed and the initial reduction and shaping of nodules into suitable cores was carried out. The small number of cores recovered from these activity areas indicates that most were removed from the site after initial trimming and reduction.

The central cluster
Tau–b values for the central cluster are presented in matrix form in Table 25. Patterns of association among the artefact class groups were found to be similar to those identified for the southern cluster and reflect the identical functions inferred for the two concentrations. Significant pairwise associations were observed to occur

between all six class groups and to indicate two patterns of artefact association. The first is also a general background pattern of association occurring between primary, secondary, tertiary, and undiagnostic pieces and reflects, as with the southern cluster, their general co-occurrence in most of the test excavation units intersecting the cluster. Their joint density distribution is shown in Figure 27d and corresponds with that identified for the concentration as a whole (Fig. 26). The second pattern is more or less the same as that identified for the southern cluster and consists of a relatively distinct pattern of association between cores, secondary pieces and the general miscellaneous class group composed on nondescript shatter, tested/flawed nodules, and core renewal flakes. This pattern also reflects the spatial co-occurrence of flaking debris related to primary flintworking activities. Figure 27e shows the joint density distribution of the three class groups with two distinct concentrations occurring with the cluster's boundaries.

Figure 27f shows the joint density distributions for the two associational patterns plotted together. Two activity areas are indicated by the concentrations identified for the second associational pattern with some overlap with the density distribution of the first pattern. This area of overlap suggests that those portions of the density distribution defined for the first pattern may belong to the two activity areas. Available data is again unable clearly to resolve this question. As with the southern cluster, both activity areas represent generalised locations where nodule testing and the initial reduction and shaping of nodules into cores were carried out. The small number of cores also recovered from this cluster indicates that most were probably removed after initial trimming and reduction.

The northern cluster
The matrix of tau–b values for the northern cluster is presented in Table 26. Patterns of association among the artefact class groups were found to be somewhat different to those identified for the southern and central clusters and reflect the different function inferred for the northern cluster. Significant associations were found to occur among all six class groups and to indicate two general patterns of artefact association. As with the southern and central clusters, the first pattern is a general background pattern of association between

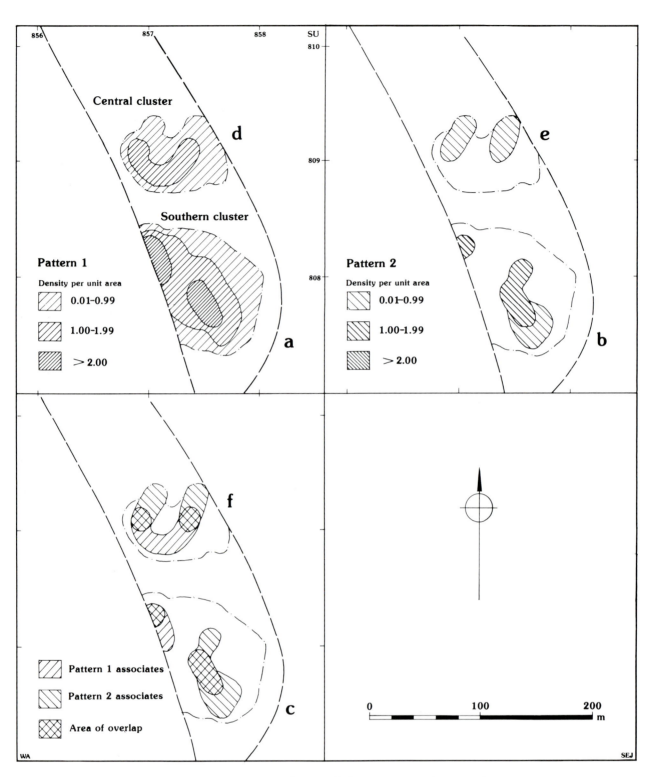

Figure 27   Maidenhead Thicket: southern and central clusters, spatial patterning

primary, secondary, and tertiary pieces and simply reflects their general co-occurrence in all of the test excavation units intersecting the cluster. Their joint density distribution is shown in Figure 28a and corresponds with that identified for the concentration as a whole (Fig. 26). The second pattern consists of significant associations occurring between primary and tertiary pieces, cores, undiagnostic pieces, and the general tool class composed of retouched and utilised

pieces. This pattern reflects the spatial co-occurrence of artefacts related to flintworking and tool utilisation. Figure 28b shows their joint density distribution with one distinct concentration occurring within the cluster's boundaries.

Figure 28c shows the joint density distributions for the two identified associational patterns plotted together and identifies a single activity area largely corresponding in location to the cluster's core area

Table 26 Maidenhead Thicket: matrix of tau–b values for the northern cluster

	P	S	T	C	U	Tool
P	–					
S	.568*	–				
T	.624*	.786*	–			
C	.490*	.321	.366*	–		
U	.471*	.256	.367*	.360*	–	
Tool	.608*	.594*	.588*	.595*	.452*	–

For key see Table 24

identified earlier. The spatial co-occurrence of flaking debris with tools appears to indicate that this activity area probably functioned as a more generalised work area where both flintworking and tool utilisation activities were carried out, probably related to a habitation area. The general absence of artefacts related to nodule testing and the initial reduction and shaping of nodules into cores, suggest that the flintworking activities carried out were primarily devoted to the production of suitable blanks for tool manufacture. It is not possible on the basis of the small number of tools recovered to infer the activities in which they may have been used.

6 Discussion

Fieldwork at Maidenhead Thicket revealed three concentrations of later Neolithic/earlier Bronze Age flint artefacts. Assemblage characteristics for the southern

and central clusters indicated that the two concentrations were probably the remains of limited activity quarry or extraction sites. Assemblage characteristics for the northern cluster suggested that it was probably the remains of a residential site. The three artefact concentrations form part of a larger distribution of broadly contemporaneous flint concentrations and isolated findspots known for the area. Immediately to the west of Maidenhead Thicket a flint concentration broadly dated to within the Bronze Age with an associated possible burnt mound was discovered by evaluation fieldwork undertaken at Stubbings House (Heaton *et al.* 1991). Further to the west within a 7–8 km distance, 15 concentrations dating to the later Neolithic and/or Bronze Age and three undated concentrations were identified by fieldwalking undertaken as part of the East Berkshire Survey (Ford 1987a; *see also below*, Chapter 4). A further 23 findspots of later Neolithic and earlier Bronze Age artefacts are known for the area and include 20 polished or flaked axes and chisels and three arrowheads (Ford 1991). Two round barrows/ring-ditches are also known for the immediate area.

The three concentrations are of interest regionally as they form part of the pattern of the later Neolithic/earlier Bronze Age settlement known for the area. Ford (1991) has convincingly argued on the basis of a major study of the middle Thames region, that the area to the west of Maidenhead was not intensively settled or exploited until the later Neolithic. Fieldwalking found later Neolithic/earlier Bronze Age flint concentrations to be more numerous and widespread in their distribution and generally without an earlier Neolithic component. The rarity of earlier Neolithic material was interpreted as evidence for the expansion of settlement into areas of the landscape not intensively exploited previously, with the occurrence of round barrows taken

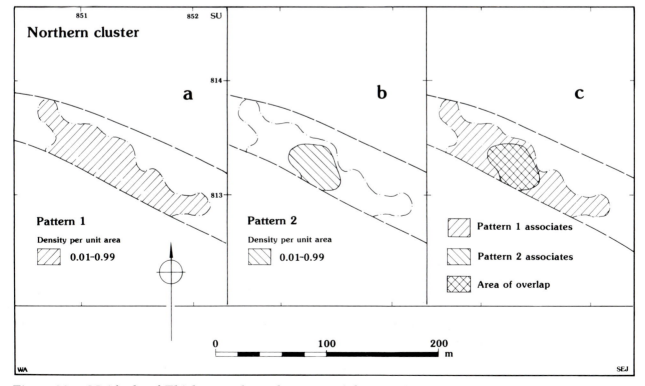

Figure 28   Maidenhead Thicket: northern cluster, spatial patterning

as an indication that a substantial proportion of the area had been brought into use by the Early Bronze Age. Although Ford (*ibid.*, 428–9) noted that the process for this expansion of settlement into areas of the landscape previously not intensively settled or exploited and its rate of occurrence are poorly understood, he identified improvements in agricultural technology and more specialised landuse strategies as the most likely underlying factors.

Assemblage composition for the later Neolithic/earlier Bronze Age flint concentrations known to occur within the area (Ford 1987a; b; 1991; Heaton *et al.* 1991) are highly variable in artefact class group representation and indicate a number of functional site types or class groups. The number of tools and diversity of class groups in the assemblage inventory from the concentrations at Stubbings House (*ibid.*, tables 1 and 7) indicate that it probably functioned as some form of residential site. Similar patterns of tool frequency and artefact class group diversity in the data for the 18 flint concentrations discovered by the East Berkshire Survey (Ford 1987a, table 23; 30–31) suggest that 14 of them were probably residential sites and four some form of indeterminate limited activity site. The southern and central clusters identified at Maidenhead Thicket have been interpreted on the basis of assemblage characteristics as limited activity quarry or extraction sites and supplement the small number of limited activity sites known for the area. Although the samples recovered from the two concentrations are relatively small, the pattern and composition of artefact class group co-occurrences indicate that their primary function was the acquisition and initial reduction of nodules into core preforms with the preforms transported elsewhere for further reduction. Whether the core preforms were moved to the northern cluster, to the concentration at Stubbings House or to some unknown site elsewhere in the vicinity of Maidenhead Thicket cannot be ascertained with the data presently available.

What can be ascertained is that these two concentrations, together with the northern cluster, functioned as part of the specialised later Neolithic/earlier Bronze Age settlement and landuse strategies identified for the area by Ford (1991) and that these strategies produced a number of types or classes of site with different assemblage characteristics. Further fieldwork and research should assist in clarifying the chronological ambiguities and the range of functional variability occurring in assemblage characteristics of flint artefact concentrations dating from this period.

3. An Early Iron Age Settlement at Dunston Park, Thatcham

By A.P. Fitzpatrick, I. Barnes, and R.M.J. Cleal

with contributions from A.J. Clapham, P.A. Harding, F. Healy, L.N. Mepham, and Elaine L. Morris

1 Introduction

In 1986 an outline planning application for the development of 50.7 ha of land on the north-east side of Thatcham, centred on SU 523 681 (Fig. 29), was submitted to Newbury District Council. The proposed development was for housing and associated services. The Kennet Valley is considered to be an area of high archaeological potential and, in accordance with Policy EN26 of the Draft *Replacement Structure Plan*, an archaeological evaluation was required prior to the completion of a Section 52 agreement relating to the development. Wessex Archaeology was commissioned

to carry out the work. A strategy for evaluation was agreed with Berkshire County Council and fieldwork took place between November 1988 and January 1989.

The evaluation fieldwork identified four areas of archaeological activity including possible prehistoric settlement in a field (evaluation Field P) in the south-east corner of the proposed development (Fig. 30). This field covered approximately 8 ha centred on SU 528 676 and it was intended that construction would start first in this field. In response to this Wessex Archaeology, in conjunction with Berkshire County Council, developed a strategy which involved two stages of excavation. These were subsequently carried out by Wessex Arch-

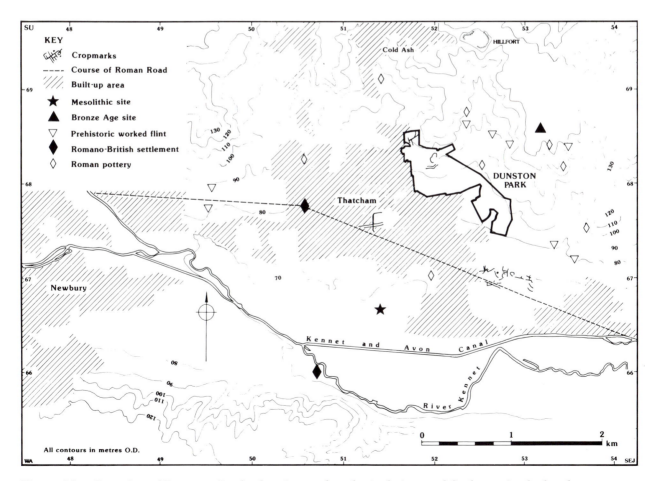

Figure 29   Location of Dunston Park, showing archaeological sites and findspots in the local area

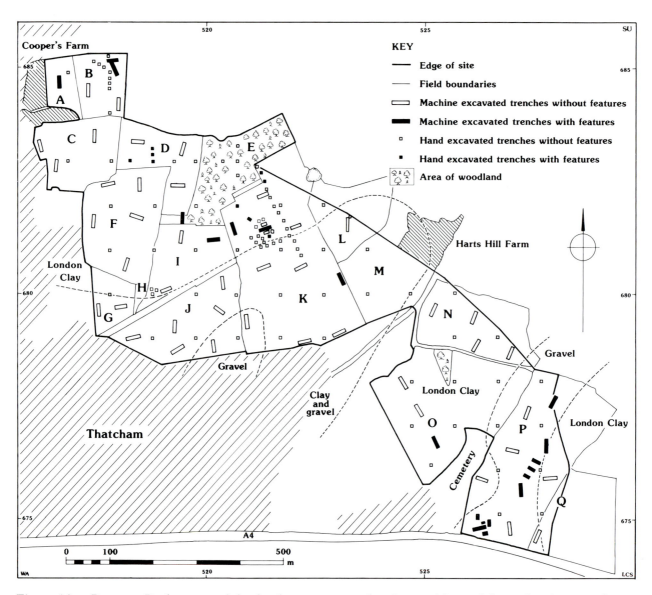

Figure 30   Dunston Park: extent of the development area, showing positions of the evaluation trenches (1988 / 1989)

aeology over two seasons in 1989 (Trenches I–V) and 1991 (Trench VI). A watching brief was also maintained over the construction of a distributor road.

Though these excavations represent only the first phase of those associated with the development it has been thought appropriate to publish the work separately as it will be many years before the construction programme is completed.

2 Topography and Geology

The site, under pasture prior to the excavations, lay to the north of the River Kennet on a south facing slope, rising from 79 m OD at the southern edge of the field to 95 m OD at the northern edge. A low ridge ran along the north–south axis of the field gradually fading away to the south and forming an almost level terrace in the south-west corner of the field.

The Ordnance Survey Drift Geology map (sheet 267) shows the lower part of the field to be composed of valley gravels with the upper portions consisting of London Clay. In reality the low ridge consisted of gravel with London Clay to either side and to the north.

3 Archaeological Background

No archaeological activity had previously been recorded on the site. Stray finds and sites in the area indicated occupation throughout the prehistoric, Romano-British, and medieval periods (Fig. 29). A Bronze Age settlement and burial site is known 0.75 km to the north, and finds of flintknapping debris in the fields to the south suggest more extensive activities dating to the later prehistoric period, as do cropmarks identified on aerial photographs (Fig. 29). The Iron Age hillfort of Ramsbury lies c. 2 km to the north, immediately east of Cold Ash. The Roman

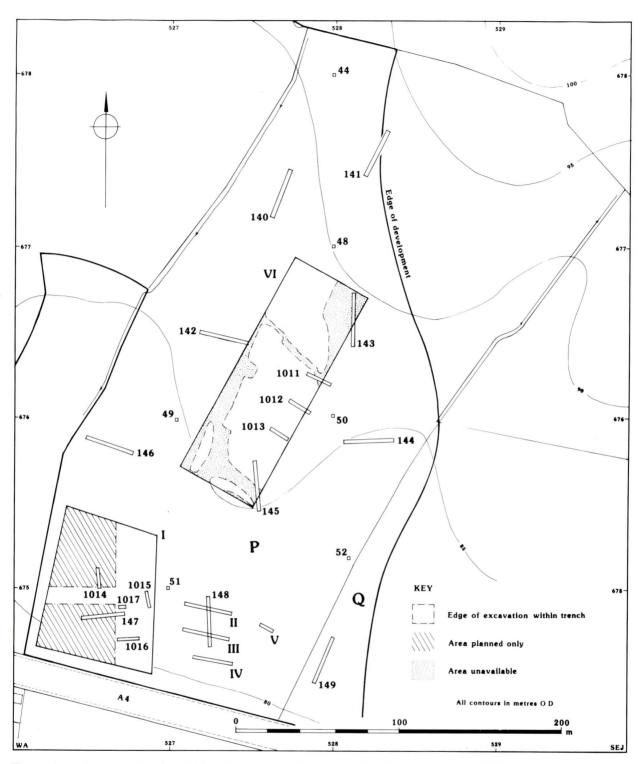

Figure 31   Dunston Park: Field P showing positions of evaluation trenches (1988/1989) and excavation trenches I–V (1989) and VI (1991) with features

road from Silchester to Cirencester passes through Thatcham and a contemporaneous roadside settlement of unknown size existed there, adjacent to the Bath road. Thatcham is known to have been a late Saxon administrative centre which subsequently developed into a medieval borough. An 18th century mansion, Dunston Park House, of which only a structural platform and garden earthworks survive today, stood 0.50 km to the west.

The Evaluation

The evaluation was carried out over a six week period during December 1988 and January 1989 and covered the whole of the 50.7 ha Dunston Park development. It consisted of 65 machine trenches, each at least 30 m long, with a minimum of one per hectare, and 97 one metre square hand trenches, one on each hectare intersection (Fig. 30). A total of 3817 m^2 was examined representing 0.75% of the development area. In addition, 24% of the area was available for fieldwalking and a survey of the extant Dunston Park House garden earthworks was also undertaken.

In all, 74 archaeological features were found across the proposed development and four areas of archaeological interest were identified. The most substantial of these, which was to prompt the excavations described below, was situated in evaluation Field P in the south-east corner of the development area. Here, as well as the statutory machine trench per hectare, a series of trenches examined the low ridge which ran up the spine of the field and the terrace in the south-west corner. Fourteen machine trenches were excavated in this field, 11 of which revealed a combined total of 48 archaeological features. Twenty-three of these features were excavated and, on ceramic evidence, three could be dated to the Late Bronze Age/Early Iron Age, one to the Iron Age, and one to the Late Roman period. These features were concentrated on the terrace in the south-west corner of the field, with a lower density on the low ridge, and were interpreted as representing a settlement site.

Another area of suspected prehistoric occupation was found at the north-western extreme of the development on the edge of a substantial dry valley in evaluation Field B (Fig. 30). From the fill of a single large pit the remains of at least five pottery vessels dating to the Early Iron Age were recovered along with quantities of ironsmithing residue. A series of hand trenches was excavated in the vicinity of this feature and a background of contemporaneous pottery along with a sherd of Early Bronze Age pottery was identified. This material is reported upon in the Appendix, below.

The other two areas of archaeological interest were in evaluation Fields D, E, and K, and were directly related to the construction and use of Dunston Park House.

5 Excavation Research Design

The analysis of the results of the evaluation led to two areas of archaeological importance being defined: the terrace in the south-west corner of Field P and the ridge in the same field. In response, two excavation areas (Fig. 31: Trenches I and VI) covering a total of c. 12,530 m^2 were sited with the aims of recording a plan of the features and to interpret the date and nature of the suspected settlement. The boundaries of the trenches were established to investigate the distribution of features found during the evaluation but with respect to modern field boundaries, and underground and overhead services. In addition, four other trenches (Fig. 31: Trenches II–V) covering a total area of 140 m^2 were opened to try to delimit the activity to the east. Trenches I–V were excavated in the autumn of 1989, Trench VI in the autumn of 1991 and the watching brief, which did not yield any archaeological data, was undertaken in the summer of 1992.

The trenches were machine stripped onto the surface of the underlying gravels or clays but considerable difficulty was experienced in 1989 in reaching the correct level because of extremely dry conditions. Apart from the southern half of Trench I the trenches were not hand cleaned as it was found that, after several days' exposure, features were readily identifiable without further cleaning.

All visible features were planned. In Trench I such a high density of features was uncovered that a sampling strategy was adopted. This involved the detailed examination of a north–south transect, 24 m wide, along the eastern side of the trench and an east–west transect 10 m wide across the centre of the trench. This sample area comprised 45.5% of the total area of Trench I; within this all the features in the north–south transect and 59% of those in the east–west transect were excavated. Outside the sample area, and in Trenches II–V, with the exception of the excavation of one ditch section, features were planned only. Only in Trench VI was it possible to plan and sample all features.

The majority of features were partially excavated. A large enough section, usually c. 50%, of each feature was excavated to allow an interpretation to be made. The majority of ditch terminals were excavated with at least one section excavated along the ditch length. All features were fully recorded using Wessex Archaeology's standard recording system. Bulk and dated samples for environmental data were taken from well sealed deposits.

6 Excavation Results

Initially it was planned to machine strip, over two seasons, an area of 12,670 m^2 but c. 1450 m^2 of Trench VI had been covered by roads and the builders compound before excavation commenced so it was only possible to examine c. 11,220 m^2.

Geology

An average of 0.20 m of dark brown sandy loam topsoil was removed by machine. Unfortunately, because of the extremely dry weather conditions prevailing during the excavation of Trench I, it was difficult to distinguish between the topsoil and underlying layers, and it subsequently became apparent that in some areas insufficient overburden had been removed. This was the case in the southern part of Trench I, but it also occurred in patches over the rest of the Trench (shown as unexcavated in Fig. 32).

The six trenches revealed a low gravel ridge, approximately 60 m wide, running south-west–north-east up the spine of the field. To either side of this ridge the geology was of London Clay, with a zone of mixed clay and gravel at the interface. The ridge ran from a height of 79.00 m OD at the south end of Trench I to 88.00 m OD at the north end of Trench VI and was little more than 0.50 m higher than the surrounding field. The London Clay was noted in the north-west corner of Trench I, in Trenches IV and V, and at the northern extreme of Trench VI.

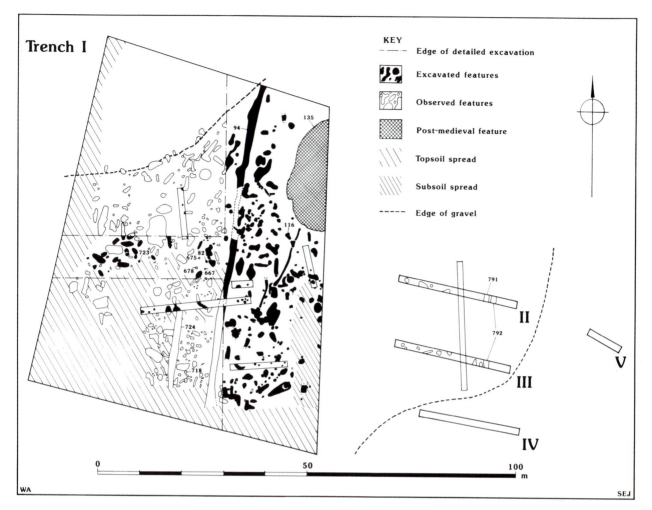

Figure 32   Dunston Park: plan of Trench I

Archaeological Features

Some 661 features were found across the site, the frequency of features varying considerably from one feature every 5 m^2 in Trenches I, II, and III to one every 60 m^2 in Trench VI. There was a marked decrease in the number of features towards the north-west corner of Trench I, the northern extreme of Trench VI, and to the east in Trenches IV and V.

The excavated features were grouped into five defined categories during post-excavation: post-holes, pits, hollows, linear features, and others. Very few of the post-holes showed post-pipes, which might suggest that posts were generally removed. Of 414 excavated features only 102 (25%) contained artefacts. From a combination of artefactual and stratigraphic evidence it is possible to postulate one undatable and six datable phases of activity. The distribution of finds other than pottery, by feature is given in Tables 27 and 28.

The excavated and unexcavated features appear to fall into three main spatial groups, which need not be contemporaneous and may themselves be composed of features of different dates. In Trench I, and possibly also Trenches II–V, there was a dense concentration of features which contained few finds. The distribution of later prehistoric pottery, probably of similar date to that in Trench VI, though more fragmentary, is shown in

Figure 33, as is that of burnt flint. A fairly low level of activity is evident, with Iron Age pottery numbering only ten sherds. Even allowing for the deposition of rubbish away from a settlement, such a low level of finds seems to be incompatible with the area having been a settlement. Many of the features are amorphous or irregular in shape and it seems likely that some at least are periglacial in origin. The smaller, well-defined features interpreted as post-holes were isolated from the background of larger features during the post-excavation analysis in an attempt to discern structures, but although it is possible to define groups of features, in general the results are irreconcilable with the clarity and quality of the data present in Trench VI. Nor, in view of the paucity of artefactual evidence can it be assumed that all these features are contemporaneous. Full details of the analyses are available in the archive. Consequently, while it is clear that there was activity which required earthfast posts in Trench I, their date and character remain poorly defined. Only group 770 (post-holes 82, 667, 675, 678) which may be a 2 x 2 m square four–post structure is felt to be a plausible grouping. This would be compatible with the Early Iron Age date of the pottery and with posts or structures spread around a farm.

In contrast to this ephemeral evidence the double ring round-house 1128 in the southern part of Trench

Table 27 Dunston Park: distribution of worked and burnt flint by feature. Evaluation and Trenches I–V (weight in g)

	Flint		Burnt flint	
	No.	Wt	No.	Wt
Evaluation	7	19	78	1515
Features (Trenches I–V)				
28	–	–	4	47
30	3	10	–	–
31	1	2	1	13
34	2	8	–	–
38	2	1	32	128
45	1	2	–	–
50	1	1	2	13
86	–	–	1	15
88	4	3	9	70
91	1	6	1	12
92	3	3	7	6
98	3	5	2	19
116	16	27	–	–
126	1	1	–	–
135	1	26	33	493
174	1	10	9	160
180	1	1	–	–
187	–	–	2	5
221	–	–	2	5
227	1	20	1	13
242	–	–	14	178
262	–	–	5	80
309	–	–	3	23
342	–	–	308	768
348	–	–	3	26
368	–	–	3	16
372	–	–	25	138
374	–	–	8	90
378	–	–	1	27
409	–	–	7	58
431	–	–	1	6
461	–	–	21	204
536	–	–	1	4
542	1	3	–	–
547	–	–	29	276
551	1	2	–	–
584	–	–	38	442
592	–	–	1	42
601	–	–	5	68
Total	51	150	657	4960

Table 28 Dunston Park: distribution of finds other than pottery from features in Trench VI (weight in g)

	Fired clay		Flint		Burnt flint		Stone
	No.	Wt	No.	Wt	No	Wt	No.
Feature							
796	–	–	–	–	1	10	–
800	–	–	1	24	2	6	–
807	–	–	1	2	4	25	–
809	–	–	2	1	1	5	–
813/4	–	–	–	–	1	6	–
826	–	–	–	–	8	16	–
828	1	16	2	5	25	296	1
830	5	22	–	–	2	112	–
832	–	–	–	–	1	18	–
862	–	–	1	2	6	32	–
864	–	–	3	49	69	2446	–
884	–	–	–	–	1	8	–
886	–	–	–	–	1	12	–
912	–	–	1	50	1	6	–
920	–	–	–	–	–	–	1
927	1	7	–	–	–	–	–
971	–	–	2	17	2	35	–
973	–	–	–	–	1	3	–
995	1	1	–	–	1	26	–
997	3	31	2	42	2	80	–
1013	–	–	–	–	1	26	–
1015	3	14	–	–	–	–	–
1022	2	6	–	–	–	–	–
1032	–	–	–	–	2	12	–
1038	–	–	–	–	3	70	–
1040	–	–	–	–	1	5	–
1056	–	–	–	–	2	12	–
1062	1	2	–	–	–	–	–
1086	–	–	–	–	5	10	–
Total	17	99	15	192	143	3277	2

VI was very clearly defined, and was clearly dated on ceramic evidence to the Early Iron Age.

The third cluster of features was in the northern part of Trench VI, and consisted of a number of small features, mainly post-holes. Three features in this area — two pits and one pit or post-hole (1054, 1056, and 1032) — were, on ceramic evidence, probably in use at the same time as the round-house 1128. Some post-holes might be interpreted as forming a circular structure (group 1129) but some features in it may be of later date, as medieval pottery was recovered from four of them (1030, 1034, 1044, 1020). Because of this range of dates it is not possible confidently to suggest the presence of an Iron Age building although it might explain the presence of pits and post-holes containing pottery of this date.

The area largely devoid of Early Iron Age features between this cluster and the round-house appears to have been an open space as there was no post-depositional disturbance to account for the lack of features, nor is it the result of a different excavation strategy in this area.

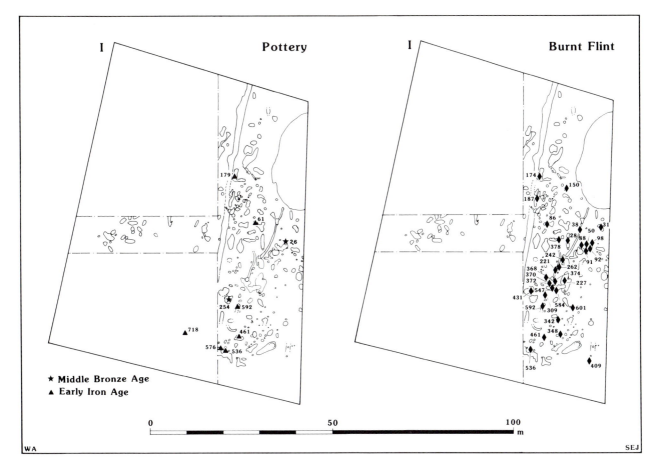

Figure 33   Dunston Park: distribution of pottery and burnt flint in Trench I

Plate 6   Dunston Park: Trench I looking south

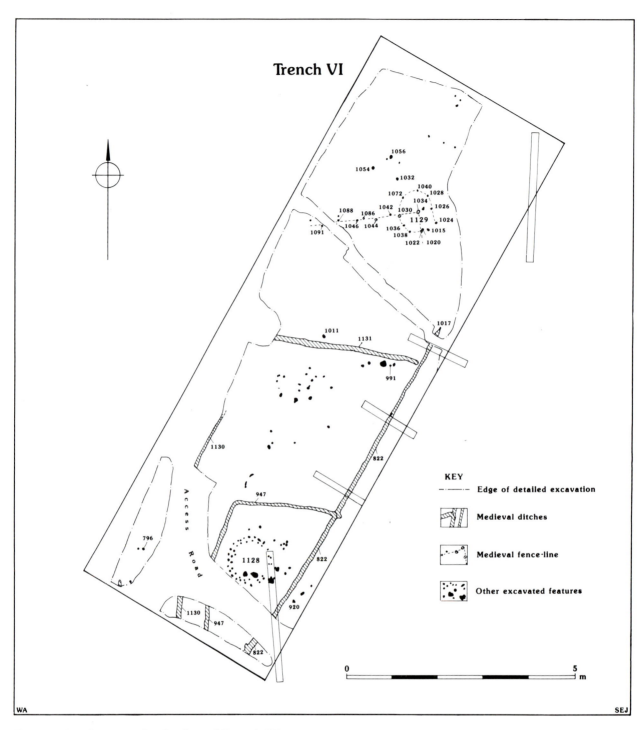

Figure 34   Dunston Park: plan of Trench VI

Phase 1: Neolithic or Early Bronze Age
A single hollow (116) in Trench I contained 16 (27 g) worked flints (Table 27) which included flakes and blades displaying platform edge abrasion and soft-hammer flaking. Both these techniques would be unusual in a later Bronze Age/Early Iron Age assemblage and are thus thought to be earlier.

Phase 2: Middle Bronze Age
Hollow 254 in Trench I contained 24 sherds (668 g) of a Deverel–Rimbury urn of Middle Bronze Age date; a fragment of worked shale found unstratified in the

immediate area may have been associated with this material. Only two other sherds (7 g) of the same fabric were found, in post-hole 26 (Fig. 33).

Phase 3: Early Iron Age
Twenty-one of the post-holes of the round-house contained Early Iron Age pottery, and apart from the round-house a total of five features in the evaluation trenches, seven in Trenches I–V, and four in Trench VI could be positively dated to the Early Iron Age on ceramic grounds. These features did not, on their own, form any coherent pattern or define areas of activity. It

Plate 7   Dunston Park: Trench VI looking north with ditch 947 in the foreground with part of round-house 1128 to the right

must be likely that many of the undated features (*below*) which are generally comparable to those of Iron Age date are also of this date.

The round-house, 1128, is the only certain structure identifiable on the site. It is possible that not all the post-holes which existed around post-hole 932 were recorded as this was where the house was discovered by machine trenching during the evaluation.

The house appears to represent a single phase with no evidence observed for repair or rebuilding other than of the porch and post-hole 892 which may have been a replacement. The house was built of double, concentric, rings of posts with a substantial porch 2.60 m wide and *c.* 2 m long facing to the south-east orientated at 120° (Figs 35 and 36). The inner ring of 19 post-holes (group 1127) was 9 m in diameter and the outer ring of 26 post-holes (group 1126) some 11 m. In both rings the post-holes were *c.* 1.25 m apart and individual post-holes ranged from 0.22 m to 0.38 m in diameter and 0.05 m to 0.28 m in depth. There was a greater diversity of diameter and depth in the inner ring (Fig. 36). Most post-holes were circular with steep or sloping sides and slightly rounded bases. They were filled with dark brown loam and gravel which varied according to the surrounding subsoil. No large packing stones were present and only two post-holes (884 and 886) showed areas of less stony fill which may indicate the position of the posts. Two irregularly shaped pits (828 and 830) were found inside the right (southern) half (viewed from within the house looking out). They contained some charcoal and a combined total of 341 sherds (2000 g) of Early Iron Age pottery, as well as fired clay (6/38 g,

worked (2/5 g) and burnt flint (27/408 g), part of a quern, plant macrofossils, and a spindle whorl (Fig. 38). Both pits appeared to have a single, homogeneous, fill.

A pair of large post-holes or pits was excavated at the entrance to the porch. The bases of both were lined with flint pebbles which were heavily burnt. There was no direct evidence that these pits had contained posts. This might suggest that they were not associated with the porch but lay next to its eaves. However, it is more likely that the large size reflects replacement of the posts, and the pebbles may be an attempt to improve drainage. The shallow scoops 764 and 862 may represent features created in repairing the porch (Harding *et al.* 1993, 102). The northern post-hole (864) contained 62 sherds (453 g) of Early Iron Age pottery, worked (3/49 g) and burnt flint (69/2446 g), and plant macrofossils. The southern post-hole, discovered during the evaluation (W292 (770)) contained three sherds (43 g) of pottery and no other finds. When examined in the evaluation pit 770 appeared to be cut by post-hole 765 of the porch, but it is more likely to be contiguous and evidence of repair: in view of the absence of evidence for more than one phase elsewhere in the house, it is possible that the features were adajacent and almost contemporaneous.

Pottery totalling 216 sherds (2229 g) was recovered from the post-holes of the round-house (excluding the porch), all except four (3 g) of which were found in post-holes in the right half of the house or around the entrance (Fig. 39, 1–9; Fig. 40). In addition, one of the structural post-holes (912) on the southern side of the round-house contained nine pieces (30 g) of a metal-working crucible (Fig. 38). A group of post-holes (848,

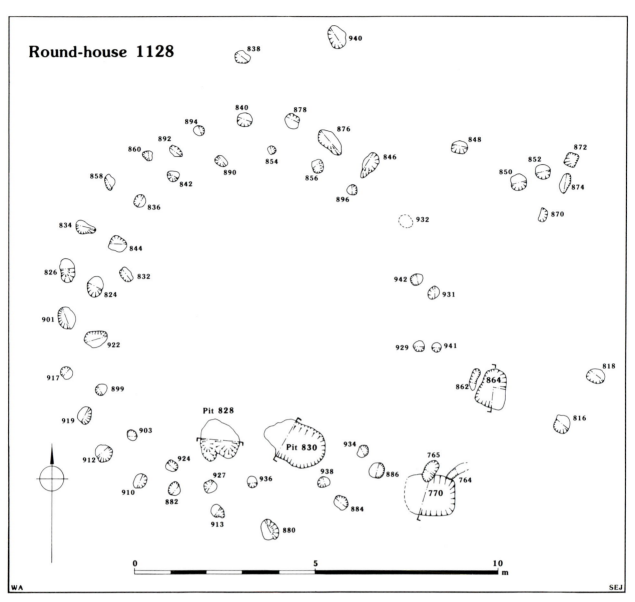

Figure 35   Dunston Park: round-house 1128

850, 852, 870, 872, 874) lay to the left of the porch, while two others (838 and 940), one of which was relatively large (940) lay next to the centre of the house's left hand side. Only one of these post-holes outside the house (818) contained any finds, five sherds of probable Early Iron Age pottery (18 g). The area next to the right hand side of the house had been destroyed by a recent road associated with the housing development so it is uncertain whether similar features had once existed there.

Approximately 75 m to the north of round-house 1128, and close to the possible round-house 1129, were two pits and one pit or post-hole (1054, 1056, 1032) which contained pottery comparable to that from the round-house. A single isolated pit, 1011, which lay between groups 1128–9 also contained Early Iron Age pottery.

Phase 4: Romano-British

When identified in the evaluation trench ditch 822 (Fig. 31) produced 36 sherds of an everted rim Black Burnish-

ed Ware I jar of late 3rd or 4th century date (Seager Smith and Davies 1993, 231–40), although the ditch itself was subsequently dated to the medieval period. A small amount of other Romano-British pottery was recovered from the site.

Phase 5: medieval enclosures

A series of four ditches (822, 947, 1130, 1131), dated to the medieval period on pottery, stratigraphic, and association grounds, was excavated in Trench VI (Fig. 34). These ditches were aligned on two axes, either northwest–south-east or north-east–south-west. They were filled with homogeneous orange brown silty gravels from which a combined total of nine sherds (64 g) of 12th–13th century pottery was recovered. In addition, where ditch 822 ran close to the Phase 3 round-house 1128, 11 sherds (103 g) of Late Bronze Age/Early Iron Age pottery, considered residual, were found. When it was first identified during the evaluation close to this point, Romano-British pottery was found in the ditch.

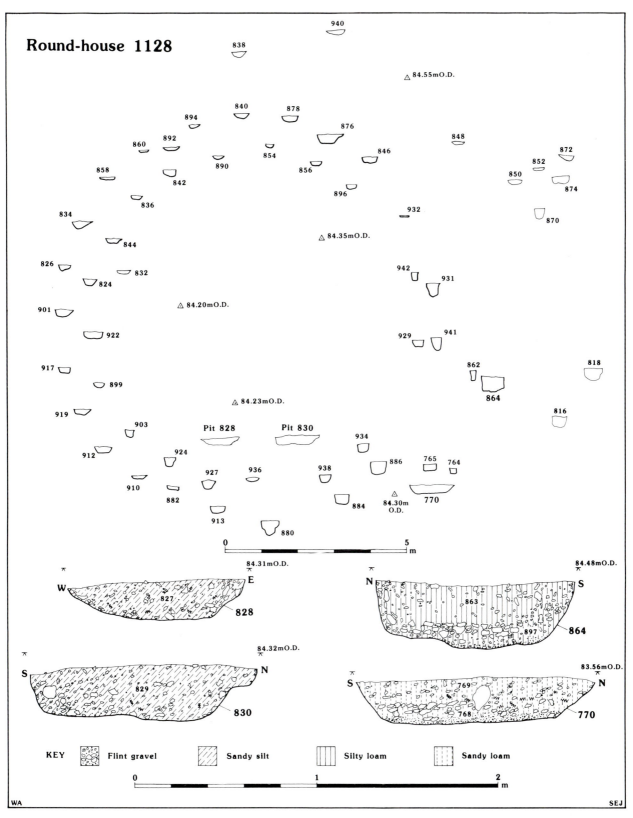

Figure 36   Dunston Park: sections of post-holes of round-house 1128

The four post-holes 1020, 1030, 1034, and 1044 containing medieval pottery appear to form a fence-line on approximately the same alignment as the ditches.

The four ditches appeared to form two enclosures of different dates; although the southern ends of neither were found. A subrectangular enclosure covering at least 2076 m^2 was defined by ditches 822, 1130, and 1131. At a later date, but still in the medieval period, ditch 947 was constructed enclosing a subrectangular area, at least 667 m^2 at the southern extreme of the

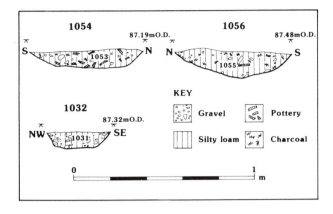

*Figure 37   Dunston Park: sections through
Early Iron Age pits 1054, 1056, and 1032*

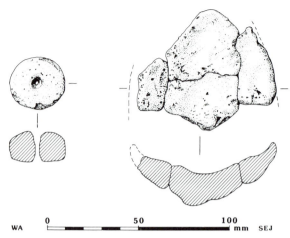

*Figure 38   Dunston Park: Early Iron Age
ceramic spindle whorl (left) and crucible (right)*

earlier enclosure. This reused the earlier ditch 822 as its western boundary and was recorded as cutting the then partially silted ditch. Apart from a low background scatter of medieval pottery — some 16 sherds (78 g) were found outside the ditches — no other evidence of medieval activity was found. In view of this the enclosures are interpreted as fields or agricultural pens. It is very likely that unphased ditches in Trenches I–III were also part of this system.

Phase 6: post-medieval
A total of 14 features could be dated to this phase by associated artefacts or stratigraphic relationship. A large semicircular feature 26 m in diameter and excavated to a depth of 1.40 m in the north-east corner of Trench I was probably a gravel quarry, and another possible gravel quarry was found at the western edge of Trench I where an engineering contractor's test-hole was observed cutting through a feature similar in character to the excavated quarry. A system of eight modern field drains was also recorded across Trenches I and VI. In addition, a small circular feature (723) in Trench I was seen to contain modern material and was assumed to be of this date, as was a narrow, straight gully (820) recorded in Trench VI.

Unphased
While strictly regarded as unphased it is likely that these features belong to two principal groups, Iron Age and medieval. The majority of the features in Trench I (270 excavated and 226 unexcavated), 12 features in Trenches II and III, and 87 in Trench VI, contained no positive dating evidence. These features, however, were either associated with, or similar in form and nature to, those dated by pottery to the Early Iron Age and it is possible that many are of this date.

Two ditches (791 and 792) found in Trenches II and III could not be dated but it seems likely that either or both of them may be a continuation of, or related to, ditch 1130 found in Trench VI. Ditches 791 and 792 were on average 1.32 m wide and 0.33 m deep with a shallow U–shaped profile. A pair of parallel ditches (94 and 724), 8.40 m apart formed a possible trackway which ran north–south across the centre of Trench I. Excavated sections through the eastern feature (94) showed it to be no more than 0.25 m deep, the fill yielded no artefacts

and it had no discernible physical relationship with any other feature. The western feature (724) remained unexcavated. The rather ephemeral nature of the features may indicate that they represent the remains of hedgerow ditches and it seems likely that they were associated with the medieval field system.

7   Finds

Metalworking Debris, by L.N. Mepham

Nine pieces (30 g) with a vesicular structure suggesting that they had been heated strongly were recovered from post-hole 912, within round-house 1128. There are three groups of conjoining sherds which derive from a single shallow, rounded vessel, probably a crucible (Object No. 518; Fig. 38, right): similar examples have been found at, for example, Aldermaston Wharf (Bradley *et al.* 1980, fig. 20). XRF analysis by J. Bayley of the Ancient Monuments Laboratory failed to detect any significant amount of metals but any original metal-rich surface is likely to have been lost.

Worked Flint, by F. Healy and P.A. Harding

The composition and incidence of the struck flint excavated during both the initial evaluation of Field P and the subsequent excavations are summarised in Table 29. Where cortex survives it is generally that of gravel flint. Much of the material is glossed, plough-damaged, or both.

The small assemblage from pit 116 is distinguished by soft-hammer struck blades and flakes with abraded platform edges, technological features more usual in Neolithic than Bronze Age industries. Similarly, early activity may be represented by a very few blades struck from regular cores found elsewhere in the area.

Otherwise the material, whether from prehistoric features or other contexts, consists mainly of hard-hammer struck flakes with little evidence of

Table 29 Dunston Park: worked flint

Type	1	2	3	4	5	6	7	8	Total	Burnt	Broken
Field P	–	–	–	–	4	–	–	–	4	–	2
Trenches I–V											
Pit 116 (no pottery)	1	–	–	1	11	3	–	–	16	–	5
Features with MBA and EIA pottery (post-hole 26, pit 174, sherd concentration 718)	–	–	–	9	4	–	–	–	13	–	10
Features with flint only (pits 30, 31, 45, 88, 534; linear features 38, 187; scoops 34, 50, 91, 92, 98, 126, 227, 542)	1	1	1	–	21	2	–	–	26	1	11
Other contexts	2	1	1	–	44	1	1	1	51	–	21
Total Trenches I–V	4	2	2	10	84	6	1	1	110	1	49
Trench VI											
Features with pottery (800, 828, 864, 862, 912)	1	–	–	–	6	–	–	–	7	1	–
Features with flint only (809, 971)	–	–	–	–	4	–	–	–	4	–	–
Unstratified	–	–	–	–	5	–	–	–	5	–	–
Total Trench VI	1	–	–	–	15	–	–	–	16	1	–
Overall total	5	2	2	10	99	6	1	1	126	2	49

1 = miscellaneous debitage; 2 = cores; 3 = core rejuvenation flakes; 4 = chips; 5 = flakes; 6 = blades; 7 = scrapers; 8 = miscellaneous retouched flakes

platform preparation. Its technology accords with that of the metal age industries, summarised by Ford *et al.* (1984). Its generally low density suggests that by the time of the Early Iron Age occupation flintworking was locally unimportant, as in broadly contemporaneous settlements at Aldermaston Wharf and Knight's Farm (Bradley *et al.* 1980, 242, 274).

Worked Stone, by Elaine L. Morris

Two saddle quern fragments were recovered: one piece (62 g) from pit 828 within round-house 1128 and one (2955 g) from pit 920, outside it. These querns are of sarsen, and the larger measures at least 130 mm thick with the smaller over 45 mm. The general appearance of these pieces suggests that they are from different stones. They could have been used for grinding grain and pulverising hard foods such as seeds and nuts.

Blocks of sarsen, suitable as raw material for the manufacture of querns, would have been available within the local vicinity during the later Bronze Age (White 1907, 102–5, 119–21). Sarsen saddle querns were recovered nearby at the Late Bronze Age settlement at Reading Business Park (Moore and Jennings 1992) but at Aldermaston and Knight's Farm querns were made from several non-local sources (Bradley *et al.* 1980, 245).

Burnt Flint, by L.N. Mepham

Burnt flint was recovered from the site in some quantity, comprising a total of 1192 pieces (13,645 g). It formed a general background scatter over much of the site, with a small number of pieces being recovered from most features (Table 29). However, concentrations were noted in three prehistoric features (461, 828, and 864), the last two within round-house 1128 where they may have been associated with the hearth, and perhaps cooking.

Pottery, by Elaine L. Morris and L.N. Mepham

A total of 1798 sherds (16,876 g) was recovered (Table 30). The bulk of the assemblage (1674 sherds; 15,095 g) is Early Iron Age in date with a small quantity of Middle Bronze Age material. There is also a small number of Romano-British, medieval and post-medieval sherds which are not considered in any detail in this report.

Pottery from the site was derived from both general clearance contexts and from features. Some of the finer prehistoric material is abraded with surface treatments often obscured or completely removed, but the sherds are generally in good to moderate condition. A small number of partially complete vessels was found fragmented and probably *in situ* and a few refitting sherds were observed between contexts within features, but none between features. The mean sherd size for the prehistoric assemblage overall is 9.3 g.

Method
The prehistoric assemblage was analysed in accordance with recent guidelines (PCRG 1992). The pottery was divided into two broad groups on the basis of the domin-

78

ant inclusion type: flint-gritted or flint-tempered (Group F) and sandy fabrics (Group Q). These two groups were then subdivided into 11 separate fabric types on the basis of the range and coarseness of inclusions, using a binocular microscope (x 20 mag.). Samples of six of these fabric types were submitted for petrological analysis, which has been carried out by D.F. Williams of the University of Southampton whose report is held in archive. The results of this analysis are included in the text where appropriate, and the sampled fabrics are indicated (P). A type series was constructed for all prehistoric rims. In a few cases these rims can be related to specific vessel forms, but in general the rims are too small for this to be possible. Details of rim form, vessel form, surface treatment, decoration, sherd thickness, firing conditions, and usewear evidence have also been recorded. The pottery was quantified using both number and weight of sherds by fabric type within each context.

The small quantities of Romano-British, medieval, and post-medieval pottery have been scanned and quantified by context but no detailed examination of fabrics or forms was undertaken. Full details are in archive.

Fabrics
The 11 prehistoric fabric types identified, one Middle Bronze Age and 10 Early Iron Age, are listed below. Fabric totals are given in Table 30. In the fabric descriptions, the following terms are used to describe frequency of inclusions: rare (<1–<3%); sparse (3–<10%); moderate (10–<20%); common (20–<30%); and very common (30–<40%). All fabrics are considered to be soft, ie, can be easily scratched with a fingernail. In all cases where firing conditions allow observation, the clay matrix appears relatively iron-rich and the majority of sherds have an unoxidised core with at least the complete oxidisation of the external surface. Other examples have both surfaces oxidised but some sherds are unoxidised.

The bulk of the Early Iron Age assemblage consists of flint-gritted fabrics (92.3% of the assemblage by number of sherds) with a smaller component of sandy and silty fabrics (7.7%) (Table 31). Fabrics can be defined as either coarsewares (F1, F3, F5, F6, F7) or finewares (all the sandy fabrics) following classes established by Barrett (1980; see below). Two fabrics (F2 and F4) do not clearly fall within either group.

Fabrics with flint inclusions (Group F)
The range of fabrics within this group includes both flint-tempered (ie, flint has been deliberately added to

the clay matrix) and flint-gritted (ie, flint occurs naturally in the clay matrix) examples.
F1 Very coarse, flint-tempered; common poorly-sorted angular flint <4 mm, some calcined in fine silty clay matrix; Middle Bronze Age.
F2 Moderately coarse flint-gritted sandy (P); rare to sparse poorly-sorted subangular flint <2 mm (most <1 mm) in clay matrix; moderate to common fairly well-sorted subrounded quartz <0.5 mm; could be part of quartz sand group (Group Q).
F3 Very coarse, flint-tempered; abundant fairly well-sorted, subangular and angular flint <3 mm in silty clay matrix; rare mica.
F4 Flint-gritted, red iron oxides (P); sparse to moderate poorly-sorted subangular flint <3 mm in clay matrix; sparse to moderate red iron oxides, rare subrounded quartz <0.5 mm, rare mica.
F5 Coarse, flint-tempered; moderate to common poorly-sorted, subangular to angular flint <5 mm in clay matrix; moderate subrounded quartz <1 mm, sparse red iron oxides < 2 mm.
F6 Coarse, flint-gritted (P); sparse poorly-sorted subangular flint <2 mm in clay matrix; sparse to moderate subrounded quartz <0.25 mm; moderate glauconite pellets or grains; quartz and glauconite similar to those of fabric Q3, suggesting a coarse version of that.
F7 Very coarse, flint-tempered; moderate poorly-sorted, angular flint <7 mm in slightly sandy clay matrix; sparse subrounded quartz <1.5 mm; sparse to moderate iron oxides <2 mm.

Quartz sand fabrics (Group Q)
Q1 Moderately fine, slightly micaceous sandy (P); moderate well-sorted rounded quartz grains <0.25 mm, rare, subangular flint <1.5 mm, sparse to moderate iron oxides in fine clay matrix; mica.
Q2 Very fine, silty (P); silty clay matrix; microscopic quartz, rare rounded quartz <1 mm, subangular flint <1.5 mm, linear strands carbonaceous material <3 mm, mica, iron oxides <2 mm.

Table 31 Dunston Park: quantification of Early Iron Age pottery by fabric type

Fabric	No. sherds	Wt sherds (g)	% by number	% by weight
Coarsewares				
F2*	33	170	2.0	1.1
F3	7	24	0.4	0.1
F4*	341	3079	20.4	20.4
F5	1105	10,910	66.0	72.3
F6*	43	174	2.6	1.2
F7	15	103	0.9	0.7
Sub-total	1544	14,460	92.3	95.8
Finewares				
Q1	42	236	2.5	1.6
Q2	64	315	3.8	2.1
Q3	7	41	0.4	0.3
Q4	17	43	1.0	0.3
Sub-total	130	635	7.7	4.3
Total	1674	15,095		

* = can be used either as coarse- or fineware

Table 30 Dunston Park: quantification of prehistoric, Romano-British, medieval, and post-medieval pottery

	No. sherds	Wt sherds (g)
Middle Bronze Age	42	1340
Early Iron Age	1674	15,095
Romano-British	39	115
Medieval	25	142
Post-medieval	18	182
Total	1798	16,876

Q3 Sandy (P); common, well-sorted, rounded quartz, moderate to common, well-sorted, rounded glauconite, both <1 mm in fine clay matrix; glauconite, altered to limonite during firing, easily identified at x20 magnification.

Q4 Moderately fine sandy; rare to sparse well-sorted sub-angular flint <1 mm in clay matrix; rare subrounded quartz <0.25 mm, rare carbonaceous matter, mica, iron oxides. All examples unoxidised throughout.

Sources

The majority of British Late Bronze/Early Iron Age pottery could have been made from clays and inclusions found within a local resource zone of up to 10 km from the settlement where the pottery has been recovered (Morris in press), and this seems also to be the case for the Dunston Park assemblage. The solid geology of the area up to 10 km around Dunston Park consists of Upper Chalk, Reading Beds, London Clay, and Barton, Bracklesham, and Bagshot Beds (White 1907). The similarities in the clay matrix of so many of the fabrics suggests that a relatively restricted source area for much of the pottery could be expected, and the results of petrological analysis show that fabrics F2, F4, Q1, and Q2 could all have been made from clays and temper obtained from the general area of the site.

The only possible indication that a second source area is represented in this assemblage is the presence of glauconite in fabrics F6 and Q3. Glauconite is commonly associated with Greensand formations, of which the nearest outcrops to Dunston Park are c. 12 km to the south-west, with larger formations 30 km to the north. However, a source nearer to hand is perhaps more likely, since glauconitic sand can be found in some of the local Reading Beds (Williams, in archive).

Vessel forms

The occurrence of certain rim types has been used in conjunction with the presence of other diagnostic features such as decoration, and recognisable parts of vessels such as carinated sherds, in order to produce a limited vessel type series.

These have been categorised according to the classes established by Barrett (1980) (Table 32). This table demonstrates that, while there is some overlap due to fabric F4 (the dominant fabric), the forms generally correspond to broad fabric divisions, with Class I coarseware jar forms confined to flint-gritted and flint-tempered fabrics, and Class II fineware jars and Class IV fineware bowls largely to the finer sandy fabrics. There are no examples of Class III coarseware bowls or Class V cups in this modest assemblage.

Jars

Type 1 Large, shouldered (Fig. 39, 12 and 13); large, upright or slightly everted, squared off or flattened rims, pronounced, high shoulder. Finger-impressed decoration on shoulder or rim. One example, with soot on ext. below rim, used as cooking vessel and has pair of post-firing holes, presumably a repair (Fig. 39, 12).

Type 2 Large, well-finished, long neck, tripartite or uncertain body profile (Fig. 39, 6); large, upright or everted, simple, rounded or pointed rims, longer neck than Type 1, either tripartite profile with carinated shoulder or uncertain profile; generally better finished appearance than high-shouldered jars, surfaces carefully smoothed. Figure 39, 10 with impressed dot or ring decoration and complex zoned triangles and Figure 39, 11 with incised hatching within possible triangle may derive from similar fineware jars.

Type 3 Small slack-shouldered (Fig. 39, 3, 9, 14); small slack-shouldered, short upright, rounded or slightly thickened rim, no neck or with neck zone. Two with fingertip impressed decoration; one burnished or smoothed on ext.

Type 4 Ovoid (Fig. 39, 18); ovoid or convex-shaped, incurved rim, no neck.

Table 32 Dunston Park: Early Iron Age vessel forms by fabric and class based on rim types

Type/fabric	Class	F2	F4	F5	F6	F7	Q1	Q2	Q3	Q4	Total
Jars (63.6%)											
Type 1	I	1	1	9	–	–	–	–	–	–	11
Type 2	II	–	2	–	–	–	1	2	–	–	5
Type 3	I/II	–	4	1	1	–	–	–	–	–	6
Type 4	I	–	1	–	–	1	–	–	–	–	2
Type 5	I	1	–	3	–	–	–	–	–	–	4
Bowls (31.8%)											
Type 6	IV	–	–	–	–	–	1	1	–	–	2
*Type 7	IV	–	2	–	–	–	1	2	–	–	*5
Type 8	IV	–	1	–	–	–	–	–	1	1	3
Type 9	IV	–	–	–	–	–	1	–	–	–	1
Type 10	IV	–	1	–	–	–	1	1	–	–	3
Uncertain (4.5%)		–	2	–	–	–	–	–	–	–	2
Total		2	14	13	1	1	5	6	1	1	44

* = vessel type recognised from body sherds only

80

Type 5   Large, long-necked, probably shouldered (Fig. 39, 1); large, uncertain profile, long necked simple, rounded rim.

Bowls

Type 6   Carinated, tripartite (Fig. 39, 11); small, tripartite carinated profile, short everted rim; excluding carinated furrowed bowls (Type 7); zoned panels with diagonal hatching, impressed dots. Decorated sherds in fabric F4 (Fig. 39, 10) could be from similar vessel, or Type 2 fineware jar (*see above*).

Type 7   Furrowed, incised, furrowed-type (Fig. 39, 2); defined on basis of decoration type and position; both true wide furrowed design above carination and incised, parallel horizontal, decoration similar to furrows but clearly not the same also above carination; presumed to belong to carinated bowl tradition but length of rim and neck uncertain. Always bears either red-slipped surface treatment or burnish, or both.

Type 8   Hemispherical (Fig. 39, 8, 15, and 17); open, half-moon shaped; either flat-topped or thin, smoothed, rounded rim. One decorated with impressed circles below rim; usually burnished.

Type 9   Round-bodied (Fig. 39, 7); round-bodied, everted rim; red-finished; some burnished.

Type 10   Long-necked (Fig. 39, 4): Long-necked, thin-walled, everted rim. Usually red-finished.

Surface treatment and decoration

The recognition of surface treatments was hampered by the poor condition of the finer sandy fabric material. However, burnishing, smoothing, and either the application of some kind of surface slip or an oxidation of a ferruginous clay body were found on many sherds of fineware fabrics F2, F4, F6, Q1–Q4 (Table 33). These treatments are not found on coarsewares fabrics F1, F3, F5–F7.

What appears to be a slip occurs on external, and occasionally on internal, surfaces. While its composition appears to be similar to the clay of the body in each case, the rich orange-red colouring often contrasts with the underlying oxidised body, apparently indicating that the possible slip or added clay surface is of a more iron-rich composition than the original vessel clay body. These slipped sherds are likely to fall within the range of 'red-finished' wares which achieved the surface effect by the application of iron-rich slips (Middleton 1987). Seven sherds were submitted to A. Middleton of the Department of Scientific Research (British Museum) for X–ray diffraction analysis and scanning electron microscopy. A full report (BM Lab. Rep. 5184) is available in the archive. The results of this analysis indicate that none of the red finishes was produced by the application of ochre/haematite but that there is clear evidence for the application of a clay slip in one sherd and possibly two cases (Fig. 39, 2); the red colouration arises from the oxidisation of a ferruginous clay body in two cases (Fig. 39, 7 and 10), and in the remaining cases the results are inconclusive.

Wiping or smearing of the external surfaces is visible particularly on the finer flint-gritted fabrics F2 and F4, where it appears that efforts were made to disguise the coarser inclusions within the clay body. The heavy flint

Table 33 Dunston Park: number of occurrences of surface treatment on Early Iron Age sherds

	F2	F4	F6	Q1	Q2	Q3	Q4	Total
BU/B	–	2	–	5	2	1	6	16
BU/E	4	25	(?1)	2	–	–	3	35
SL/B	–	3	–	2	12	–	–	17
SL/E	2	115	–	12	28	1	–	158
SM/E	–	1	–	1	–	–	2	4
SM/I	–	21	–	–	–	–	–	21
WP/E	–	82	–	–	–	–	–	82
Total	6	249	(?1)	22	42	2	11	333

BU = burnished; SL = slipped/clay body; SM = smoothed; WP = roughly wiped; E = exterior; I = interior; B = both surfaces

gritting noted frequently on the bases of Late Bronze Age vessels in the area (eg, Longley 1980, 65), is also present here, in coarse flint-gritted fabrics only.

The frequency of decoration within the assemblage is considerable (Table 34). A total of 65 sherds carries some form of decoration representing *c.* 20 separate vessels. Half of the decorated vessels have fingertip or fingernail impressions which only occur on the rims and, more frequently, shoulders of jars in coarseware, flint-gritted fabrics (Fig. 39, 3, 5, 13). One probable fineware jar in fabric F4 has elaborate decoration of impressed circles within vertical panels of incised lines and horizontal bands of triangles infilled with diagonal incising (Fig. 39, 10). Decoration on bowls consists of three types: impressed circles or dots, incised lines, and wide, tooled, furrows. The circles occur on two types of bowls, a very large hemispherical vessel with only circles (Fig. 39, 15) and a small tripartite vessel bearing other decoration (Fig. 39, 11). These vessels not only have similar designs to the likely fineware jar discussed above, but are also made in the same fabric, F4. Incised lines occur on the tripartite bowl and in imitation of the wide, furrowed design in fabrics F4 and Q3. Furrowed decoration (Fig. 39, 2) is found on sherds in both sandy (Q1 and Q2) and the finer flint-gritted (F4) fabrics.

Table 34 Dunston Park: decoration types on Early Iron Age pottery represented by number of identifiable vessels

Decoration	F4	F5	Q1	Q2	Q3	Total
Furrows	2	–	1	3	–	6
Fingertip/nail	2	5	–	–	–	7
Incised lines	1	–	1	–	–	2
Impressed circles	–	–	–	*3	–	*3
Hatched triangles	–	–	–	*2	–	*2
Parallel incised	1	–	–	–	1	2
Total	6	5	2	*8	1	*22

* = one vessel represented twice

Usewear evidence

As a result of the poor surface condition of some sherds it is only possible to comment on the presence rather than presence and/or absence of evidence for use. This evidence, either as soot on the exterior or burnt residues internally, was recorded on four vessels, suggesting that they were used for cooking. All of the pots are in the flint-gritted or flint-tempered fabrics F4 and F5, including Figure 39, 12.

Chronology and affinities of the assemblage

Comparison of the fabrics, forms, and decorations with other assemblages shows that the majority of the pottery from Dunston Park fits well within the known range of the later part of the Early Iron Age, dated to the 7th century BC. A small element of the assemblage is earlier in date. Fabric F1 is represented by sherds which are probably derived from a single, thick-walled vessel. Only base sherds and plain body sherds are present, and these were recovered from Trench 1 only (Table 35). These thick-walled sherds in a very coarse flint-tempered fabric are characteristic of Deverel–Rimbury urn material recovered elsewhere in the Kennet Valley, for example at Sulhamstead Abbots (Woodward 1992).

The remainder of the assemblage is similar to a number of sites in the regions, some of the closest parallels for fabrics, forms, and decorations occurring in the assemblages from Rams Hill (Barrett 1975), Knight's Farm, subsite 1 (Bradley *et al.* 1980) and Blewburton Hill (Bradford 1942; Collins 1947) and slightly further afield from Runnymede Bridge (Longley 1980; 1991), Petters Sports Field (O'Connell 1986), Winklebury (Smith 1977), and Brighton Hill South, Site X/Y (Morris 1992). Several aspects of this assemblage would indicate a broad date of the 8th–7th century. They include the presence of sandy fabrics which have been observed to increase at the expense of the coarse flint-gritted fabrics towards the end of the Late Bronze Age and into the Early Iron Age (Longley 1980, 65; O'Connell 1986, 72), the relatively high proportion of fineware jars and bowls, and the frequency of decorated vessels.

However, it is possible to assign a more precise date of the 7th century, or later, to this assemblage. The presence of a furrowed bowl was not unexpected given the known distribution which includes west Berkshire (Cunliffe 1984, fig. 6.21). The Berkshire examples are flared rim types (Bradford 1942, fig. 3, 42; Barrett 1975, figs 3:6, 60; Mepham 1992, fig. 19, 33), a form assigned to the Later All Cannings Cross style of Early Iron Age (Cunliffe 1978, fig. A:6; 1984, 254); the Dunston Park sherd may be similar to these. There is also a long-necked bowl of Later All Cannings Cross style. However, there are no biconical bowls, a typical element of the Early All Cannings Cross style (Cunliffe 1978, 31–3) and found at Knight's Farm 1 (Bradley *et al.* 1980, fig. 35, 43–7). There are two examples of round-bodied bowls. This simple type is characteristic of the 6th-5th centuries in Hampshire, along with red-finished, scratch-cordoned wares (Cunliffe 1984, 254, fig. 6.22). Plain and decorated, round-bodied bowls appear in the later Early Iron Age in this area and in Oxfordshire (Cunliffe 1978, A:9–10). Therefore the presence at

Table 35 Dunston Park: prehistoric pottery from Trench I (no finewares or surface treated sherds present)

Context / feature type	Context / feature No.	MBA		EIA coarse-wares		Mean EIA sherd Wt(g)
		No.	Wt	No.	Wt	
Clearance	16	–	–	1	3	3.0
Clearance	17	16	665	16	63	3.9
Clearance	18	–	–	1	1	1.0
Post-hole	26	2	7	–	–	–
Pit	61	–	–	1	6	6.0
Hollow	254	24	668	–	–	–
Post-hole	433	–	–	1	12	12.0
Pit	461	–	–	2	9	4.5
Post-hole or hollow	536	–	–	3	11	3.7
Post-hole	576	–	–	1	2	2.0
?Gully	592	–	–	1	3	3.0
'Scatter'*	718	–	–	85	940	11.1

* = also 1 decorated sherd

Dunston Park of a furrowed bowl, a long-necked bowl, and round-bodied bowls, and the absence of biconical bowls, indicate a date in the 7th century, or possibly slightly later.

The occurrence of mainly locally produced pottery with a small amount of non-local vessels in the assemblage is typical of the Early Iron Age period (Cunliffe 1984, 259; Morris 1991; in press). The significance of this is that although suitable vessels were being produced from resources found in the immediate area, everyday pots in fabrics similar to the local wares were being acquired from elsewhere. This probably reflects the simple maintainance of social networks (Halstead and O'Shea 1982; Morris in press). The occurrence of both decorated bowls and jars at this site and at similarly dated sites in the wider region suggests that there is little to indicate social differences between them in the Early Iron Age.

Spatial distribution of the pottery

Apart from the material from house 1128, pottery was recovered from Trench I to the south-west (Table 35), from isolated features (991, 1011) to the north, and from three pits (1032, 1054, 1056; Fig. 39, 12–16) to the north of Trench VI which may be associated with a circular structure (1129; Table 36). These pits, like those within house 1128 (pits 828, 830) and that of 920 to its east, contained both larger quantities and larger pieces of pottery (Table 36). The sherds from pits 1032, 1054, and 1056 largely derive from fragmented but substan- tial parts of both coarsewares and finewares, decorated and undecorated vessels. These include two Class I and one Class II jars from pit 1054 (Fig. 39, 12, 13) and sherds of the large Class IV bowl with impressed decoration and an incised fineware vessel from pit 1056 (Fig. 39, 15, 16). The third pit, 1032, contained only the base of a

Table 36 Dunston Park: Early Iron Age pottery from Trench VI by feature

Structure and feature type	Feature No.	Coarsewares		Finewares		Decoration		Surfaces treatment (finewares)	Mean sherd wt (g)
		No.	Wt (g)	No.	Wt (g)	Coarse	Fine	No.	
House 1128: left hand (northern) side									
Post-hole	860	–	–	2	1	–	–	–	0.5
Post-hole	854	1	3	–	–	–	–	–	3.0
Post-hole	941	1	1	–	–	–	–	–	1.0
House 1128: right hand (southern) side									
Post-hole	901	–	–	3	7	–	–	1	2.3
Post-hole	917	–	–	1	3	–	–	1	3.0
Post-hole	919	4	6	–	–	–	–	–	1.5
Post-hole	912	27	73	5	24	1	–	1	3.0
Post-hole	903	2	5	–	–	–	–	–	2.5
Post-hole	910	10	52	3	13	–	–	–	5.0
Post-hole	924	3	8	2	7	–	–	1	3.0
Post-hole	882	9	25	2	18	–	1	2	3.9
Pit	828	106	942	36	288	1	3	7	8.7
Post-hole	927	18	181	23	180	–	2	2	8.8
Post-hole	913	69	1448	3	8	1	–	–	20.2
Post-hole	880	15	80	–	–	–	–	–	5.3
Pit	830	161	580	37	154	1	–	6	3.7
Post-hole	938	–	–	1	1	–	–	–	1.0
Post-hole	884	2	6	3	6	–	1	1	2.4
Post-hole	886	1	1	1	3	–	–	1	2.0
Post-hole	770	2	39	1	4	1	–	–	14.3
Post-hole	764	1	2	2	13	–	–	1	5.0
Post-hole	765	8	36	5	22	–	1	4	4.5
Post-hole	862	3	25	–	–	–	–	–	8.3
Post-hole	864	70	395	9	42	–	1	2	5.5
Post-hole	816	5	118	–	–	–	–	–	23.6
Post-hole	818	5	18	–	–	–	–	–	3.6
East of round-house 1128									
Pit	920	4	26	31	209	–	2	1	6.7
North of possible round-house 1129									
Pit	1032	82	824	–	–	–	–	–	10.0
Pit	1054	713	6975	1	9	1	–	1	9.8
Pit	1056	5	114	27	408	–	2	3	16.3

coarseware jar in fabric F5. The majority of these sherds are in relatively good condition, and many joins were noted. The mean sherd size from these three features together is 10.1 g.

The majority of the prehistoric pottery was found in or near round-house 1128 (Table 36), predominantly from the post-holes and pits of the right hand side of the building (Fig. 40). Only three small sherds were found in the left hand side. The quantities of finewares and coarsewares were investigated to determine whether there was any groupings of either jars or bowls or finewares or coarsewares. This analysis showed that

when at least five sherds were present in a feature both finewares and coarsewares, and bowls and jars, were present. The sole exception was post-hole 880 which contained only undecorated body sherds of fineware fabric F6. This suggests that although the pottery may have been found in the right hand or southern side of the house, all types were deposited in the pits, or eventually recovered from the post-holes, without any apparent selectivity.

In contrast to the material from elsewhere on the site, the sherds from round-house 1128 are generally in poorer condition, some being abraded and there are few

Extent of sooting

WA

0   100   200
mm

SEJ

Figure 39   Dunston Park: Early Iron Age pottery: pots 1–9 are from round-house 1128

84

conjoining sherds. The exception is a substantial group from post-hole 913, similar in nature to the pottery from the northern features described above. The mean sherd size for the features of, and within, round-house 1128, is 7.4 g, and if post-hole 913 is omitted the figure falls to 5.7 g. The explanations for this probably lie in more activities taking place within a confined space and the simple fact that larger quantities of less fragmented material can be incorporated within pits. Otherwise the range of fabrics at the two possible buildings is similar (F2, F4, F5, Q1, Q2), as is the presence of both decorated and undecorated, jars, and bowls.

Conclusions

With the exception of the Deverel–Rimbury-type Middle Bronze Age sherds from Trench I, the evidence indicates a date for the prehistoric pottery from Dunston Park in the Early Iron Age, probably contemporary with the later part or end of the Knight's Farm sequence. It seems likely that the assemblage represents a fairly limited chronological range. Although relatively small, the assemblage is significant in that it both complements and extends our knowledge of the Early Iron Age ceramics in west Berkshire. Several substantial assemblages are now known from sites on the river gravels to the south-west of Reading; Dunston Park extends that group westwards along the Kennet valley towards Newbury. The most likely date for this material is the later part of the 7th century BC. The pottery was probably made locally for the most part, but a small amount of both coarse and finewares may have been acquired through intra-regional exchange. The deposition of this material was specifically concentrated in the southern half of structure 1128, and in pits in the northern area of this trench. There does not appear to have been any deliberate selection of material occurring in these deposits though they may be diffentiated by the size range of vessel fragments present. This, however, could be at least partly a matter of preferential preservation within cut features.

Illustrated pottery

1. Large Type 5 jar; fabric F2. 926, post-hole 927, structure 1128 (PRN 71).
2. Carinated furrowed Type 7 bowl; fabric Q2; wide, tooled furrows; red-slipped. 926, post-hole 927, structure 1128 (PRN 73).
3. Small Type 3 jar; fabric F4; fingertip impressions around rim. 907, post-hole 912, structure 1128 (PRN 52).
4. Long-necked, flared Type 10 bowl; fabric F4; red-slipped both surfaces. 827, posthole 828, structure 1128 (PRN 12).
5. Large shouldered Type 1 jar; fabric F5, finger impressions around shoulder. 1111, pit 828, structure 1128 (PRN 147).
6. Large, tripartite Type 2 jar; fabric F4, red-slipped ext., well-smoothed or burnished int.; 1111, pit 828, structure 1128 (PRN 144).
7. Rounded Type 9 bowl; fabric Q1; red-slipped ext., burnished both surfaces. 1111, pit 828, structure 1128 (PRN 157).
8. Simple hemispherical Type 8 bowl; fabric Q4; burnished ext. 1111, pit 828, structure 1128 (PRN 202).
9. Small slack-shouldered Type 3 jar; fabric F6. 863, post-hole 864, structure 1128 (PRN 31).
10. Carinated vessel, ?Type 2 jar; fabric Q2; zoned decoration, vertical row of impressed circles and horizontal bands of incised hatched triangles; red-slipped. 911, pit 920 (PRN 64).
11. Tripartite, carinated Type 6 bowl; fabric Q2; single, horizontal row of small impressed circles around neck above bands of diagonal incised hatching at shoulder; one row of impressed finger or tool points below carination. 911, pit 920 (PRN 178).
12. Large shouldered Type 1 jar; fabric F5, poorly manufactured, spalling visible on surface; sooted; pair of post-firing repair holes below rim. 1053, pit 1054 (PRN 93).
13. Decorated vessel, ?Type 1 jar; fabric F5; fingernail impressions on carinated shoulder point. 1053, pit 1054 (PRN 94).
14. Small Type 3 jar; fabric F4; burnished or well-smoothed ext. 1053, pit 1054 (PRN 96).
15. Large Type 8 bowl; fabric F4, impressed rings or circles below rim edge, red-slipped ext., well-smoothed or burnished int. 1055/1104, pit 1056 (PRN 98/118).
16. Body sherd, ?Type 2 jar; fabric F4; diagonal incised hatching. 1055, pit 1056 (PRN 99).
17. Flat-topped, hemispherical Type 8 bowl; fabric Q3; burnished both surfaces. 863, pit 864/1100 (PRN 30).
18. Ovoid Type 4 jar; fabric F4. 808, ditch 807 (PRN 5).

Fired Clay, by L.N. Mepham

A total of 17 fragments (99 g) of fired clay was recovered from the site, all from Trench VI. Of this total, 16 are featureless fragments of unknown date and function. These were recovered from seven features (Table 28), two of which (830 and 927) are associated with round-house 1128 and can be dated to the Early Iron Age.

The other piece is a complete cylindrical spindle whorl (Object No. 516; Fig. 38, left), recovered from pit 828 in round-house 1128. The spindle whorl is made from a flint-gritted fabric, corresponding to pottery fabric F2. It has a diameter of 30 mm, a thickness of 15 mm, and a weight of 16 g.

Plant Remains, by A.J. Clapham

Thirteen samples were studied for charred plant macro-remains (excluding charcoal), 10 from Early Iron Age contexts, and three from two medieval boundary ditches.

The samples were processed using Wessex Archaeology standard flotation procedures. The analysis consisted of identification of the preserved charred plant macro-remains using a Wild M5 stereo-microscope, with critical identifications carried out using a modern reference collection based at the Pitt-Rivers Room in the Department of Archaeology, University of Cambridge. Nomenclature follows that of Stace (1991).

The charred plant remains were very poorly preserved, enabling identifications to specific level in only one case. The samples also contained modern roots and, in many cases, modern uncarbonised intrusive seeds due to the shallow nature of the features sampled. Altogether, there were very few plant remains found in the samples from either period studied (Table 37).

Early Iron Age

A pair of pits in the right hand side of round-house 1128 (828 and 830) contained charred plant remains. Both

Table 37 Dunston Park: plant macro-fossils from Early Iron Age contexts

	1101	1102	1103	1104	1106	1108	1109	1110	1111
Cultivated plants									
Hordeum sp. (barley) rachis fragment	–	–	–	–	1	–	–	–	–
Cerealia indet.	2	14	14	6	24	18	31	19	20
Wild plants									
Papaver sp. (poppy)	–	–	–	–	–	–	–	–	1
Corylus avellana (hazel)	–	–	–	1	–	–	–	1	–
Chenopodiaceae indet.	1	–	1	–	–	–	–	–	–
Polygonaceae indet.	2	–	–	–	–	–	–	–	–
Brassicaceae indet.	1	–	–	–	–	–	–	–	–
Vicia/Lathyrus (vetch/vetchlin) cotyledons	–	–	–	–	–	–	3	1	–
Miscellaneous remains									
Chara sp. *oogonia*	1	–	–	–	–	–	–	–	–
Parenchymatous tissue	–	–	2	–	–	–	–	–	–
Charred root	–	–	–	1	–	–	–	–	–
Stem fragments	–	–	–	–	–	2	–	–	–
Fungal sclerotia	13	–	5	2	–	–	–	–	1

pits contained indeterminate cereal fragments (Table 37), and included very few other charred remains; poppy (*Papaver* sp.); cabbage family (Brassicaceae), goosefoot family (Chenopodiaceae), knotgrasses (Polygonaceae) and a stonewort oogonium as well as fungal sclerotia. Small fragments of charcoal (primarily >1 mm) were common in both samples.

Four post-holes forming part of the round-house also contained macro-remains. Post-hole 912 contained 31 fragments of indeterminate cereals and three cotyledons of Vetch/Vetchling (*Vicia/Lathyrus* sp.). Post-hole 913 contained one Barley (*Hordeum* sp.) rachis fragment, which was fused to a piece of charcoal, and 24 fragments of indeterminate cereal grain. Post-holes 886 and 927 contained little carbonised material but included a number of indeterminate cereal remains and other plant macro-remains (Table 37).

One of the pair of large post-holes (864) of the porch of the round-house was sampled but no plant remains, except for a large quantity of unidentifiable charcoal, were recovered from the upper fill; the lower (sample 2004) contained 14 fragments of indeterminate cereal grains.

The paucity of plant remains from the pits and the post-holes make any specific interpretation difficult. The lack of cereal remains in the pits suggests that if, for example, they were used for storage, they may have been cleaned out before the round-house was abandoned. Nevertheless from this sparse evidence and that from the post-holes it is possible to state that crop processing was probably occurring in the area with the presence of the barley rachis, although this could be extraneous material. The discovery of the vetch remains suggest the presence of ruderal or segetal habitats, that is disturbed ground, perhaps fields. These results, while modest, are not untypical of the Iron Age or the local regional context.

Medieval
Two medieval ditches were examined but due to the paucity of plant remains it was not possible to determine which habitats were present around the ditches or the surrounding area. Full details are in archive.

8 Discussion, by A.P. Fitzpatrick

Although there are isolated features of Middle Bronze Age date, and what appears to be a medieval field system and fences, the principle interest lies in the Early Iron Age.

The evidence points to a dispersed, unenclosed, Iron Age settlement running up the low gravel ridge. Although only one certain house (1128) and one possible one (1129) were identified, it remains possible that others lie outside the areas examined, making it uncertain whether activity to the south-west, and perhaps the north, should be associated with house 1128. Similarly the scatter of post-holes in Trench I may be associated with tasks away from house(s) and with which the small quantities of worked flint, burnt flint, and pottery were associated.

A variety of activities is indicated by the Early Iron Age artefacts. The pottery assemblage consists of jars suitable for the cooking, storage, or presentation of foods, and an impressive array of fineware, plain and decorated bowls which, with one unusual exception, are generally small. Other domestic activities, food processing and spinning, are indicated by the recovery of the saddle querns and the spindle whorl respectively.

The scope of the environmental evidence is limited by the poor preservation of animal bone, but the plant macrofossils show that barley was grown. The barley may have been processed on the site and the uncleaned crop is likely to have contained those weeds of arable land or disturbed places such as poppy, goosefoot, and

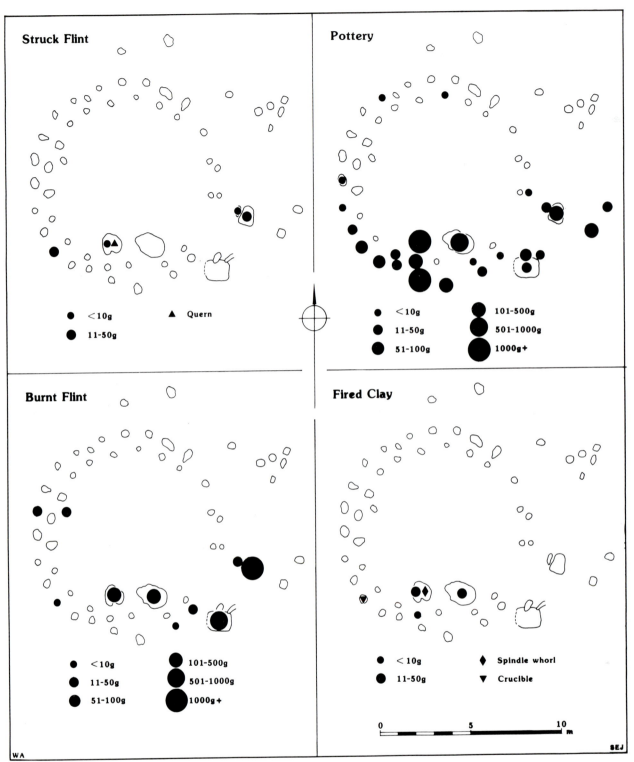

Figure 40   Dunston Park: distribution of finds by weight within round-house 1128

knotgrasses which were recovered. The data is too limited to do more than show that cereals were grown and to endorse the supposition that a typical Early Iron Age farming regime of small-scale, mixed farming which exploited a range of habitats was practised.

The settlement will not, however, have been socially or biologically self-sufficient and the exchange of animals and peoples may be envisaged (Jones 1986), and it is in this context that the small scale exchange of

goods contained in pots made of glauconitic clays may be seen.

Despite the limited evidence for farming practices, the evidence from 7th century BC house 1128 is of particular interest in its own right. The two post-rings of the house give an internal diameter of 9 m and an area of 64 m^2. As with most Iron Age houses the entrance is aligned to the east/south-east (Hill 1993, 66–8, fig. 3a), and the plan of the house displays symmetry of planning

(Guilbert 1982). Only relatively large features were identified in excavation and less substantial features such as internal screens, or external weatherboarding may not have survived ploughing. Only one post-hole (932) does not appear to be part of the walls, and while it could be a repair, it seems more likely to be a carefully placed internal feature. The post-hole is opposite the porch from where the post or furniture it supported would have been clearly visible.

It has been shown that the distribution of all categories of material culture is generally restricted to the porch and the right hand side of the house (when viewed from inside looking out of the porch), not just in the two pits next to the wall but also in the post-holes themselves. It would be inappropriate to explore the full significance of this in the present report, but some observations are appropriate.

Clearly these distributions reflect not only what objects were in use, but also the values ascribed to them which determined how they were disposed of. Decay and other formation processes, and excavation methods also contribute. The poor preservation of bone at Dunston Park may reduce the representation of some finds and perishable goods such as wooden bowls might also be lost (Evans 1989). Even so, the rarity of the discovery of such a large number of finds from an Iron Age house should be emphasised; most Iron Age houses seem to have been kept very clean (Hingley and Miles 1984, 64). While the smaller and abraded pottery sherds from the post-holes of house 1128 could be associated with the use of the house (eg, Hodder 1984, 55), it seems more likely that the finds relate to the abandonment and final decay of the house, and the mean sherd size is not dissimilar to that from Brighton Hill South (Morris 1992), where the house was burnt down. But this does not mean that the distribution at Dunston Park can be interpreted readily. It is possible that the left side was the living area which was kept clean and that the finds in the right side indicate storage there or the presence of furniture behind which parts of broken pots accumulated. The disposal of material when a house was abandoned may also have been different from when it was in use. It is easier to identify such caveats than to accommodate them; for the purposes of discussion the distribution of finds is taken here to relate to the ways in which the house was used.

The presence of two pits in the right half of the Dunston Park house and their absence from the left half emphasises the binary distribution which may have been symbolised by the post visible from the entrance. There are also hints of subtle patterning, in that while there are no significant differences between the distribution of coarse and fine wares, there is a suspicion that both fine and coarse decorated wares are restricted to the area next to the porch.

At one level this division might be interpreted as indicating that day time activities took place in the right half of the house. If we can associate the decorated pottery assemblages of the Late Bronze Age and Early Iron Age with the serving of food individually (Barrett 1980), then it is possible that there was an activity/group specific area towards the front of the house. The fact that the crucible and quern fragments and the spindle-whorl were found in pit 828 and post-hole 912 provides in-

sufficient evidence to suggest that there was a working area towards the back of the house, and it might be thought unlikely that metal-smelting would be undertaken inside.

The presence of burnt flint, and perhaps fired clay also, could suggest that cooking took place within the house but there was no structural evidence for any hearths or any other evidence for a distinction between cooking and eating areas. The general absence of finds in the left hand side of the house may indicate that this was a sleeping area. The three coarseware sherds from post-holes 854 and 860 could suggest items were stored in there or that, for example, there was a toilet there.

At another level, social space was clearly structured. The architecture of the house and the nature and distribution of the activities which took place within it with its clear left/right distinction will almost certainly incorporate cosmological referents (Fitzpatrick 1991; Parker Pearson in press), and the precise orientation of Iron Age house (including house 1128) and enclosure entrances towards sunrise should be noted here (Hill 1993). It may be that it was this orientation which helped define the left/right distinction and the post (932) could have signified these distinctions to people as they passed through the porch, crossing the threshold of the house, and entering the household. By contrast, the distribution of finds in the two pits outside the porch is reversed, with more finds from the left hand one, which may suggest a different order outside the home.

This left/right division is echoed by the distribution of finds from the comparable, and broadly contemporary 7th–6th century BC house at Longbridge Deverill Cow Down, Wiltshire. The double (or less likely triple) ringhouse was burnt down and the distribution of finds within it indicated that all the 'domestic refuse was confined to this (right) side of the house' (Chadwick 1960, 19; Chadwick Hawkes 1994). The finds included pottery, querns, bone tools, burnt flint, animal bones, spindle-whorls, and two pits in a similar situation to those at Dunston Park, which are interpreted as having supported a dresser. Chadwick Hawkes also interprets this as a separate living area and sleeping quarters. Interestingly the presence of a small amount of pottery in post-holes 854 and 860 in the left side of the Dunston Park house is paralleled at Longbridge Deverill (Chadwick Hawkes 1994, 67–8, fig. 4, and pers. comm.). Such a distinction is not so clear cut at Pimperne but assessed from the published data, the ratio of findspots between the right and left of the house is approximately 2:1 (Harding et al. 1993). This distinction in use may occur elsewhere in Britain later on in the Iron Age (Hill 1982, 27, fig. 1), but at present, in Wessex at least, there is little evidence to support Hingley's suggestion of a central 'public' area in round-houses (1990, 128–35).

While the Dunston Park house is of a well known type, there is some variability within the double ringhouses (ibid.) and the Dunston Park house finds its best parallels both in its very large size, and in the presence of a clearly recognisable second ring within Wessex where a number of similar houses are known (ibid.). It seems likely that the porch was not structural rather than symbolic; helping define the orientation of the house, and perhaps of time, and emphasise the threshold. Closely comparable houses are known at

Plate 8   Dunston Park: house 1128 under excavation, view from the north-west

Pimperne, Dorset (Harding and Blake 1963, 64, pl. viii; Harding *et al.* 1993) which the excavator considers to date to the 5th century, but which may be slightly earlier in date, Brighton Hill South, Site X/Y (Coe and Newman 1992, 10–13, fig. 5) and Old Down Farm (Davies 1981, 102, fig. 14), Hampshire, Little Woodbury House II, Wiltshire (Bersu 1940), and Longbridge Deverill Cow Down (Chadwick Hawkes 1994); all of which date between the 7th and 5th centuries BC, with the emphasis on the 7th century. It is notable that these houses do not appear at Danebury where major occupation commenced in the 6th century BC. When Guilbert first discussed double ring round-houses (1981), comparatively little dating evidence was available, but in Wessex at least it is now possible to stress the short time for which these houses were in fashion. These houses are found in both enclosed and unenclosed sites. Dunston Park appears to be unenclosed and the same may be true for both Little Woodbury and Longbridge Deverill Cow Down (McOmish 1989, 102–3). At Old Down Farm and Pimperne the houses and enclosures appear to be contemporaneous.

The size of the house should also be emphasised. In comparison with houses of Middle Bronze Age or Middle and later Iron Age date in general the type is very large (Hill 1984, fig. 2; Strang 1991). It is this size which contrasts clearly with the smaller buildings of the

Middle–later Bronze Age and which have been suggested to occur in pairs as the standard settlement module; one building being residential, the other ancillary for more specialised uses (eg, Drewett 1982; Ellison 1987). This module may also be present at some Early Iron Age sites, for example, Winnall Down (Fasham 1985, 142). It may be that the increased size reflects a change in the location of activities which now all occurred under one roof or it may reflect a different emphasis on the categorisation and presentation of residential groups, for example in the ways that gender and lineage were defined (Barrett 1989, 312). Groups might now have lived as extended families under one roof. However, ancillary buildings might still exist at this time (Fisher 1985), and this is also true for Dunston Park.

Few Iron Age houses were rebuilt and this is also the case with these large houses which may support the observation that the style of house and perhaps also the living arrangements it represents, spanned a comparatively brief period when the emphasis was on encompassing the household rather than belonging to the clan. This change would have affected not just the household but the ways in which daily life was organised. It may not be coincidental that the houses at Brighton Hill South X/Y, Dunston Park, and Longbridge Deverill Cow Down all appear to have been abandoned, and without indications of repair or renewal. Chadwick

Hawkes suggests that the burning of a series of Early Iron Age houses at Longbridge Deverill Cow Down represents the deliberate destruction of the house as part of the mortuary rites (1994, 68).

Although their contemporaneity and association should not be pressed, these changes in domestic architecture occurred at approximately the same time as other developments in Wessex. The changes included an increase in the deposition of the products of the 'bronze industry', greater emphasis on the enclosure of settlements, even though they may be as much symbolic as functional constructions (McOmish and Bowden 1987), the appearance of iron, an increase in the number of hillforts (Thomas 1989, 274), and the creation of vast middens such as at East Chissenbury Warren and Potterne (Brown et al. 1994; Lawson 1994). The association of hillforts with earlier 'ranch boundaries' dividing parts of the Wessex landscape, perhaps into domestic and agricultural areas, has been well rehearsed (eg,

Cunliffe 1990). Within the Kennet Valley the comparative rarity of Early Iron Age settlements in comparison with ones of later Bronze Age date (Butterworth and Lobb 1992, 172–5; Moore and Jennings 1992, 118–20) is also noteworthy.

The reasons for these changes and their relationships — if any — are not clearly understood. Population pressure and, in particular, an increase in agricultural productivity have been suggested (eg, Barrett and Bradley 1980b, 202–4). However, the redefinition of land, settlements, and houses as well as an increased emphasis on decorative motives on other sorts of material culture suggest a major shift in the social order and the ways in which it was presented. The similarities between Dunston Park and Longbridge Deverill show that these changes were enacted precisely over considerable distances (c. 80 km); it is in this context that the evidence for intra-site patterning within the Dunston Park settlement should be seen.

Appendix: an Early Iron Age (7th century BC) Pit with Ironworking Debris from Cooper's Farm, Dunston Park

A.P. Fitzpatrick, with contributions from I. Barnes, Peter Crew and Elaine L. Morris

Introduction

During the evaluation of the whole of the proposed development of Dunston Park, Trench (or test-pit) 2, situated in Field B near to Cooper's Farm (Fig. 30, *above*), produced a quantity of prehistoric pottery. This area was further examined by a series of machine trenches (1003–7), one of which, 1007, revealed an Early Iron Age pit containing ironworking slag (Fig. 41), probably indicating an Early Iron Age settlement (SU 517 685). As it will be some time before the development proceeds in this area, the opportunity is taken to publish here this important evidence for early ironworking. The site is called Cooper's Farm to distinguish it from the contemporaneous settlement at Dunston Park, described above, c. 1 km to the south-east.

Fieldwork, by I. Barnes and A. P. Fitzpatrick

The site lies at the western end of a ridge of higher ground which has commanding views to the south and west. Trench 1006 ran along the western edge of a spur of this higher land while trench 1007, 50 m long and 2 m wide, was aligned parallel to the north slope of a small dry valley which falls away from the ridge. The mechanical excavator cut through pit 661 which was c. 1.5 m in diameter and cut into the base of colluvial deposits;

health and safety considerations precluded further examination.

The upper edges of the pit were difficult to define, but it was seen to cut into silty clay layers (654) which were sandier near to the base of the section (655). Layer 652 was similar to 654 but did not contain any finds suggesting that it post-dates the pit. The finds were recovered from pitfill on the trench side. The homogeneity of the pottery and its close parallels with that from Dunston Park suggest that the pit can be regarded as a single, closed, group.

Finds

Metallurgical Debris, by Peter Crew

A small collection of slag, originally in nine pieces, weighing 316 g was found. A further 1236 g of what was described as 'ironstone' was also recorded, but unfortunately, in the assessment phase, this was not retained for examination. Charcoal was also noted.

Slags

S1 Part of a heavily vitrified and glazed clay plate, 3 joining pieces, 87 g. Overall dimensions 70 x 50 x 35 mm. Vitrified zone 25 mm thick, lustrous and vesicular in fracture. One surface is essentially flat, with a thin coating of pale green to black glass, partially spalled off, with a distinct semi-

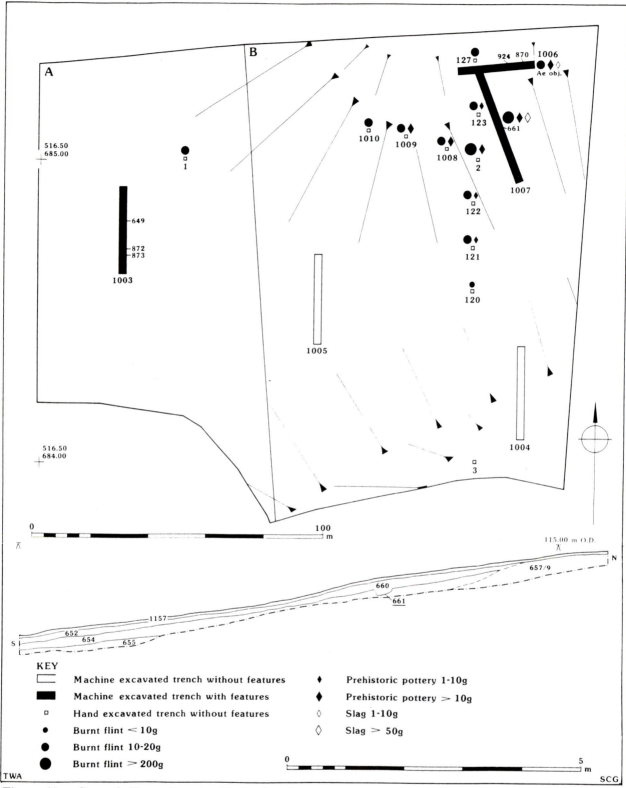

Figure 41   Cooper's Farm, Dunston Park: site plan

circular hollow on one edge, 15 mm diameter and about 15 mm deep. The opposite surface is very irregular due to losses of less fired clay.

S2 Fragment from the edge of a small cake of slag, 2 joining pieces, 71 g, 60 x 40 x 27 mm. Lower surface irregular, upper surface relatively flat, both coated in pale to dark brown secondary concretions and corrosion products.

S3 Amorphous fragment of slag cake, 61 g, 40 x 37 x 28 mm. Lower convex surface of clean grey contorted slag, char-

acteristic of cooling in a charcoal bed. Upper surface irregular with red–brown cooling surface.

S4 Amorphous broken fragments of slag similar to S2, total weight 34 g.

S5 Fragment of a thin slag cake, 2 joining pieces, 61 g, 28 x 28 x 34 mm. Lower zone of friable pale brown concretion, upper zone of 14 mm depth of relatively homogeneous, slightly vesicular slag, with a smooth red–black cooling surface.

S6 Small broken rounded fragment of grey/black fuel ash slag. 2 g.

Microstructure

Samples from S3 and S5 were cut and polished for microscopic examination. Both samples are typical fayalitic slags, consisting of wustite and fayalite in a glass matrix, with rare small particles of iron of both rounded and angular shape.

In S3 the fayalite crystals are rather amorphous and show no orientation. The wustite is exclusively in the form of very fine dendrites, with an even distribution throughout the slag. One edge of the sample merges with fired clay, which has zoned ?hercynite crystals and rare small particles of iron.

In S5 the fayalite crystals are small but well formed. They are evenly distributed throughout the glass matrix, with no orientation except near the cooling surface. The slag has a high proportion of wustite (over 50% of the surface area) in both a massive form and as globular dendrites, with some very fine dendrites near the cooling surface. There is one notable zone of subrectangular concentrations of wustite, up to 2 x 0.01 mm, which are probably the remnants of flakes of hammer scale not fully absorbed into the slag.

Discussion

This small collection of slag is a typical collection of smithing debris. S1 is part of a hearth lining from just above the blowing hole. The degree of vitrification indicates that the hearth was held at a high temperature for some time. S2 and S3 are fragments of small cakes of smithing slag which form just below the blowing hole. S5 is a small cake of slag which might be mistaken for a flow of smelting slag, but under the conditions indicated by S1 such a flow could occur in the base of the smithing hearth. The high wustite content of this piece is typical of a smithing slag.

The 'ironstone' recorded during the excavations might indicate that some smelting had taken place on the site, but this is not supported by the collected slags. The very small quantity of slag recovered could only be part of the debris of, at most, two smithing operations and it is therefore only an indication that some iron-smithing was carried out.

Pottery, by Elaine L. Morris

A total of 288 sherds (1421 g) of Early Iron Age pottery was recovered from the upcast fill of pit 661. The sherds are generally quite fragmented and many are in a soft condition with no surfaces and rounded edges, but a few sherds are in fact quite hard-fired. The assemblage was analysed and recorded in the same way as the finds from Dunston Park and the range of fabric, form, and decoration is generally consistent with the assemblage from round-house 1128 and associated features (Tables 38 and 39).

Fabrics

Six fabrics were identified, five of which are similar to those already defined (F4, F5, F6, Q2, and Q3). One additional fabric, Q5 is presented below. The number

Table 38   Cooper's Farm, Dunston Park: quantification of Early Iron Age pottery by fabric

Fabric	No. sherds	Weight (g)
F4	210	949
F5	1	7
F6	18	86
Q2	50	174
Q3	3	15
Q5	6	190
Total	288	1421

and weight of sherds by fabric type is presented in Table 38.

Q5 Coarse sandy fabric with detritus (6 sherds/190 g); common, poorly-sorted rounded–subangular quartz grains < 1 mm; rare amount of one or more very large, poorly-sorted inclusions, apparently naturally occurring in uncleaned clay matrix; < 10 mm, may be patinated, subangular and angular flint or rounded unidentified, non-calcareous pebbles; unoxidised but possibility of rare glauconite; coarseware.

Form and decoration

The vessel forms identified consist of several Class I coarseware, shouldered jars, one of which is a Type 1 vessel (Fig. 42, No. 1), with several probable Type 1 vessels consisting of only shoulder zones (eg, Fig. 42, Nos 2–4), and bodysherds from at least one possible Class IV fineware, round-bodied bowl with a long neck, which may have been a variation on the Type 9 or Type 10 vessels (not illustrated). Four of the Class I jars are decorated with fingertip impressions, all on the shoulder zone with one also on the rim edge. No other types of decoration occurred in the assemblage. The correlation of fabrics to vessel forms and decorations is presented in Table 39.

Surface treatment and evidence of use

The presence of various fine surface finishes on sherds is limited due to the nature of the deposit and recovery conditions of the assemblage. The possible round-bodied bowl in fabric Q3 displays the remnants of burnishing

Table 39   Cooper's Farm, Dunston Park: correlation of pottery fabric, form, and decoration

	F4	F6	Q3	Q5	Total
Jar					
Type 1	3	1	–	1	5
Bowl					
?Type 9/10	–	–	1	–	1
Decoration					
Fingertip	2	–	–	2	4

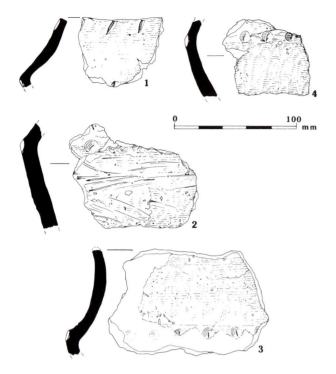

*Figure 42   Cooper's Farm, Dunston Park:
pottery from Pit 661*

on both the interior and exterior surfaces of the neck
sherd from this vessel. Two Class I jars (Fig. 42, Nos 2
and 4) have rough wiping marks on the exterior. Only
one vessel (Fig. 42, No.1), displays evidence of use in the
form of burnt residue on the interior of the vessel at the
shoulder zone.

Discussion

This small assemblage contains coarse and fineware
fabrics similar to those at Dunston Park. The addition
of a new, coarse sandy fabric with detritus inclusions is
consistent with fabrics found amongst other Early Iron
Age assemblages in Wessex. The range of vessel forms,
dominated by sherds from Class I shouldered jars decorated with fingertip impressions, is also similar to the
material from Dunston Park, including the presence of
a possible round-bodied, long-necked bowl. The absence
of incised or furrow decorated vessels may be due to the
relatively small quantity of material present or to a
slightly different date for this group than that from
Dunston Park.

The frequency of decoration, however, is high (*c.*
36%), with at least four decorated vessels out of a total
of approximately 11–12 identifiable examples.
Therefore there is no reason to doubt that the use and
deposition of this pottery were contemporary with the
settlement at Dunston Park, ie, the 7th century BC.
Quantitatively and qualitatively the range of material

is also comparable to those from the pits at Dunston
Park (Table 36).

Illustrated sherds (Fig. 42)

1. Large, shouldered Type 1 jar. Fabric Q5. Inward curving
    rim; fingertip impressions on rim edge and shoulder. (PRN
    253).
2. Shoulder from probable Type 1 jar. Fabric Q5. Fingertip
    impressions on shoulder; one sherd has wiping marks.
    (PRN 252).
3. Shoulder from probable Type 1 jar. Fabric F4. Fingertip
    impressions on shoulder. (PRN 239).
4. Shoulder from probable Type 1 jar. Fabric F4. Fingertip
    impressions on shoulder; vertical finger-smearing or wip-
    ing marks. (PRN 241).

Other finds

Five pieces of worked flint, included a scraper and a
fractured core which would not be out of place in a later
Bronze Age context (Ford *et al.* 1984) were found. Thirty-
six (625 g) fragments of burnt flint and seven (45 g) of
charcoal were also recorded. Some of these finds may be
associated with the metalworking activity.

Discussion

The importance of the group lies not just in indicating
the presence of an Early Iron Age settlement or of one
in the vicinity, probably on the westernmost spur of the
ridge, but in the relatively early date for the ironworking
debris. Much of the debate concerning the adoption of
iron in Britain has been set in the context of explaining
changes in the patterns of deposition of bronzes in
hoards, with relatively little attention being paid to iron
(Thomas 1989).

Analysis of early iron in its own right has, however,
indicated that iron was manufactured and used at a
seemingly constant level throughout Britain through
the 9–7th centuries BC, usually in areas close to sources
of iron (Turnbull 1984, 279). Most of this evidence for
early ironworking does not come from hoards.

The evidence from Wessex and the Thames Valley,
areas where there are no major sources of ores has been
slight, with few sites yielding evidence for ironworking
in or before the 7th century BC (Winklebury, Hampshire; Smith 1977; and Brooklands, Surrey; Hanworth
and Tomalin 1977 (which may be 6th century BC or even
later); Turnbull 1984; Salter 1989, 266).

At Cooper's Farm only a small quantity of smithing
slag was found, but the 'ironstone' might indicate that
it was also a production site. This is, however, valuable
evidence for the working of iron in the region within the
Llyn Fawr phase, and gives an indication of the potential
of the site.

4. Excavations at Park Farm, Binfield, Berkshire, 1990: An Iron Age and Romano-British Settlement and Two Mesolithic Flint Scatters

by M.R. Roberts

with contributions from Paul Booth, Mark Robinson, and Steve Ford

1 Introduction

Excavations at Park Farm, Binfield, were conducted by the Oxford Archaeological Unit in 1990 in advance of development by Bryant Homes, Beazer Homes, and Luff Developments Ltd. The sites had been identified in the course of the East Berkshire Archaeological Survey (EBAS) carried out by Berkshire County Council (Ford 1987a) and an evaluation carried out by the Oxford Archaeological Unit (Oxford Archaeological Unit 1989).

Location and Topography

Binfield is situated in east Berkshire on a band of London Clay between the Chalk to the north and Plateau Gravel to the south (Fig. 43). The parish lies in the south-west centre of a northward loop of the River Thames. Park Farm lies east of the village. Area E, the Iron Age and Romano-British settlement, lay at SU 853 705 on the east side of Park Farm next to a stream known as the Cut, although its course at this point appears to be natural (Fig. 44). The site sloped gently, from 48 m OD in the north-east to 51 m in the south-west, rising towards the highest point of the parish at Amen Corner. The natural subsoil consisted of lenses of clay and concreted iron-rich gravel. Areas A/M and B, the Mesolithic sites, lay west of Park Farm on the east side of the ridge occupied by the modern village of Binfield, on the lip of the slope at SU 846 706 and SU 847 704. The natural subsoil of both was clay.

Previous Investigations

No cropmarks are visible on the aerial photographs of the excavated areas. The East Berkshire Archaeological Survey recorded three flint scatters (Areas A–C) and two finds of Roman pottery (Areas D and E; Ford 1987a). In 1989 the Oxford Archaeological Unit carried out an evaluation of some 85 ha on behalf of Bryant Homes and Beazer Homes in advance of the construction of housing, a hotel, a golf course, and a road. This demonstrated a low level of prehistoric and post-medieval activity over most of the area and tentatively identified a palaeo-channel north of Area E, which subsequently proved to be disturbance from the laying of sewer mains.

In Area E, shovel test-pitting identified a scatter of medieval or post-medieval tile and brick and one medieval sherd. Trenching, however, revealed two parallel ditches and other features containing 1st–2nd century AD pottery. These were interpreted as representing a Romano-British settlement, the approximate limits of which were established by negative evidence from surrounding trenches. Shovel test-pitting recovered struck and burnt flint from the areas of the known scatters. The only feature identified within them was an undated pit in Area C.

Following the evaluation the County Archaeologist specified that Area E and the apparent palaeo-channel beside it were to be excavated and that the Area B flint scatter, now demonstrated to be confined to the plough-soil, should be fieldwalked, shovel test-pitted, and sieved. Similar investigations would be extended to other scatters if they were to be disturbed during golf course construction. In the event this applied only to Area A/M.

Documentary Evidence

The Binfield area is not ideal for settlement, as it lies on heavy clay soil away from large rivers. Nevertheless, by the time of the first documentary evidence in 1167, when the priest witnessed a document (E. Mosses pers. comm.), Binfield was already a flourishing community with a church. In the 13th century the parish was part of Windsor Forest, within whose boundaries there were many small villages. Binfield was part of Cookham Manor, perhaps as a woodland/pasture outlier, owned by the Crown, forming a portion of the lands awarded to the Queens of England on their marriage.

On Pride's map of 1790 the area of Park Farm is called Binfield Common. The areas of medieval common land in parishes around Binfield are flat. Although probably wooded, with mature oak trees interspersed with coppices, these commons would have been more accessible than the heavily wooded clay hills and may represent the most easily exploited land in the forest.

Just to the north-east of Area E is Binfield Manor. An independent manor at Binfield seems to have been a late development; it is first mentioned in 1544 and should probably be seen as part of the 16th and 17th century pattern of division into smaller portions of manors which had been previously been parish-sized or larger.

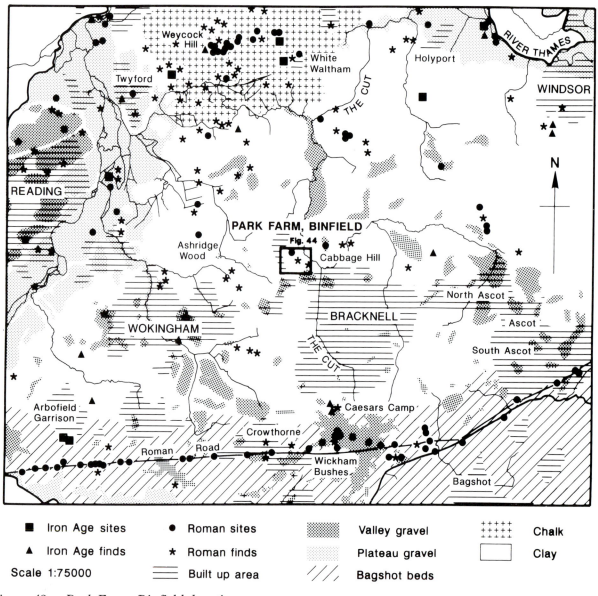

Figure 43 *Park Farm, Binfield: location*

The area of Park Farm is next mentioned in the mid 18th century, when one Francis Wilder owned a small enclosure to the west of Binfield Manor. This enclosure was north of Tippets Lane, which ran from the ford at the south of the manor grounds to the Golden Cross south of what is now Park Farm. This lane and Wilder's enclosure are clearly visible on Rocque's map of 1761 and Pride's map of 1790 and can be seen to the north of Area E on Figure 44; Tippets Lane forms the north-east/south-west field boundary starting at the footbridge and the enclosure is represented by the lozenge shaped fields immediately to the north of the Area E and west of the Cut.

The wood which lies to the south-west of Park Farm changed its name between 1761 and 1790, as the two maps name it as Hawkswood and Popeswood respectively. This commemorates the poet Alexander Pope (1688–1744), who lived in Binfield as a boy. The village of Binfield is thought to have shifted south from its original focus (*Victoria County History of Berkshire*, 119).

2 Area E, the Iron Age and Romano-British Settlement

Method of Excavation

Ploughsoil was stripped using a 360° excavator. The modern ploughsoil and a slightly older but still recent ploughsoil were removed in three trenches, 107, 108, and 109, over an area which eventually totalled 10,300 m² (Fig. 44). The surface of the natural clay thus revealed was hand cleaned to clarify features cut into the natural, and the site was planned immediately while these were still fresh. This strategy was not totally successful, as it transpired that visibility was at its best three to six weeks after stripping; this led to further features (eg, ditch 1246) being identified on the penultimate day of the excavation.

The initial excavation was planned to take place over six weeks on an area of 7500 m², corresponding to the extent of the settlement as indicated by the evaluation,

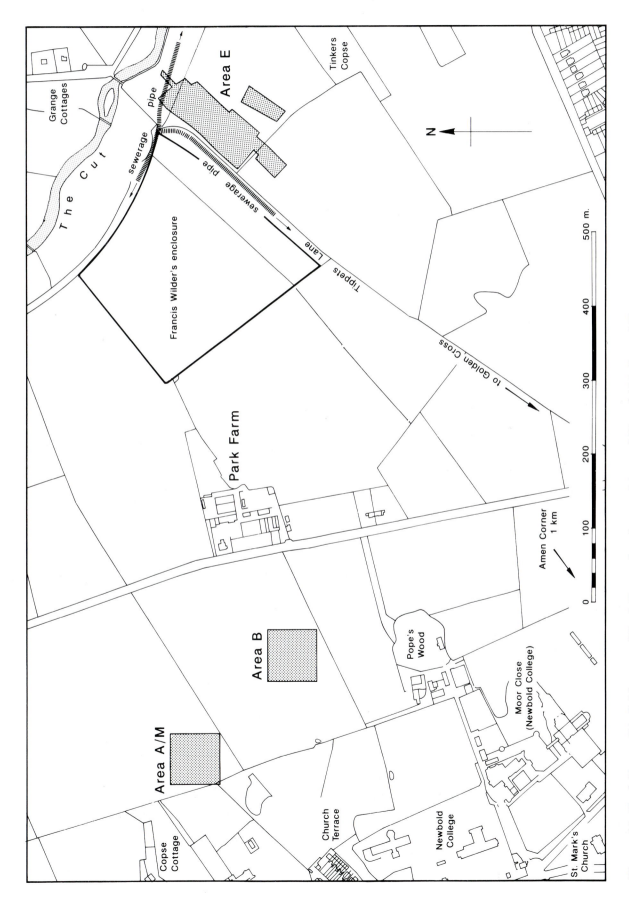

Figure 44 Park Farm, Binfield: area of Park Farm showing positions of Sites A/M, B, and E

with a further two weeks' contingency funding available for an additional area of 2500 m^2, which was taken up. The number of features revealed meant that the site had to be sampled selectively, some of it during stripping to aid in the formulation of the excavation strategy. The strategy adopted was as follows (*see Fig. 45 for distribution of features*).

i. A large boundary ditch running north-west–south-east across the site and rectilinear enclosures to the south-west of it were sampled for stratigraphic relationships and dating evidence.

ii. A large single penannular gully (1020) in the south-west was investigated to see if it ed part of a house.

iii. An area of pits in the centre of the site north of two intersecting ring-gullies was examined to determine whether they formed an aisled building (this possibility was subsequently excluded).

iv. The two intersecting ring-gullies (Houses 1 and 2) were excavated.

v. A post-built round-house (House 3) was defined, although the complete set of post-holes was not found until the area to the south-east was stripped during the contingency phase.

vi. A concentration of small circular and subcircular gullies in the angle of a ditch in the south-west was cleaned and excavated, resulting in the definition of a further post-built round-house (House 4).

vii. A complex of rectangular enclosures north-east of the boundary ditch was sampled for stratigraphic relationships and dating evidence.

viii. Furrows to the north-east of the boundary ditch were investigated and were found to be later than the 15th century.

ix. Large, round, charcoal-filled features in the north-east were excavated and found to date from the 15th century.

x. The contingency funding was used to strip another 2800 m^2 of overburden to see whether and how far features extended beyond the limits of the original trench. These areas can be seen to the south-west and south-east of the original trench on Figure 44 and were hand cleaned. The very few archaeological features identified were sampled to determine their nature and date.

xi. A small trench was dug towards the Cut to locate the apparent palaeo-channel and to determine its relationship, if any, to the settlement.

Problems of Phasing

Stratigraphic relationships were not as useful, nor as numerous, as might have been expected. This has entailed reliance on the three principal ceramic phases (CPs) defined in detail by Paul Booth in the pottery report. They are:

CP1 'Middle Iron Age'
CP2 Late Iron Age–early Romano-British ('Belgic type')

CP3 Romanised, probably dating from the later 1st century AD

Features ascribed to each are shown in Figures 58–60. There are anomalies between stratigraphy and ceramic phasing, especially in the successive cuts of the central boundary ditch. These may be attributed largely to the redeposition of material in the course of the silting and recutting of the ditch over at least a couple of centuries. Many features produced little or no datable material. The site is therefore described by elements or areas rather than phase-by-phase.

Site Description

Four main elements were identified within an organised layout: a large boundary ditch, up to four houses with their domestic areas, an extensive area of circular enclosures, and a network of rectangular enclosures (Fig. 45).

It is possible that the northern and north-western edges of the settlement may have been destroyed by the construction of sewerage mains (Fig. 44). The effect of ploughing on its peripheral areas can only be guessed at.

The central boundary ditch

There was a long-term boundary, consisting of at least 10 cuts on the same alignment, running roughly north-west–south-east between the domestic area and the rectangular enclosures. The northern terminals of three cuts, 1017, 1040, and 1154, were identified, but the southern terminal of only one, 1051, was recorded. Stratigraphic relationships indicated that the ditch 'moved' southward, ie, that each successive recut started south-east of the previous one.

Three cuts (1011) were visible in section at the north-west edge of the site (Fig. 46). They were just over 1.0 m deep and just under 2.0 m wide (Fig. 48e). Overlying their fills was a top layer of silting (1155 in Fig. 48e) containing large quantities of domestic debris. In one section (1011/D) this layer contained 1.75 kg of burnt flint, as well as the only stratified metal small find, a copper alloy brooch pin. All the layers of the ditch, from top to bottom, contained pottery of CP3. 16 m to the south-east was the north-west terminal of a second cut (1154), again with a topmost silting layer (1155, Fig. 48d and e), both containing pottery of CP3. Ten metres to the south-east again, these four cuts, of which only one was visible in section (1087), were cut in turn by the north-west terminal of a third cut (1040: Figs 48c and 49) the upper fills of which contained pottery of CP3 and the lower fills a small amount of pottery of CP2 — one of the potential anomalies between stratigraphy and ceramic phasing noted above. The upper fills of 1040 contained hawthorn and abundant oak charcoal dumped with a large amount of pottery and loomweight fragments. Sixteen metres to the south-east, 1051, the earliest of three cuts visible at the north-west edge of the excavation, terminated. It contained no finds. The terminal was visible as it lay slightly south-west of the rest of the cuts (Fig. 46).

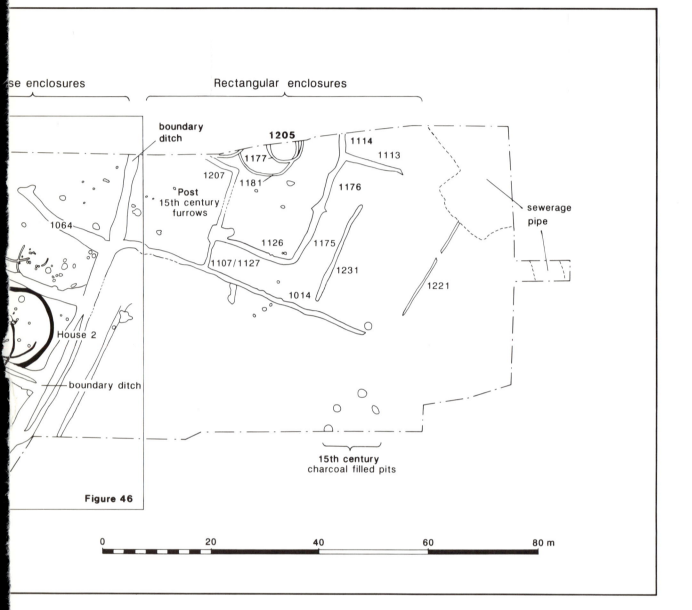

se enclosures

Rectangular enclosures

boundary
ditch

1205

1114

1177

1113

1207

1181

1176

Post
15th century
furrows

1064

1126

1175

1107/1127

1231

1014

1221

House 2

boundary ditch

sewerage
pipe

15th century
charcoal filled pits

Figure 46

0   20   40   60   80 m

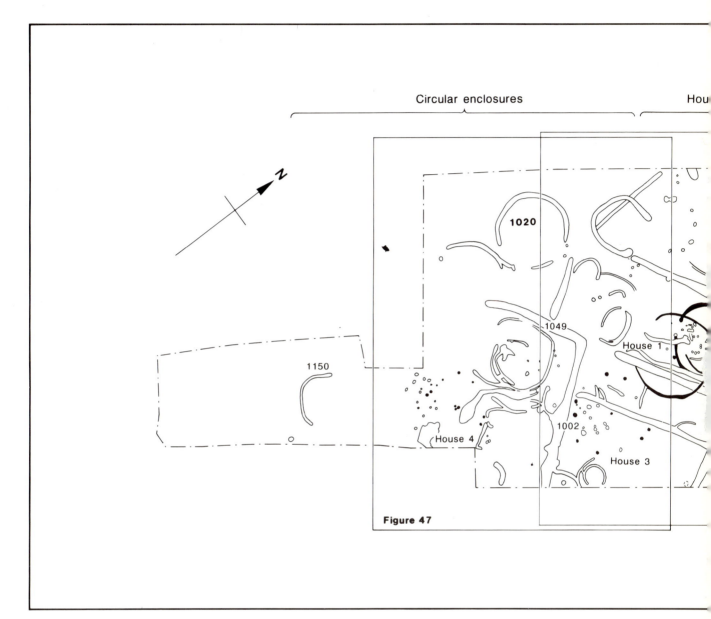

Circular enclosures   Hou

Figure 45   Park Farm, Binfield: all features plan

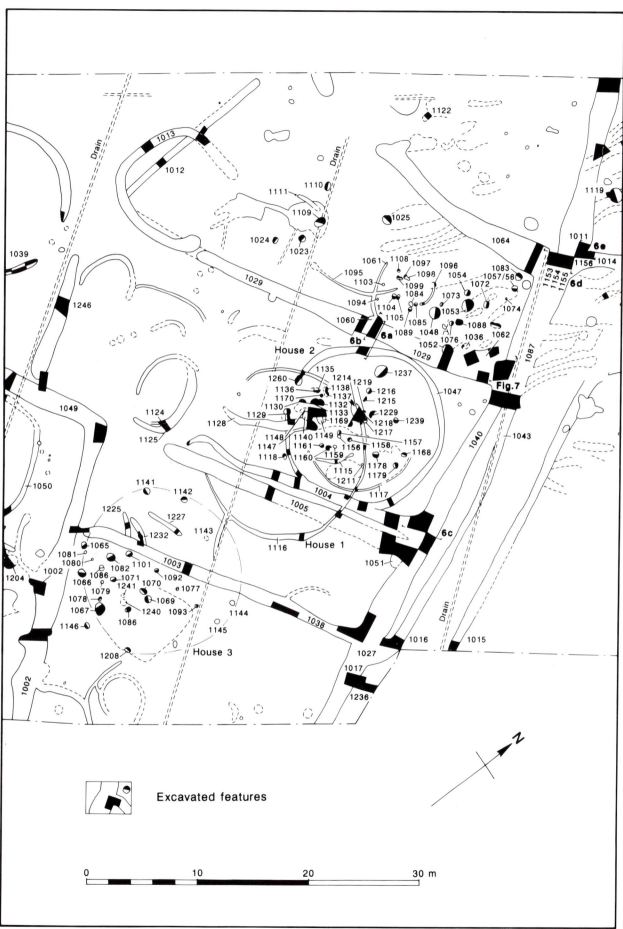

Figure 46   Park Farm, Binfield: Area E, detail

Seven metres to the south-east these phases of the ditch were cut by the terminal of the fourth cut, 1017, which continued off the site to the south-east. It contained pottery of CP3. Just visible in the section at the south-east edge of the site was an earlier cut (1018) which also contained pottery of CP3. At this point 1027 had as one of its upper fills a layer of burnt flint: over 100 kg were excavated from two sections. This part of the ditch also contained abundant oak charcoal and possible loomweight fragments.

No gaps with opposed terminals, permitting passage across the ditch were identified. Earlier gaps may have been removed by later cuts.

North-east of this complex of ditches and parallel to it was a small ditch, 1015, which terminated just south-east of the terminal of 1154. It had no stratigraphic links to any other features, and the single excavated section contained no pottery.

Enclosures south-west of the central ditch

A series of shallow gullies and one large ditch (1064) were aligned at right-angles to the boundary ditch (Figs 46 and 47). All were cut by the successive terminals of the boundary ditch and contained loomweight fragments. They are described from north-east to south-west.

1064 was the largest of these features, 3.00 m wide and 1.00 m deep. Its east terminal was just cut by the boundary ditch (Figs 46 and 48e).

1029, 1.28 m wide and 0.55 m deep, was cut by the terminal of ditch 1040 (Fig. 48a and b). It could not be determined from the sections whether 1029 turned to run within the line of the boundary ditch or terminated at the intersection (Fig. 49). This feature contained many finds of CP3 and its dark fill suggested domestic activity nearby. It had two cuts, an earlier shallow gully and a later, deeper, V–shaped one which may not have extended much further south-west than pit 1060, which it cut (Fig. 48b). Loomweight fragments were found in 1029 and 1060.

1004 and 1005, two almost parallel gullies, lay 1.0 m north-west of the terminal of boundary ditch cut 1051. Gully 1004 was 0.82 m wide and 0.16 m deep, 1005 1.32 m wide and 1.31 m deep, with two cuts. Both contained pottery of CP 1/2 and 1004 contained abundant alder/hazel and hawthorn charcoal. They were cut by boundary ditch cuts 1051 and 1040 (Fig. 48c). The gully of House 1 (1116) cut both 1004 and 1005 while the gully of House 2 (1047) was cut by 1004.

The most south-easterly of these features consisted of an initial cut, 1003, replaced by and/or extended in its north-east part by 1038. 1003 ran through House 3 but no stratigraphic relationship was discernible. 1038 lay at right-angles to and was cut by the terminal of boundary ditch cut 1017 and apparently turned at this point to become 1016/1043, running parallel to the boundary and slightly north-east of it. Both 1003 and 1038 were of similar dimensions, 0.90 m wide and 0.30 m deep; 1016/1043 was slightly larger, 1.20 m wide and 0.42 m deep. 1016 contained a substantially complete samian bowl.

Structures

Post-pipes could not generally be distinguished. The dimensions of post-holes are given here where appropriate.

House 1 (Figs 46 and 50) consisted of penannular gully, 1116, with an internal diameter of 14.10 m and a central post-hole, 1118. The gully was very slight, at most 0.09 m deep and 0.26 m wide, and the only break in its circuit suggested a south-west facing entrance. The gully also contained a large quantity of burnt material which was presumably domestic in origin, consisting of alder/hazel, oak and ash charcoal (Table 43). The gully cut gullies 1004 and 1005 as well as 1047, the ring-gully of House 2, and 1117, an arc of gully parallel to 1047 and within it. The location of the 'central' post-hole 1118 may be entirely fortuitous, since there were numerous nearby post-holes (Fig. 46), but it lay slightly to the south of them and contained pottery of the same ceramic phase (CP3) as the gully. The post-hole was 0.40 m in diameter and 0.24 m deep.

The section of the boundary ditch (1040) next to House 1 contained carbonised plant remains likely to represent the dehusking of grain (Robinson *below*). This was the only context to contain carbonised plant remains, suggesting that this activity was localised.

House 2 (Figs 46 and 50) was formed by two concentric features, penannular gully 1047, 0.70 m wide and 0.23 m deep with an internal diameter of 13.2–13.6 m, and 1117, an arc of gully, perhaps a wall slot, 0.12 m wide and 0.09 m deep, 1.55–1.20 m inside 1047. 1047 contained pottery of CP1. Among the many post-holes within the circuit, 1217, 1218, or 1219 may have been central to the structure, but this is conjectural. These post-holes ranged from 0.20 m to 0.35 m wide and from 0.10 m to 0.14 m deep. The gap in the circuit of 1047 provided a south-west-facing entrance on a similar alignment to that of House 1. Post-holes 1129 and 1260, cut into the terminals, may mark a later modification of the entrance. Both were rather larger than the possible internal post-holes. 1260 contained abundant oak charcoal, 1129 contained loomweight fragments, and one small, possibly intrusive, sherd of CP3.

House 3 (Figs 46 and 50) has been tentatively identified within a cluster of post-holes south of Houses 1 and 2. It was represented by a subcircular setting of nine post-holes (1065, 1066, 1141, 1142, 1144, 1145, 1146, 1208, and another, unnumbered, between 1145 and 1208), 13.9 m in internal diameter with a central post-hole 1092. The post-holes in the circle ranged from 0.12 m to 0.36 m deep and from 0.25 to 0.80 m wide. Only one, 1208, contained pottery, of CP1. A west or south-west facing entrance may have been destroyed by ditches 1002 and 1003 (Fig. 47); alternatively, 1145 and 1144 might represent a north-east facing entrance, especially as they lay slightly outside the line of the other post-holes.

House 4 (Figs 47 and 51) was identified among a cluster of post-holes south-west of House 3. It seems to have had

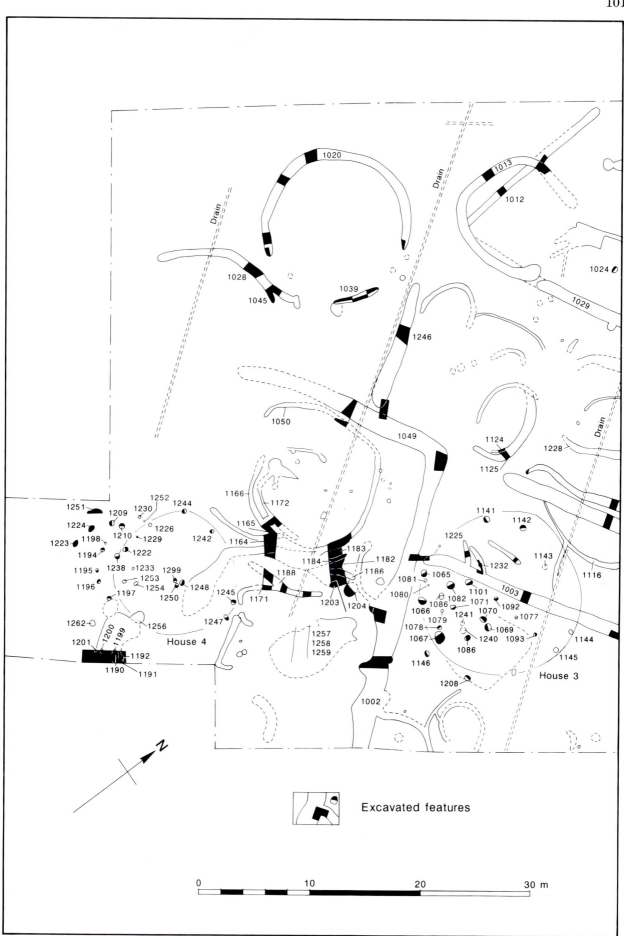

Excavated features

0   10   20   30 m

Figure 47   *Park Farm, Binfield: Area E, detail*

102

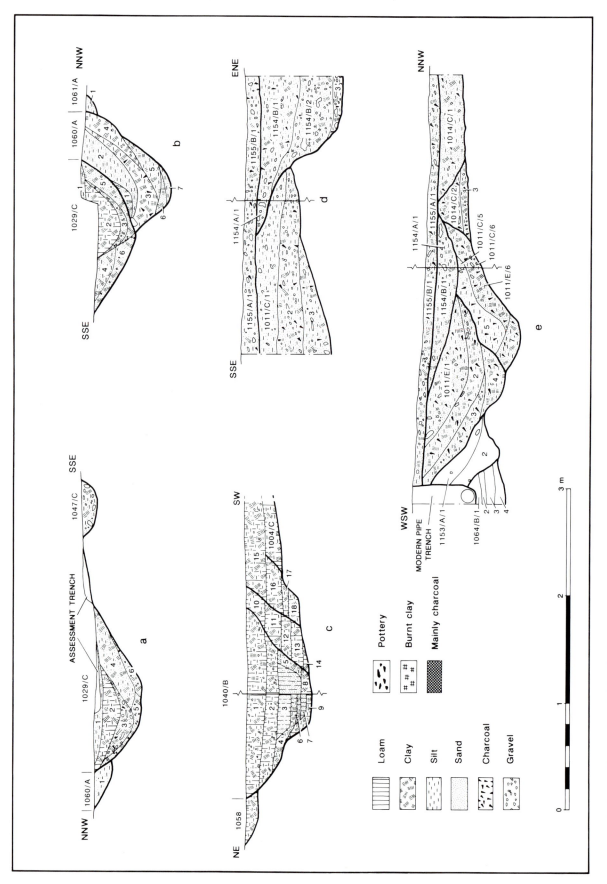

Figure 48 Park Farm, Binfield: ditch sections

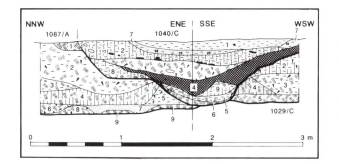

Figure 49   Park Farm, Binfield: ditch section

an inner ring 10.20 m in internal diameter, surviving as eight post-holes (1222, 1226, 1229, 1238, 1242, 1244, 1245, and 1247) which ranged from 0.20 to 0.40 m wide and 0.12 to 0.37 m deep. An outer ring or the remains of another structure may be represented by the arc of 1194, 1195, 1196, 1197, 1198, 1209, 1210, and 1230, post-holes between 0.18 and 0.60 m wide and 0.05 and 0.24 m deep. There appeared to be three central post-holes, 1248, 1249, and 1250, which were 0.35–0.55 m wide and c. 0.10 m deep. In the inner ring, post-hole 1222 contained 0.25 kg of burnt flint and 1210 contained 0.50 kg.

In the outer arc, post-hole 1209 contained 1.00 kg of burnt flint and post-hole 1194 pottery of CP1. 1245 and 1247 may have formed a north-east facing entrance, alternatively, a west or south-west facing entrance may be reflected by the disposal of rubbish in the form of charcoal and large quantities (3.625 kg) of fired daub in pits 1223 and 1224, immediately to this side of the structure.

Internal and external features There was a dense group of 35 pits and post-holes within the area of House 2 (Fig. 46), but these did not appear to form any recognisable structures. There were also two short lengths of gully (1115 and 1128) where the circuits of Houses 1 and 2 intersected. Gully 1128 cut the gully of House 2. Two of these features and both the gullies contained pottery of CP1, three contained pottery of CP2, six of CP 2/3 and three of CP3. Gully 1128 contained a small amount (0.25 kg) of burnt flint. Loomweights were found in 1128 and in several small pits and post-holes (1129, 1130 and 1147).

Within the area of House 3 (Fig. 47) there were 13 features (1067, 1069, 1070, 1071, 1078, 1079, 1080, 1081, 1082, 1086, 1101, 1240, and 1241) in the south-west quadrant, three short lengths of gully (1225, 1227, and 1232) in the north-west quadrant and two post-holes to the south-east (1077 and 1093). 1070 and 1086 contained pottery of CP1 and 1071 of CP3. 1067 and the gully 1237 contained a small amount of burnt flint (together 1 kg). Two post-holes (1086 and 1070) within the circle contained pottery of CP1.

North-west of Houses 1 and 2 was an area of 30 pits and post-holes extending about 20 m south-west from the boundary ditch (Fig. 46). Noteworthy among them were three large, round, charcoal-filled pits (1048, 1052, and 1053). They varied in depth from 0.09 m to 0.52 m, and were between 0.96 and 1.40 m wide. Pit 1048 contained abundant alder/hazel and oak charcoal and 1052 and 1053 contained oak charcoal. There were also

three short lengths of curved gully (1095, 1096 and 1061). Two post-holes (1097 and 1104) contained pottery of CP1, two pits pottery of CP2 (1048 and 1056) and one pit (1088) pottery of CP2 or 3. One post-hole (1054) and two large pits (1060 and 1052) produced pottery of CP3, as did two of the gullies (1096 and 1095). The other gully (1061) contained pottery of CP2. Loomweight fragments were found in 1060, 1083, 1088, and 1096. Posthole 1054 yielded abundant oak charcoal. Post-hole 1083 contained 2.25 kg of burnt flint.

North-west of House 4 (Fig. 47) were three small pits (1223, 1224, 1251). 1223 and 1224 contained charcoal and burnt daub and 1251 contained 1.50 kg of burnt flint. 1223 contained pottery of CP2. Inside House 4 were three post-holes (1233, 1253, and 1254). Just to the south-west of House 4 were several closely intercut features, one gully aligned roughly north-west–south-east (1190), another aligned north-east–south-west (1191), and a pit (1192). These had been filled by later silting (1202), which was very dark and contained 2.50 kg of burnt flint. It was subsequently cut by stake-holes or animal burrows (1199, 1200, and 1201). Gully 1190 contained pottery of CP1, 1202 pottery of CP3.

Domestic focus
All the features described so far lay south-west of the boundary ditch. In contrast to the numerous small pits and post-holes in this area, there was only one small pit (1119) north-east of the boundary. The pit itself was 1.20 m wide by 0.38 m deep and contained pottery of CPs 1 and 2, abundant alder/hazel and oak charcoal and 4.25 kg of burnt flint. The combination of small, non-linear features and probable houses in a single area of the site corresponds to a concentration of artefacts, food remains, charcoal, and burnt flint — the debris of occupation, exemplified by the distribution of daub, loomweights, and charcoal (Fig. 57). No domestic debris was found to the north of 1064, the most north-westerly of the ditches running at right-angles to the central boundary. There is a distinct impression of domestic focus defined by 1064 to the north-west and the central ditch to the south-east, with an outlier in the area of House 4.

Circular and subcircular enclosures
Most of the south-west of the site was occupied by large, shallow, subcircular enclosures, roughly the same size as the gullies of Houses 1 and 2, but with no internal features and little domestic debris, and sometimes with more than one entrance (Figs 45 and 47).

1013 was horseshoe-shaped with a diameter of about 8.0 m and was 1.65 m wide and 0.62 m deep. Its entrance was quite large and faced north-east. It was the only circular enclosure which clearly had only one entrance and the only one of these enclosures to post-date linear features, cutting both the south-west (earlier) end of 1029 and 1012, which ran north from the end of 1029.

1020, south-west of 1013, had an internal diameter of 11.2–12.0 m and two entrances, to the north-east and south-east. It was 0.60 m wide and 0.22 m deep. The larger, south-east entrance was overlapped and divided

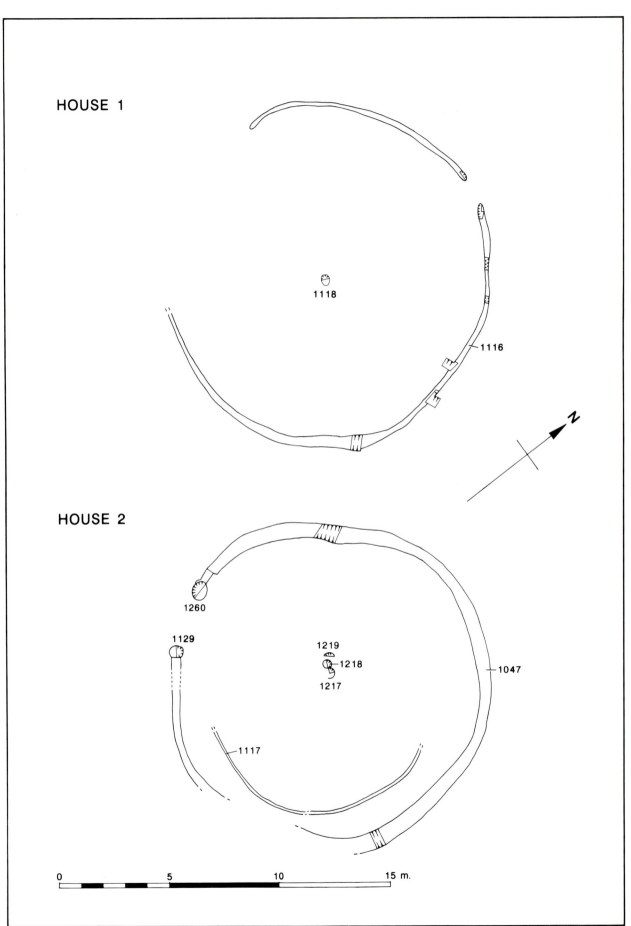

HOUSE 1

1118

1116

N

HOUSE 2

1260

1129

1219
1218
1217

1047

1117

0   5   10   15 m.

Figure 50   Park Farm, Binfield: Houses 1 and 2

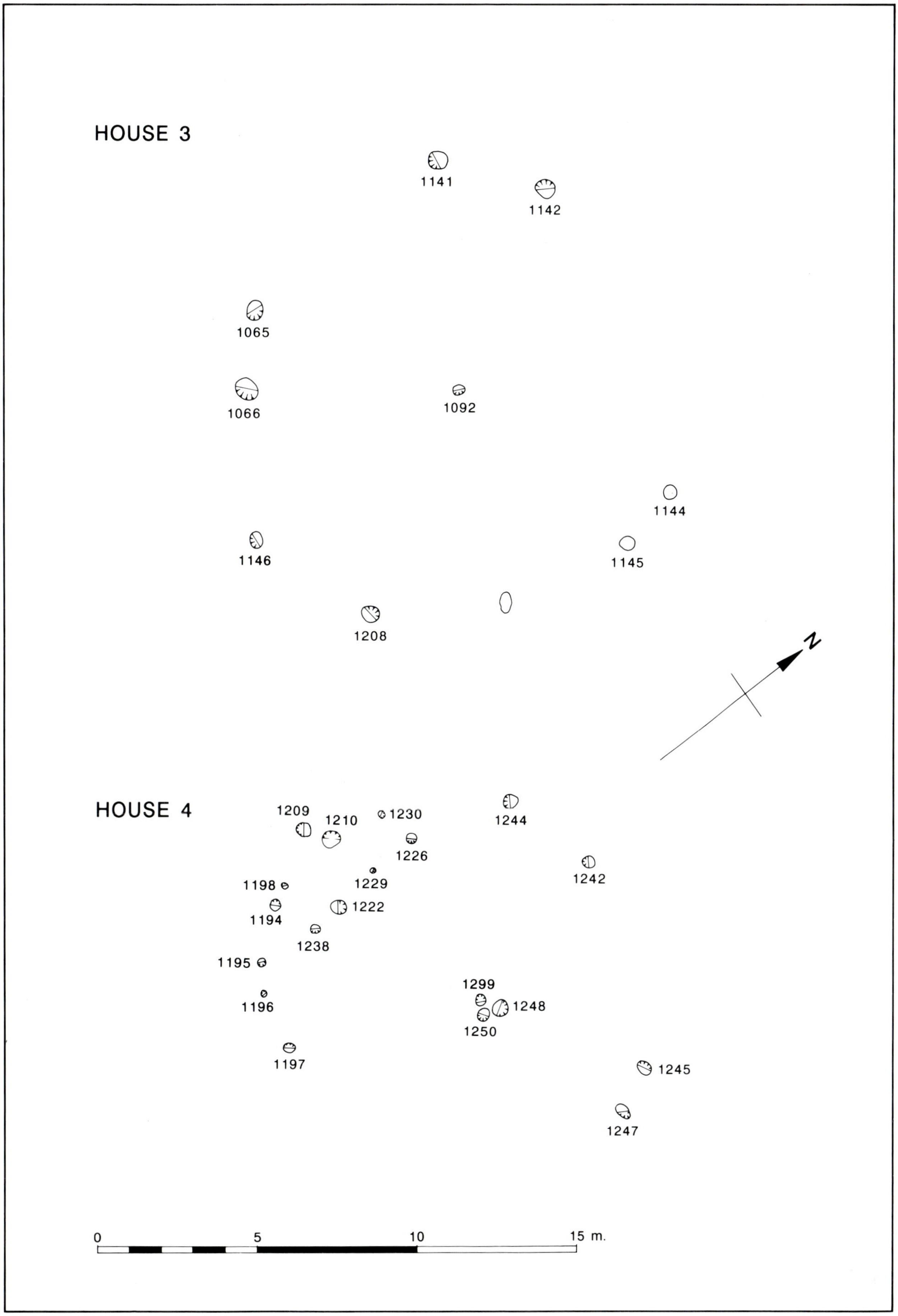

Figure 51   Park Farm, Binfield: Houses 3 and 4

into two by an arc of gully (1028). 1039, the western arc of the circuit between the entrances, contained pottery of CPs 1 and 2 as well as loomweight fragments.

1050, south-east of 1020, was an almost circular gully 0.40 m wide and 0.18 m deep, with an internal diameter of 10.2–12.8 m, which formed two-thirds of a circuit. The missing arc was formed by either 1166 or 1172, making entrances to the south-east and north-west. This gully and others to the south-east of it lay in the angle of ditches 1002 and 1049. Both 1002 and 1049 contained loomweight fragments and may have marked the division between this area and that of Houses 1–3.

South-east of 1050 was an area of very shallow gullies, on average only 0.10 m deep, which probably formed a series of superimposed circular features. They contained pottery of all three ceramic phases. They were poorly preserved, and there was not time in which to excavate them fully. They seemed superficially similar to 1020 and 1050.

1150 at the south-west edge of the excavated area (Fig. 45), was a semicircular gully. No finds were recovered from it.

Smaller subcircular gullies, not easily visible in plan, were grouped north of ditch 1049. Not all of these were excavated, but two of the larger features, 1124 and 1125, were sectioned and were found to be 0.22 m and 0.60 m wide and 0.08 m and 0.20 m deep respectively.

Rectangular enclosures north-east of the boundary ditch
The north-eastern half of the site comprised a southern part consisting of one large area and a northern part divided into several smaller plots by rectilinear ditches and gullies (Fig. 45). These two areas were separated by ditch 1014, which ran north-east from the junction of the boundary ditch and ditch 1064. It was 1.44 m wide and 0.44 m deep and was cut by the boundary ditch.

Ditch 1107/1127 ran at right-angles to, and was cut by, 1014. 1107/1127 was 0.41 m wide and 0.30 m deep. Its line was continued by a ditch 0.43 m wide and 0.20 m deep which turned south-west just before the edge of the excavation as 1207. The enclosure bounded by these ditches and the boundary ditch measured 16 x 18 m.

1126 cut 1107/1127 and ran north-east at right-angles to it for 15 m then turned north-west as 1175, continued by a recut, 1176, which turned slightly east again as 1114. This feature gained in depth and width, eventually becoming 1.40 m wide and 0.45 m deep. The dimensions of this second enclosure were at least 24 x 15 m.

1113 ran north-east from the junction of 1176 and 1114, at right-angles to and of the same dimensions as 1114. Its north-east end was destroyed by a 19th century drain and the main line sewer.

The area north-east of 1176 was subdivided by two gullies, 1231 and 1221, at right-angles to 1014. Their only relationship to the other features is a spatial one.

1231 was 0.65 m wide and 0.35 m deep, 1221 0.40 m wide and 0.18 m deep.

In trench 109, south-east of the main excavation (Fig. 44), were two north-west–south-east ditches, only one of which was excavated (1167). The excavated section did not contain any finds.

The small quantity of pottery from ditches in this half of the site, less than 30 sherds in all, is of CP3. Intersections such as those of 1014 and 1107 and 1107/1127 and 1126 indicate more than one phase in the layout. Once 1107/1127 was silted up, the gaps between 1014 and 1126, 1231 and 1221 could have provided an entranceway.

Curvilinear features north-east of the boundary ditch
Within the second of the two enclosures described above were three intersecting curvilinear gullies, 1177, 1181, and 1205, running into the north-west edge of the excavated area (Fig. 45). Their internal diameters ranged from 4.8 m to 9.8 m and they were 0.60–0.40 m wide and 0.25–0.11 m deep. Finds were very few. 1181 contained three sherds of CP1, 1177, which cut it, one small sherd of CP3.

Sewerage pipes
The small trench excavated to the north-east of the main area revealed a gently sloping bank with evidence of tree roots. This was undated and could have been recently buried by the construction of the sewerage pipe. The bank overlay iron-concreted natural gravel. The entire edge of the field had been built up about 1.5 m by the soil dumped when the Bracknell sewerage pipe trench (which was 2.5 m deep and up to 12 m wide) was backfilled. Further north-west the sewer pipe was 50% larger, as the Wokingham sewerage pipe ran parallel to the north-west edge of the trench in the next field and joined the Bracknell sewer. Any archaeology in this area would thus have been destroyed.

3 Finds

Iron Age and Romano-British Pottery, by Paul Booth

The 1990 excavations at Binfield produced 1712 sherds of Iron Age and Romano-British pottery, weighing 29 kg and totalling c. 18.52 EVEs (*see below*). The pottery ranged from handmade material of Middle Iron Age type to a Romanised assemblage of about the middle of the 2nd century AD. There was very little material which need have been later than this date.

All the sherds were examined macroscopically, and many fabrics were checked under a microscope at x20 magnification. Quantification was by sherd count, weight, and estimated vessel equivalents (EVEs: based on the sum of percentages of rim circumference represented by the surviving sherds). Details of fabric, manufacture, and ware (*see below*) were recorded, as well as information relating to vessel form, and rim, base, and decoration types, etc. Soil conditions on the site were not favourable for the preservation of pottery;

many sherds were badly eroded, with the result that evidence for surface treatment and decoration was generally lacking.

The pottery bears out the more-or-less continuous development suggested by the stratigraphic sequence. Three principal ceramic phases (henceforth CP) were defined, which probably followed one another in close succession and may be subdivided on the basis of the stratigraphy. These are:

CP1   a 'Middle Iron Age' phase,
CP2   a Late Iron Age-early Romano-British 'Belgic type' phase, and
CP3   a Romanised phase probably dating from the later 1st century AD.

These are discussed in greater detail below. Representative vessels are illustrated in Figures 52–6.

Fabrics

Fabrics were defined on the basis of their principal inclusion types and an indicator of the fineness of these inclusions (on a scale of 1 (fine) to 5 (coarse)). The principal inclusion types were A: quartz sand; F: flint; G: grog or clay pellets; I: ?iron oxides; M: mica; and V: vegetable or organic material. Z was used for voids of uncertain origin (eg, organic or calcareous) and N to indicate an absence of obvious inclusions, particularly for some of the finer Roman fabrics. For the purposes of coding the fabrics only the two most common inclusion types were used, though many fabrics contained three or more inclusion types (*for detailed descriptions see Table Mf. 7*).

Individual fabrics were assigned to 'ware groups'. These were less objectively characterised than the fabrics themselves but were felt to provide meaningful groupings of fabrics for the purposes of interpreting the assemblage. Fabrics were thus assigned to, for example, groups of oxidised or reduced coarse wares, or specialist ware types such as mortarium fabrics or white wares. In the case of the handmade Iron Age pottery, in particular, there was quite a wide range of variation of fabric within what were considered to be individual 'wares'. The Roman material, on the other hand, was more consistent in its production, though even here some wares combined sherds in several different fabrics. In some cases, however, an individual 'ware' had only one fabric definition, the two thus amounting to the same thing.

Table Mf.8 shows the correlation between individual fabrics and wares, expressed as numbers of sherds. Some fabrics occurred several times in different 'wares' — eg, Fabric AI2 in M22, Q25, 26, and 31, E22, O33, O51, and R21, 22, 32, and 33 as well as the Iron Age ware P12. This reflects the ubiquity of sand as a tempering agent and the occurrence of iron oxides in the clays used for potting. It also indicates the general suitability of moderately fine sand-tempered fabrics for a variety of purposes, from ordinary domestic pottery (for cooking?) of Iron Age date through to specialist Romanised vessels such as flagons and mortaria.

The breakdown of ware by fabric also shows the technological trends suggested by the ceramic phases

mentioned above and discussed in more detail below. For the handmade Middle Iron Age pottery quartz sand was almost always the dominant tempering agent, and there were only two sherds (of fabric VG4) in which sand was not one of the two principal inclusion types. The incidence of grog/clay pellets was uncommon and these probably never occurred as deliberate inclusions. The same was true of iron oxides. Deliberately used inclusion types were organic material and, to a lesser extent, flint, though even in P14, the only Iron Age ware to contain flint, the flint inclusions were usually uncommon.

In the Late Iron Age and Romano-British periods there was a greater variety of fabrics. Sand tempering was still dominant, but only *c.* 56% of the sherds had sand as the major inclusion type. Grog-tempered fabrics amounted to almost 30% and flint tempering also became quite significant, up to 12%. Both these inclusion types were particularly common in the Late Iron Age–early Romano-British phase. The use of flint tempering continued in the Romanised reduced ware R22, but here it was always secondary to sand temper, and this was probably the only flint-tempered fabric to have outlasted the 1st century AD.

Fifty-two wares were identified at Binfield, including five ascribed to the Iron Age. Twenty-seven of these were of relatively minor importance, with less than 10 sherds of each. 'Fine and specialist' wares (samian, fine wares, mortaria, white, and white-slipped fabrics) were rare, amounting to only 5% of the total sherds.

Samian (S) and fine (F) wares
15 sherds, 0.9%; 692 g, 2.4%; 1.65 EVEs, 8.9%.
There were only 14 sherds of samian ware from the site, nine ?South Gaulish and the remainder probably from Lezoux. Most of the sherds were badly eroded. There were no decorated pieces, although one base sherd might have been from a Dragendorff (Drag.) 37. Other forms represented were 18, 18/31, 33, 38 ?Curle 11, and possibly 15/17. None of these vessels is likely to have been of pre-Flavian date. The only vessel of note was a substantially complete Drag. 38 inverted in the fill of feature 1016/A. This may have been one of the latest vessels on the site, but even so was probably of early rather than later Antonine date. The sole fine ware sherd was a tiny fragment, probably of Central Gaulish 'Rhenish' ware.

Mortaria (M) and white (W) wares
49 sherds, 2.8%; 702 g, 2.4%; 0.31 EVEs, 1.7%.
There were two sources of mortaria at Binfield, the *Verulamium* region and Oxfordshire industries, with five and four sherds respectively. Each industry was represented by a single rim of late 1st–early 2nd century type. The *Verulamium* region was probably also the principal source of white wares, the majority of which were in the sandy fabric AN3. These included several thick-walled sherds which must have been from a very large flagon or (perhaps more likely) from a Dressel type 2–4 amphora such as were produced at Brockley Hill (cf Castle 1978). The sources of the other white wares are uncertain. W25 was not distinctive. W31 was a fine ware used for a bowl with a small bead rim and rouletted decoration (No. 54), but there was also the base of a ?butt

beaker in this ware. Fine butt beakers in this type of fabric were often imported (Rigby 1989, 137), but it is uncertain if this was true of W31.

White-slipped (Q) wares
20 sherds, 1.0%; 137 g, 0.5%; 0.51 EVEs, 2.8%.
Four distinct wares were represented, of which one (Q26) was probably the same as the oxidised coarse ware O51 with a white slip. This and the other wares in this group were mainly fairly fine sandy fabrics with iron inclusions. Q25 was characterised by its fine sand temper; Q27 was similar but with the addition of sparse organic inclusions. Both Q25 and the reduced ware Q31 occurred in indeterminate ?jar forms, but nevertheless the principal vessel types in these wares were probably flagons. Examples were the ring necked form No. 55 and a substantial two-ribbed handle, both in ware Q25. None of these wares can be ascribed to a known source.

'Belgic type', etc, (E) wares
354 sherds, 20.7%; 5261 g, 18.1%; 4.14 EVEs, 22.3%.
This term has been used for a generally distinctive group of wares, mainly dating to the 1st century AD, comprising principally fabrics and forms of 'Belgic' character (cf Thompson 1982). Such fabrics were mainly wheel-thrown, although the method of manufacture could not always be determined owing to the poor surface condition of many of the sherds, but several handmade flint-tempered fabrics in a rather different tradition (the E60 wares) were included in this group, mainly because they seemed to share a similar chronological range.

The E ware group had three main subgroups; E20 wares, which were principally sand-tempered, the flint-tempered E60 wares, and grog-tempered E80 wares. E20 wares were the smallest component. E21 was the most important of these; it was tempered chiefly with sand and organic material, though grog and occasional iron inclusions were also characteristic. E22 and E23 did not contain grog, but both had occasional flint temper. Vessel types in these wares consisted entirely of jars, mostly of forms with curving everted rims but also including simple bead rim jars.

It was in the E60 wares that flint was of major importance. In all except a few sherds of E63 such tempering was common and the inclusions were often large and obtrusive on the surface of the sherds. There was considerable variation among the E60 wares, however. E61 contained quartz sand, grog and (particularly) organic material as well as flint. E63 was similar but usually rather finer. E62, E64 and E65 all contained sand in addition to flint. The sand grains varied considerably in size and frequency; in E62 they were small and sparse, in E64 larger and more common, and E65 contained very large (up to *c.* 2 mm) quartz sand grains. Only ware E66 appears to have been tempered with flint alone. Despite the variations in fabric, however, there can be little doubt that all the E60 wares were variants on a common theme. All appeared to have been hand-made.

Vessels in these wares were consistently of bead rim and related types with the exception of No. 11, a fairly straight-sided bucket/barrel-like vessel of Middle Iron Age type. This vessel, in ware E62, can probably be seen as a link between the Middle Iron Age and Late Iron Age–early Romano-British traditions. The E60 wares may therefore have developed out of the former, though the evidence does not suggest that this development was a lengthy process (*see below*). There are some similarities between the E60 wares and fabrics classified as 'Silchester ware' (Fulford 1984, 135; Timby 1989, 85), but most of the E60 fabrics were more mixed in composition and the rim forms were less well-defined than classic Silchester ware (J. Timby pers. comm.). The only exception was E66, with the clean matrix characteristic of Silchester ware. This fabric was rare at Binfield. The E60 wares and Silchester ware nevertheless seem to derive from a common tradition. The E60 wares are likely to have pre-dated the floruit of Silchester ware around the middle of the 1st century AD.

The E80 wares were characterised by dominant grog inclusions. The most common, E82, also contained sand and organic temper, and E83 was distinguished by the presence of small amounts of flint in addition to these. As with the other E wares the range of vessel types was restricted entirely to jars, but there seems to have been a slightly wider variety of forms in the E80s, including narrow mouthed and bead rim types as well as a range of medium mouthed jars. These types are all found within the 'Belgic' ceramic repertoire of south-east England.

The sources and overall date range of the E wares remain uncertain. Local production seems likely but cannot be proven. It is impossible to determine when the E20 and E80 wares came into use, though this is likely to have been some time before the Conquest. Nevertheless there is some evidence that E80 wares in particular might have been in use generally rather later than the E60 wares (*see discussion of CP2 below*).

Oxidised (O) coarsewares
417 sherds, 24.3%; 1065 g, 36.4%; 0.85 EVEs, 4.6%.
These wares formed a somewhat heterogeneous group, emphasised by their widely varying importance as a proportion of the whole assemblage, depending on the quantification method used. Only four wares (O26, O51, O71, and O73) were of any numerical significance.

O20 and O30 wares were sand-tempered, of varying coarseness; O26 was consistently moderately sandy with iron inclusions. The O20 wares were unsourced, but the O30s are paralleled in north Wiltshire at kiln sites such as Purton (Anderson 1980) and may have originated in that area. This would probably account for their relative rarity at Binfield. The single sherd of O43 may have come from even further afield; it was thought to be a Severn Valley ware, although this identification was not certain. The fabric of this sherd was distinct from those of the other oxidised wares in the assemblage. The only vessel rim in these wares was from a flagon (No. 64) in O33. It is unclear, however, if such vessels were among the repertoire of the north Wiltshire potters (cf Anderson 1980, 57), although this is possible.

O50 wares were generally fine. O51, with very fine sand and occasional clay pellet and iron inclusions, was numerous in terms of sherd count, but the sherds were extremely small, weighing on average *c.* 5.5 g (the average sherd size for the site was *c.* 17 g). Rims, which

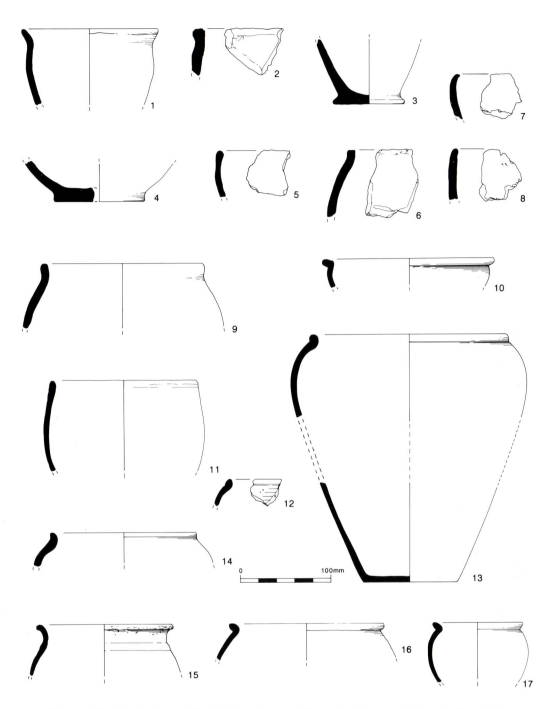

*Figure 52   Park Farm, Binfield: pottery of Ceramic Phases 1 (Nos 1–8) and 2
(Nos 9–17). Scale 1:4*

were scarce, were consequently not identifiable to specific types.

The major part of the O ware group was taken up with O70s — coarse-tempered wares. O71 was much the most important of these, and was the commonest single ware at Binfield both in terms of sherd count and weight (respectively 16.4% and 31.2% of the assemblage, but only 2.1% of EVEs). O71 was characteristically tempered with grog and organic inclusions, though in a small number of sherds quartz sand was the most common inclusion type. Iron also appeared infrequently. O71 was the same in composition and character as the reduced ware R81. Some sherds in both wares were unevenly fired, and the distinction between O71 and

R81 probably had no real significance, reflecting accidental rather than deliberate variations in firing conditions. O71/R81 was used exclusively for large storage jars, and it was the only important ware to span CP2 and CP3 (*see below*).

Like O71, O72, and O74 had grog tempering, associated with flint and organic material respectively. Both were scarce. O73 was slightly more common and was characterised by coarse sand inclusions, with no other inclusion types evident. Of these three wares only O73 was represented by a rim sherd — from a substantial bead rim jar (No. 38) closely comparable to those found in the flint-tempered E60 wares. The remaining oxidised ware was a single sherd of O81, perhaps pink grogged ware with a source in the Milton Keynes area (Booth and Green 1989). The fabric of the Binfield sherd was, however, atypical in containing some organic inclusions, so the identification is uncertain.

Reduced (R) coarsewares
608 sherds, 35.5%; 7137 g, 24.6%; 9.58 EVEs, 51.6%.
These wares were the most important component of the Romano-British assemblage except in terms of weight. The date of their earliest appearance is unknown, but as there are similarities in fabric, for example between some sherds of E21 and R24, and R22 contained flint inclusions in the same way as E22 and E23, a development of at least some of the R wares out of the E20 ware group can be postulated. This development is likely to have been under way by the Flavian period at the latest, and could have commenced rather earlier.

The principal R wares were all sand-tempered. In the most common, R21, sand was probably the only deliberate tempering agent since the iron oxides also found in this ware are likely to have occurred naturally in the clay body. Clay pellets and organic inclusions were found only very rarely in R21. In R24 and R31 organic inclusions were more common and were second only to sand in importance, although even they were fairly sparse. Although both R24 and R31 were relatively fine wares the sand in R31 was consistently less common and slightly smaller grained, thus allowing the distinction to be sustained.

Only the R80 wares differed from the remainder of this group in being principally grog-tempered. R81, the most common of these, has been discussed above.

The R ware vessel type repertoire was dominated by jars of various forms, totalling over 90% of the vessels in these wares. Beaker (in R31), bowl (R21 and R22), dish (R22 and R31), bowl/dish (R24 and R31), and lid (R21) forms also occurred, but all were rare.

Black Burnished Ware (B)
10 sherds, 0.6%; 281 g, 1.0%; 0.21 EVEs, 1.1%.
The small quantity of Black Burnished Ware at Binfield is consistent with occupation at the site having ceased before the end of the 2nd century AD. Most of the sherds came from some of the stratigraphically latest features (eg, 1002 and 1029). Identification of the fabric was hampered by the poor surface condition of the sherds, but all seemed to be BB1 of Dorset origin. The three vessels represented, two cooking pots (eg, No. 35) and a flat rimmed bowl/dish, were all 2nd century types.

Handmade Iron Age (P) wares
239 sherds, 14.0%; 4227 g, 14.6%; c. 1.27 EVEs, 6.9%.
Five wares were distinguished, of which P13 and P15 were of minor importance. Sand tempering was dominant in these wares, and in P11 was often the only visible inclusion. Although P12, in particular, apparently exhibited fairly wide variations in fabric there was nevertheless still considerable consistency within the ware. The principal inclusions were sand and organic material, but iron and clay pellets were also present to the extent that they occasionally formed the second most important inclusion type.

P11 and P12 dominated the assemblage in the 'Middle Iron Age' phase (CP1). P13 (1 sherd) and P14 (2,

or possibly 3 sherds), were rare in this phase and were found mainly in CP2, while sherds of P15 occurred only in the fully Romano-British phase (CP3), though they must have been residual there. It is possible, therefore, that P14, in which flint was important as well as sand, and P13 and P15, with particularly prominent organic, iron or clay pellet inclusions, were only late introductions to the repertoire in CP1. The small numbers of sherds concerned, however, make this uncertain, except perhaps in the case of P14, of which there were sufficient sherds (34) for its almost total absence in CP1 to be considered significant.

P ware vessel forms were very simple, consisting almost entirely of barrel shaped jars with, at most, slightly everted rims. One vessel in P12 was rather more globular and had a slightly beaded rim. This form is typologically later than the other P ware vessels and was common in CP2, particularly in the flint-tempered E60 wares.

Ceramic phasing
The three ceramic phases were defined without reference to the stratigraphic sequence (*see above*). Each context assemblage was assigned to one of these phases — or, in a few cases, to transitional phases 1/2 and 2/3 — on the basis of its ceramic content. The allocation of context groups to ceramic phases took no account of the possibility that some groups of CP1 and CP2 were contaminated by later material. A few groups may therefore have been assigned to a phase later than that of their deposition. Nevertheless, the percentages of material from earlier ceramic phases occurring in deposits of CP2 and CP3 were not particularly high, suggesting that there was relatively little contamination of this kind and, moreover, that the inevitable occurrence of residual material was not a major problem here. This is perhaps surprising in view of the fact that many of the largest assemblages derived from ditches — a context type which tends to produce mixed groups with a large proportion of redeposited material.

The contents of the ceramic phases are presented in summary form in Table 39. Their definitions and characteristics are discussed below.

Phases 1 and 1/2
CP1 consisted of those groups which contained only handmade pottery of Middle Iron Age character (in effect, P wares). Almost two-thirds of all P ware sherds occurred in this phase. As noted above, wares P13–P15 were not common in this phase and it is possible that they were later developments in CP1, supplementing the sand-tempered wares P11 and P12, and being thus more likely to occur in contexts of the following phase. The few vessel types in wares P13–P15 do not, however, indicate any typological development over those in P11 and P12.

This, and the relatively low percentage of P wares in groups assigned to CP2, suggest that the replacement of the P wares by 'Belgic type' and related wares may have been a fairly rapid process. Only one very small group was assigned to the overlap between CP1 and CP2. Here a single sherd of E21 was very small and may have been intrusive.

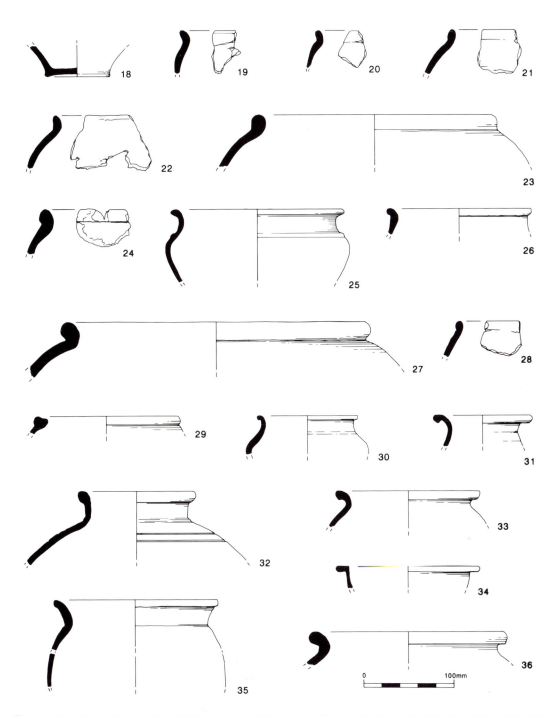

Figure 53   Park Farm, Binfield: pottery of Ceramic Phases 2 (Nos 18–27), 2/3 (Nos 28, 29), and 3 (Nos 30–36). Scale 1:4

Phases 2 and 2/3

CP2 consisted of groups which contained principally 'Belgic type' wares, those assigned to the E ware group. Such groups amounted to 12.4% of the total site assemblage but comprised 72.9% of this phase. Apart from P wares, which totalled 17.8% of the sherds in CP2, and of which not all were necessarily residual, the only other significant component of the assemblage was sherds of O71/R81. There seemed no good reason to suppose that these were not contemporary with wares of the E group, particularly as they shared with some of the latter the characteristic of grog tempering. The majority of sherds in these wares occurred in the following phase, however.

The pottery in this phase was dominated by E60 wares, which make up 54% of the total sherds while E20 and E80 wares together amounted to only 21.7% of the assemblage. Almost two-thirds of all E60 sherds were found in this phase, whereas less than half the E20 sherds and only 16.8% of E80 sherds occurred in CP2. These data can be interpreted in several ways. They could suggest that groups which should have belonged to CP3 were assigned to CP2 because their sole or principal contents were E60 sherds, wrongly thought to have been restricted to CP2. Alternatively, and more probably, CP2 may have been genuinely dominated by E60 wares. These are likely to have been the earliest E wares in use in this phase. The occurrence of 77.6% of all E80 sherds in CP3 suggests that these grog-tempered wares continued in use in that phase. This need not necessarily imply that E80 wares were only introduced late in CP2, although this could have been the case.

CP2 was thus characterised by two very different ceramic traditions. The flint-tempered (E60) one, while still handmade, contrasts with the earlier P ware tradition in fabrics and forms, though there are hints which point to its development from the P wares. In its turn it seems to have been supplemented and then supplanted by the wheelthrown and largely grog-tempered Belgic tradition. There is apparently, therefore, a contrast between the trend observable at Binfield and that seen at Silchester, where flint-tempered 'Silchester ware' seems to have largely replaced grog-tempered wares 'by the Claudian period' (Timby 1989, 84). The significance of this contrast is uncertain. It could reflect sample bias arising from the relatively small size of the Binfield assemblage; alternatively it could represent a genuine difference in the development of pottery supply to higher and lower status sites.

A few groups, with a total of 53 sherds, were assigned to CP2/3. These were groups where there was some uncertainty about their character. Most of them were small, but were dominated by E wares and (in particular) sherds of O71/R81. In several cases the groups consisted solely of the latter wares. Since most sherds in O71/R81 were found in CP3 contexts it is likely that some of these groups were of that date, but as this could not be certain it was decided to assign them to the transitional either/or phase.

Ceramic Phase 3
Pottery groups assigned to this phase accounted for 75% of the sherds on the site. They were characterised by the presence of 'Romanised' reduced coarsewares, which amounted to *c.* 47% of the assemblage, and other Romanised wares such as samian and mortaria, though these were never numerous. The degree of overlap between the CP2 and CP3 assemblages is uncertain, but it has been suggested that some R wares developed out of E20 sand-tempered wares, and as the majority of E80 wares were found in CP3 some at least of these may have been in contemporary use with more Romanised fabrics. Nevertheless, E and P wares only totalled 17.3% of the CP3 assemblage, so at worst the residual component of the assemblage is unlikely to have been more than *c.* 20% (this figure allows for the possibility that some sherds of O71/R81 may have been residual from CP2) and was probably rather less.

Sherds in O71/R81 were the main component of the assemblage apart from those already mentioned, although their importance was probably exaggerated as the result of the occurrence of large numbers of sherds, probably from a single vessel, in 1040. There is no doubt, however, that such vessels were in use alongside sand-tempered and other wares. The long term persistence of the grog-tempered tradition for the manufacture of large storage jars can be paralleled elsewhere (eg, in the Oxfordshire industry; Young 1977, 202).

Table 39 Park Farm, Binfield: incidence of ware groups by Ceramic Phase (quantification by no. of sherds)

Ware	Ceramic Phase					Sherd total	%
	1	1/2	2	2/3	3		
S	–	–	–	–	14	14	0.8
F	–	–	–	–	1	1	0.1
M	–	–	–	–	9	9	0.5
W	–	–	–	–	40	40	2.3
Q	–	–	–	–	20	20	1.2
E20	–	1	23	2	24	50	2.9
E60	–	–	115	5	59	179	10.5
E80	–	–	18	7	100	125	7.3
E sub-total	–	1	156	14	183	354	20.7
O20	–	–	–	–	37	37	2.2
O30	–	–	–	–	11	11	0.6
O40	–	–	–	–	1	1	0.1
O50	–	–	1	1	48	50	2.9
O70	–	–	12	25	280	317	18.5
O80	–	–	–	–	1	1	0.1
O sub-total	–	–	13	26	378	417	24.4
R10	–	–	–		3	3	0.2
R20	–	–	1	3	466	470	27.5
R30	–	–	–	–	102	102	6.0
R80	–	–	6	7	20	33	1.9
R sub-total	–	–	7	10	591	608	35.5
B	–	–	–	–	10	10	0.6
P	152	3	38	3	43	239	14.0
Total	152	4	214	53	1289	1712	
%	8.9	0.2	12.5	3.1	75.5		

Vessel Forms
The vessels were divided into a number of major classes (flagons, jars, beakers, etc) which were then subdivided where possible. Classes and their subtypes were designated by letter codes (Table Mf. 9).

The range of vessel forms at Binfield is quite narrow. The assemblage is dominated by jars, which amount to 80.2% of all vessels (figures for vessel types are expressed as a percentage of EVEs), with a further 1.9% of uncertain jar/bowl types. While a number of other vessel types occur, all are poorly represented and the range of forms within these types very limited. These facts reflect the date range of the site, since jars tend to be rather more common in Late Iron Age and early Romano-British assemblages than in those of the later Romano-British period (cf Millett 1979, 37–9). All the identifiable Middle Iron Age vessels were classified as jars or jar/bowls, but their removal from the overall figures makes very little difference to the overall representation of jars.

There was considerable variation of form within the jar category, but the main types were the barrel-shaped Iron Age forms (type CB), narrow mouthed (type CC), medium mouthed (type CD; a general category), and bead rim jars (type CH). Uncertain types (where insufficient of the body survived to allow specific identification) constituted 42% of all jars.

The correlation of vessel types with particular wares or ware groups shows that the barrel-shaped forms occurred exclusively in P wares, as might have been expected. Bucket-shaped, globular and squat, high-shouldered jars (types CA, CG, and CE) were found solely in E wares, which also accounted for about two-thirds of the bead rim (type CH) jars. The latter type was also found in wares P12 and O73. Since there were only two examples in R wares (both in R21) the type may be considered characteristic of CP2. It was the most common individual jar type in E wares.

With one possible exception in ware E82, narrow-mouthed jars were confined to R wares, and about 85% of the general 'medium-mouthed' jar class were also in R wares. Carinated and angled everted rim types (types CF and CI), both rare, were found solely in R wares. Jars of 'cooking pot' form (type CK) were also scarce, with a single example in R21 and two in Black Burnished Ware (B11). The rarity of this type may be a result of chronological factors, and indicative of the absence of late Antonine (and later) occupation, by which time the type would be expected to be quite common. Storage jars (type CN) occurred exclusively in grog-tempered fabrics (O71/R81 and E83), with the exception of a single example in the flint-tempered ware E62.

Apart from jars, only bowls amounted to more than c. 2% of the assemblage (8%), and this figure was inflated by the presence of an almost complete Drag. 38, emphasising the extent to which relatively small assemblages can be distorted by a few substantial rim sherds when quantified as EVEs. Bowls occurred mainly in samian ware, but were also found in reduced wares R21 and R22 and in white ware W31. The only obvious chronologically aberrant sherd in the assemblage was the rim of a bowl (No. 74) in ware R31 (though the fabric was atypical) from 1112/A/1, a medieval furrow nonetheless containing an otherwise 2nd century group. This vessel was of a characteristically late 3rd–4th century type, closely comparable to, for instance, the Alice Holt type 5B.8, dated AD 270–420 (Lyne and Jefferies 1979, 46). The fabric does not seem to indicate an Alice Holt origin, however.

Like bowls, the majority of dishes were also of samian ware, of forms 18 and 18/31, with occasional examples in reduced wares. Indeterminate bowl/dish forms were found in reduced wares and Black Burnished Ware. Of the remaining types, flagons totalled 2.1% of the total EVEs, but there were only two vessels, in Q25 and O33. There were likewise only two mortaria. Beakers, cups, and lids were each represented by a single vessel, in R31, samian ware and R21 respectively.

Discussion and conclusions

The date of the earliest occupation at Binfield is uncertain. The site seems to have been continuously settled up to approximately the middle of the 2nd century AD. Pottery from the latest ceramic phase, which probably commenced in the 3rd quarter of the 1st century AD, comprises the bulk of the material. The handmade fabrics of Middle Iron Age tradition characteristic of CP1 amount to only 14% of the total sherds. Allowing for the fact that the overall level of pottery use may have been lower in CP1 than later, and that the extent of settlement (ie, the number of households present) could have been less, it is still possible to interpret this figure as indicating that CP1 was of relatively short duration. In this case occupation of the site may have commenced no earlier than the 2nd century BC at the earliest.

There are few assemblages within the region with which Binfield can be compared. At Ufton Nervet, north of Silchester, a Middle Iron Age component was not explicitly identified in the assemblage, though handmade vessels of Middle Iron Age type did occur (eg, Thompson and Manning 1974, 33–34, nos 116, 119, 120, 123, and 124). A date 'perhaps not long before the Roman Conquest' was suggested for this material (ibid., 33). At Aldermaston Wharf Middle Iron Age pottery, all to a greater or lesser degree flint-tempered, was broadly dated to the 3rd–1st centuries BC (Cowell et al. 1978, 3). A later group, dominated by grog-tempered wares, was dated c. AD 1–30, although it was thought that it could have started as early as c. 50 BC (ibid., 25–6). This evidence complements and does not contradict that from Binfield, but it does not allow refinement of the dating. The more westerly sites such as Ufton Nervet contrast with Binfield in that the Conquest period groups are dominated by Silchester Ware which is almost totally absent at Binfield.

The traditions of the Binfield pottery are therefore comparable with other assemblages in the region, but are not exactly the same. In particular, the use of flint as a tempering agent is less prevalent at Binfield, especially in the Middle Iron Age. Quartz sand remains a major temper type throughout the period, though its importance was diminished for a while in the Late Iron Age/early Romano-British period (CP2). Much of the pottery in all periods must have come from local sources, although in most cases these are not known in detail. One possible source for some of the flint-tempered fabrics is Knowl Hill, some 9 km north of Binfield, where coarse flint and sand-tempered pottery tentatively dated to the first half of the 1st century AD was associated with a possible pottery kiln (Over 1973, 66). A source in the Staines area is thought possible for both fine and specialist ware fabrics and types such as the flagon, No. 55, (and perhaps the dish, No. 53, if it was mica dusted) as well as reduced wares such as the Surrey bowls, Nos 10 and 52, and the biconical jar, No. 44. If most or all of the other R21 and R31 vessels were from the same general area it would have been a major source for Binfield. This remains to be confirmed, however. The other likely major local source for Binfield pottery is the Alice Holt industry. The extent of its contribution is, however, uncertain, although fabric D (Lyne and Jeffer-

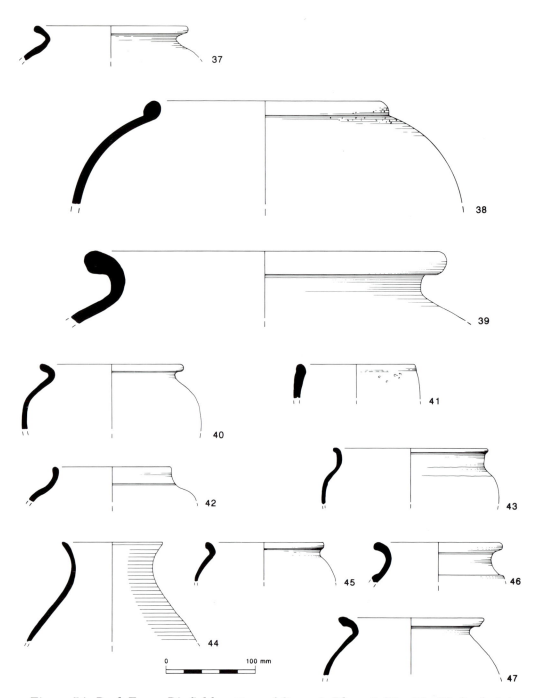

Figure 54 Park Farm, Binfield: pottery of Ceramic Phase 3 (Nos 37–47). Scale 1:4

ies 1979, 18) has been tentatively identified here (*see wares O73 and R23*).

The various extra-regional sources represented only provided a small proportion of the total pottery. Samian and a single sherd of Lezoux ware were the only cross-channel imports. Mortaria were from Oxfordshire and the *Verulamium* region, the latter also producing white wares, and non-local oxidised wares included possible north Wiltshire, Severn Valley, and Milton Keynes area products. All of these were found in very small quantities and presumably cannot indicate direct trade from these diverse sources, but rather occasional purchases from a local market centre.

The overall level of prosperity indicated by the pottery evidence is quite low, with a total fine and specialist ware component of only 5% of the sherds (*see above*). The low representation of samian and fine wares and the total absence of amphorae are indicators of a low status assemblage. This conclusion is supported by the breakdown of vessel types (*see above*). While the high representation of jars (80%) is to be expected in a group of this chronological range, the paucity of other vessel types also suggests that this is a somewhat conservative assemblage. There is nothing in the range of vessel types to suggest that the assemblage had distinctive functional characteristics.

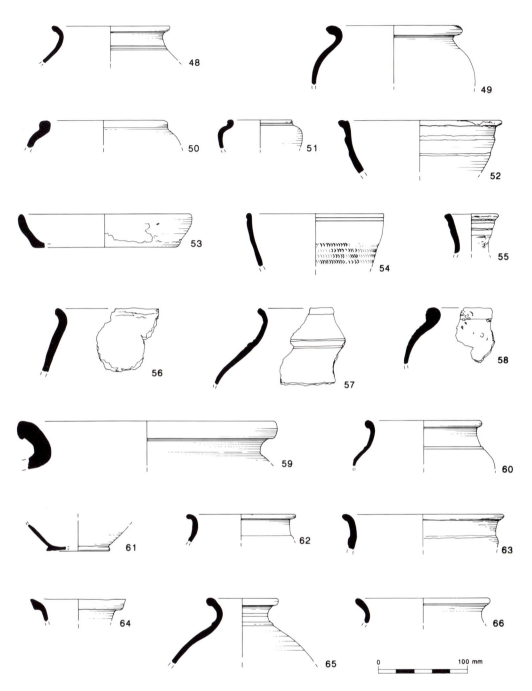

Figure 55 Park Farm, Binfield: pottery of Ceramic Phase 3 (Nos 48–66). Scale 1:4

Illustrated pottery

The illustrated vessels are arranged in groups by ceramic phase. Within each CP group the contexts are arranged in an approximate geographical sequence across the site, from south-west–north-east. Sherds have not generally been illustrated where there was clear stratigraphic evidence that the groups to which they belonged must have been later in date than the CP to which they were assigned. Some clearly residual pieces are included, however, if they represent, for example, otherwise unparalleled ware/type combinations which amplify the range of material from the site. Detailed descriptions of individual sherds are not provided, but fabric, ware, and type classifications (all

explained and discussed above) are given for each piece and unusual characteristics are commented upon.

Ceramic Phase 1 (Fig. 52)
1 Type CB, Fabric AN3, ware P11, 1179/A/1
2 Type CB, Fabric AV2, ware P12, 1208/A/1
3 Fabric AI2, ware P12, Base, 1070/A
4 Base, Fabric IA2, ware P12, 1239/A
5 Type CB, Fabric AI2, ware P12, 1128/A/1
6 Type CB, Fabric AV2, ware P12, 1097/A/2
7 Type D, Fabric AV2, ware P12, 1104/A/2
8 Type CB, Fabric AN3, ware P11, 1119/A/2

The small group from this phase contains typical vessels to which can be added Nos 14, 19, and 20 from CP2, and 41 and

116

56 from CP3. These vessels are mostly from features comprising or adjacent to Houses 2 and 3.

Ceramic Phase 2 (Figs 52 and 53)
9   Type CH, Fabric FA4, ware E62, 1223/A/1
10 Type H, Fabric AI3, ware R21, 1257/A
11 Type CA, Fabric FA5, ware E62, 1039/C/2
12 Type CH, Fabric FA4, ware E62, 1004/C/1
13 Type CH, Fabric FA5, ware E62, 1004/C/1
14 Type CH, Fabric AI2, ware P12, 1061/B/1
15 Type CD, Fabric AV2, ware E21, 1061/B/1
16 Type CH, Fabric AI2, ware E22, 1084/A/1
17 Type CG, Fabric VG3, ware E63, 1013/A/6
18 Base, Fabric GV3, ware E82, 1011/B/10
19 Type C, Fabric AI3, ware P11, 1027/B/2
20 Type C, Fabric AV2, ware P12, 1027/A/2
21 Type C, Fabric FA4, ware E62, 1027/B/2
22 Type CG,Fabric FV4, ware E62, 1027/A/2
23 Type CH, Fabric FA5, ware E64, 1027/A/2
24 Type CH, Fabric FA5, ware E65, 1027/A/2
25 Type CE, Fabric GV3, ware E82, 1040/C/8
26 Type C, Fabric AV2, ware E21, 1040/C/6
27 Type CH, Fabric FV5, ware E61, 1040/A/5

Numbers 9–11 are from the south-western part of the site. The remaining vessels derive from features to north-west and south-east of House 2 (Nos 12–17) and from the fills of ?early components of the main boundary ditch complex through the centre of the site (Nos 18–27). It is possible that all of these ditch contexts belonged to CP3, but the contents of the lower fills were quite consistently distinguishable from those of the upper fills which were clearly of CP3, they are therefore regarded as CP2 assemblages. The only R ware vessel amongst this material (no. 10) is a 'Surrey bowl' (cf Marsh and Tyers 1978, 576–7). Although sometimes considered to be of Flavian and later date a pre-Flavian date is also possible. The fabric of this vessel suggests an origin in the vicinity of Staines rather than the known production centre at Alice Holt (K. Crouch pers comm). This piece may be intrusive in this phase.

Ceramic Phase 2/3 (Fig. 53)
28 Type CH, Fabric AV2, ware E21, 1140/A/1
29 Type CH, Fabric GA4, ware E83, 1140/A/1

Two vessels from a pit in the area of House 2.

Ceramic Phase 3 (Figs 53–56)
30 Type CD, Fabric AF3, ware R22, 1182/A
31 Type C, Fabric AI3, ware R21, 1002/A/2
32 Type CC, Fabric AI3, ware R21, 1049/C
33 Type CD, Fabric AI3, ware R21, 1002/D/1
34 Type H, Fabric AF3, ware R22, 1002/A/2
35 Type CK, Fabric AN3, ware B11, 1002/C/2
36 Type CN, Fabric GA4, ware E83, 1246/A
37 Type CD, Fabric AI3, ware R21, 1013/B/3
38 Type CH, Fabric AN4, ware O73, 1088/A/2
39 Type CN, Fabric GV4, ware O71, 1060/A/2
40 Type CL, Fabric AF3, ware R22, 1060/A/2
41 Type CB, Fabric VA4, ware P15, 1029/G/2
42 Type CD, Fabric AF3, ware E23, 1029/G/3
43 Type CD, Fabric GA3, ware E81, 1029/G/2
44 Type C, Fabric AV2, ware R31, 1029/C/2
45 Type CD, Fabric AI3, ware R21, 1029/B/3
46 Type CD, Fabric AI3, ware R21, 1029/C/2
47 Type CD, Fabric AF3, ware R22, 1029/C/1
48 Type CD, Fabric AV2, ware R24, 1029/G/3
49 Type CD, Fabric AV2, ware R24, 1029/C/2
50 Type CH, Fabric AI3, ware R21, 1029/B/2
51 Type D, Fabric AV2, ware R31, 1029/G/3
52 Type HC, Fabric AI3, ware R21, 1029/G/2
53 Type JA, Fabric AV2, ware R31, 1029/B/5
54 Type H, Fabric AN1, ware W31, 1029/B/2
55 Type BA, Fabric AI2, ware Q25, 1029/B/1
56 Type CB, Fabric IA4, ware P13, 1011/B/1
57 Type CC, Fabric GA3, ware E82, 1011/B/4
58 Type CH, Fabric FA5, ware E65, 1011/D/1
59 Type CN, Fabric GV4, ware O71, 1011/B/2
60 Type CD, Fabric AV2, ware R31, 1011/B/4
61 Base, Fabric AV2, ware R24, 1011/D/1
62 Type CD, Fabric AV3, ware R22, 018/A/1
63 Type D, Fabric AV2, ware E21, 1040/A/1
64 Type BB, Fabric AI2, ware O33, 1040/A/2
65 Type CC, Fabric AV2, ware R24, 1040/C/3
66 Type CK, Fabric AI3, ware R21, 1040/C/2
67 Type C, Fabric AI2, ware Q31, 1040/C/2
68 Type CH, Fabric FA5, ware E62, 1043/A/2
69 Type C, Fabric AF3, ware E22, 1043/A/3
70 Type CG, Fabric GV3, ware E82, 1154/B/2
71 Type CF, Fabric AI3, ware R21, 1154/B/2

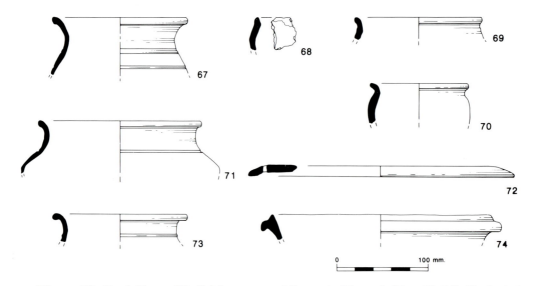

Figure 56 Park Farm, Binfield: pottery of Ceramic Phase 3 (Nos 67–74). Scale 1:4

72 Type L, Fabric AI3, ware R21, 1154/B/2
73 Type C, Fabric AF3, ware R22, 1175/A/1
74 Type IA, Fabric AV2, ware R31, 1112/A/1

Numbers 30–36 are from features in the south-west part of the site, including Nos 31–35 from ditch 1002/1049 south-west of House 1 and No. 36 from adjacent, related ditch 1049. This group includes the first occurrence of Black Burnished Ware on the site (No. 35). Numbers 37–40 are from features north-west of (and in the case of 1060, Nos 39 and 40, cut by) ditch 1029, which defines the north-west side of the House 1 compound and Nos 41–55 are from the ditch itself. This is one of the most varied groups from the site, including a flagon, bowls (of which No. 52 is a second 'Surrey' type), and a dish (No. 53). The surfaces of this last vessel are in poor condition but might possibly have been mica-dusted, in which case an origin in the Staines area is likely.

The remaining material derives from the principal boundary ditch complex (Nos 56–72) and a ditch bounding one of the enclosures to the north-east of it (No. 73). The exact form of No. 72 is uncertain but it is probably a lid, and if so is the only example from the site. Number 74, from a post-Roman plough furrow, is the only certain late Romano-British piece in the assemblage.

Fired Clay, by M.R. Roberts

The excavations at Binfield produced fired clay weighing 23.205 kg from 78 stratified contexts of various types — 40 ditch or gully sections and 38 pits or post-holes. All the pieces were examined macroscopically. Quantification was by fragment count and by weight within context. Details of fabric and type were recorded as far as they could be determined.

Fabrics and types

The range of fabrics is not wide (Table 40). Three main fabrics were defined by variations in the amounts of sand and small (up to 10 mm) flint inclusions. This definition was fairly subjective, as the fabrics thus distinguished represented shades within a continuous spectrum. Fabric is not always consistent within each fragment, as might be expected with such 'low technology' artefacts.

Fabric 1   few sand inclusions and occasional pieces of flint
Fabric 2   common sand inclusions and occasional pieces of flint
Fabric 3   the same level of sand inclusions as fabric 2, but with common flint inclusions.

Table 40   Park Farm, Binfield: weight in grammes of fired clay by type and fabric

Fabric	Loom-weight	?Loom-weight	Daub	?Daub	Other
1	2550	3350	3625	150	1025
2	3025	1605	–	–	2150
3	1650	300	–	–	225

The main categories recorded were loomweights, daub (probable structural fragments), and unidentifiable fragments. If a context contained several identifiable fragments, unidentifiable fragments from it were recorded as belonging to the identified type.

Loomweights were defined as fragments with one or two holes for the attachment of vertical threads and one or two flat sides or faces, or as having three sides but no holes. Possible loomweight fragments were identified as having one flat side with a corner/edge or two flat sides. Daub was recognised by three or more wattle impressions in two directions or impressions of larger stakes/timbers. Possible daub had wattle/twig impressions in two directions. The unidentifiable fragments of fired clay were amorphous or had one flat side but no other distinguishing features (Table 40).

Loomweights

There were 17 definite and 31 possible loomweight fragments (Tables 40 and 41), plus over 200 small fragments of baked clay which, from their fabrics, may have been from loomweights. These three categories weighed 7.225 kg, 5.255 kg, and 3.400 kg respectively. Where the shape of the loomweight fragments could be discerned they were triangular. One large loomweight from ditch 1002 was 60 mm thick and 130 mm high: the sides were about 180 mm long. It seems to have only two holes, at angles of 60° to the sides. Of two loomweights from 1040 in the central boundary ditch, one has a hole at 60° to its side and the other a corner where three sides join, two of which are at 60° to each other. The side of a loomweight from post-hole 1142 in House 3 is 180 mm long. One from post-hole 1147 in the area of House 2 has two 60° corners and a side measuring 180 mm.

Daub

The only recognisable daub came from two adjacent pits, (contexts 1223 and 1224) west of House 4. It weighs 8.175 kg and is very fragmented, consisting of over 213 pieces. Although some pieces are quite large (90 x 80 x 40 mm thick), with clear impressions of wood, many of them are too small for any characteristics to be recognised.

The impressions in the daub are of two types: wattles and larger timbers. The wattles were c. 15–22 mm in diameter and in some cases seemed to be arranged in a

Table 41   Park Farm, Binfield: loomweights/possible loomweight fragments, fabric by Ceramic Phase

	Loomweight/possible loomweight fragments				
Fabric	*CP1*	*CP2*	*CP2/3*	*CP3*	*Undated*	*Total*
1	–	3/0	–	5/4	0/1	8/5=13
2	–	–	1/0	1/20	4/3	6/23=29
3	0/2	–	–	0/1	3/0	3/3=6

Note: of the 31 possible loomweight fragments, 8 were found in context 1011 and 4 in context 1154, both of CP3. Each of these 12 fragments appeared to derive from a different loomweight.

very loose weave with (in a few measurable instances) spaces of at least 40 mm between them. In other instances there was evidence for two wattles lying immediately next to one another. The other impressions are of abutted stakes or timbers *c*. 50 mm in diameter. These may represent a stake wall or the abutting ends of two wattle hurdles. None of the pieces is large enough to show this clearly; the stakes may have lain horizontally rather than vertically.

Evidence for weaving

Including the possible fragments, 48 identifiable loomweight fragments were recovered from the site. Their occurrence in features of all types and ceramic phases (Fig. 57) indicates that weaving went on throughout the occupation of the site. Where shape could be reconstructed the loomweights were large and triangular, an Iron Age type which differs from Romano-British forms (Wild 1970, 63).

Given the small proportion of feature fills excavated at Binfield (Figs 46–47), the loomweight fragments recovered must be a fraction of the total discarded there. Comparable sites on different terrains in Oxfordshire do not seem to have had such a high frequency of loomweights. A 1:36 ratio of loomweight fragments to sherds at Park Farm (48:1712) stands out from ratios of 1:1600 for Iron Age contexts at Ashville Trading Estate (5:8000; Parrington 1978, 40, 37), 1:85 for Iron Age features at Farmoor (15:1275; Lambrick and Robinson 1979, 35, 57), 1:120 for Watkins Farm (12:1446; Allen 1990, 34, 53), and 1:1549 for Mingies Ditch (2:3098; Allen and Robinson 1993, 70, 78). This disparity in frequency must surely indicate differences in economy.

Weaving would have been a labour intensive activity. The fibres, of whatever origin, had to be gathered and prepared. Preparation included retting, pounding and hackling for hemp and linen and scouring, washing, cording, combing, and dyeing for wool. The fibres were then spun into threads by hand using the spindle and the distaff. The spin direction, either left-hand or right-hand spin, made a difference to the quality of the thread and thus to its potential use. The warp or vertical threads were sometimes of a right-hand spin direction and the weft, or horizontal, threads left-hand to improve the durability (the warp needs to be harder wearing as the weft is beaten over it) or felting properties of the cloth (the left-hand spin produces softer thread which mats together and also fills the spaces in the warp quickly: Nyberg 1990, 76). This required sorting and storing the correct quantities of thread required for each piece of cloth, complicated by the fact that different threads were required for the starting band or selvedges, which probably needed to be stronger than other parts of the weave. Checkered patterns and borders were produced inside and outside the Roman Empire (Wild and Jørgensen 1988, 76–82), and these too must have required organisation of the necessary threads.

Spinning with a drop spindle uses both hands; it can be carried out while standing or walking (Nyberg 1990, 79–80), but obviously other manual tasks cannot be performed at the same time. It takes many hours of spinning to produce the yarn for a single garment, and spinning probably took up much of the spare time of the adult female population even in settlements which were not producing a surplus of textiles.

In Iron Age and Roman Britain the sorted threads were woven on two main types of loom, a warp-weighted loom and an upright beam loom. The principal technical difference was that the weft was beaten upwards on the weighted loom and downwards on the upright beam loom; the principal archaeological difference is that no evidence is likely to survive of the use of an upright beam loom, since the tension was provided by the lower beam, whereas the stone or clay weights from the warp-weighted loom are commonly found during excavation. Numbers of weights vary depending on the size of the loom, but around 50 are usual. The beating was done with bone combs, solid or pin beaters, all of which may survive archaeologically, or by hand. Wild cites Seneca (*c.* AD 63) and Julius Pollux (*c.* AD 180–192) as evidence that the warp-weighted loom was displaced by the upright loom by the 2nd century, although he points out that according to Festus linen continued to be woven on the weighted loom in the late 2nd century (1970, 67).

It is generally assumed that since baked clay loomweights were a low technology artefact they were disposable. However, the correct weighting of the warp would have been excessively time-consuming if the weights had to be weighed and rematched for each use, and suitable sets of well matched weights may have acquired an heirloom value. Hoffman describes the use of a set of soapstone weights which had belonged to the weaver's great-aunt, although these would have had a longer life than baked clay weights (1964, 39–46).

The loomweights were the only evidence recovered for weaving. The acid, dry conditions would have destroyed organic artefacts such as combs or pin beaters of bone or wood.

Carbonised Plant Remains, by Mark Robinson

A total of 23 soil samples from throughout the site were investigated for carbonised plant remains. They ranged in size from 2–10 litres. Each sample was broken up in water and the light fraction washed over onto a 0.5 mm mesh sieve. The material recovered was then dried and sorted under binocular microscope for carbonised plant remains. The remains were identified with reference to the collections of the Environmental Archaeology Unit in the University Museum, Oxford. The results from those samples from which identifiable material was recovered are listed in Table 42 (carbonised seeds and cereal chaff) and Table 43 (charcoal). Spikelet forks have been enumerated as two glume bases. Charcoal has been recorded as + present and ++ abundant. In addition, a single glume of *Triticum dicoccum* or *spelta* was recovered from ditch 1002 and an unidentifiable cereal grain was present in 1055, a pit cutting ditch 1029. All the samples from which carbonised remains were identified were Romano-British in date.

The only two samples to contain abundant carbonised plant remains other than charcoal were from 1040, the boundary ditch. The remains are mostly comprised glumes of *Triticum spelta* (spelt wheat) and *T. dicoccum*

Table 42 Park Farm, Binfield: carbonised seeds and chaff

Sample	1040/ A /2	1040/ C /3
Sample volume (litres)	5	5
Cereals		
Triticum sp. (wheat)	–	6
Avena sp. (oats)	–	5
cf. *Avena* sp.	–	2
Cereal indet.	3	36
Total grain	3	49
Chaff		
Triticum dicoccum Shüb (emmer wheat, glume bases)	–	2
T. spelta L. (spelt wheat, glume bases)	2	94
T. dicoccum Shüb or spelta L. (glume bases)	21	151
T. dicoccum Shüb or *spelta* L. (glume bases)	1	4
Avena sp. (oats, awn fragments)	4	32
Total chaff	28	283
Weed seeds		
Lathyrus nissolia L. (grass vetchling)	–	1
cf. *Vicia* or *Lathyrus* sp. (vetch, tare)	–	1
Polygonum persicaria L. (red shank)	–	1
Rumex sp. (dock)	–	4
Total weeds	–	7

Table 43 Park Farm, Binfield: charcoal

Context	A/C	F	P	Q
1004/A/3	+	–	+	–
1027/B/3	–	–	–	+
1040/C/3	–	–	+	+
1048/A/4	+	–	–	+
1053/A/2	–	–	–	+
1053/2	–	–	–	+
1054/A/2	–	–	–	+
1055/A/2	–	–	–	+
1116/A/1	+	+	–	+
1119/1	+	–	–	+
1260	–	–	–	+
1500/A	–	–	–	+

A/C = *Alnus*/*Corylus* (alder/hazel); F = *Fraxinus* (ash); P = cf. *Pomoideae* (hawthorn, etc); Q = *Quercus* (oak)

or *spelta* (emmer or spelt wheat). They greatly outnumbered the grain and even fewer weed seeds were present. It is probable that these two samples represented waste from the de-husking of spikelets of spelt wheat prior to the milling of the grain. Two glumes of *T. dicoccum* were identified and it is possible that emmer was growing as an impurity amongst the spelt. Some oat remains were present. They could not be identified to species but it is likely that wild oat was a weed in the wheat crop.

Over half the samples contained significant quantities of charcoal, the amount of *Quercus* (oak) charcoal being particularly high. The ratio of charcoal to carbonised cereal remains was greater than is usual on low status Romano-British settlement sites. This suggests that there could have been a non-domestic activity taking place which involved burning. Some of the charcoal was from pits in which burning had occurred but it is not possible to relate this to any particular process.

4 Discussion

Dating

It is not possible to date the first occupation of the site with any precision. The site produced a small quantity of Middle Iron Age pottery (250–50 BC), with which three of the four houses were associated (Fig. 58). The Romano-British pottery continues up to the third quarter of the 2nd century AD, at which point the site went out of use. A nearby site at Cabbage Hill has little 1st century pottery but seems to have continued through the 2nd–4th centuries, perhaps indicating a change of settlement location.

Layout, Development, and Structures

The evidence of the evaluation, summarised above (*Previous Investigations*), suggests that most of the settlement plan was recovered, although sewer construction may have destroyed some of it to the north and north-west (Fig. 44), and the effect of ploughing on peripheral areas can only be guessed at.

The concentration of artefacts, building material, charred cereals, burnt flint, and charcoal south-west of the central ditch and south-east of transverse ditch 1064, coinciding with three of the four probable houses and with almost all the small pits and post-holes on the site (Figs 57–60), indicates a single domestic focus throughout the life of the site. Further, unidentified structures may be represented among the gullies, post-holes, and pits in this area, especially between transverse ditches 1064 and 1004 (Fig. 46). This consistent division between the north-east and south-west of the site indicates an early origin for the boundary represented by the central ditch, itself apparently of Late Iron Age/early Roman date.

The large post-hole circles (Houses 3 and 4) are probably to be dated to the Iron Age on typological grounds, even though the associated pottery was sparse, only one post-hole in each containing pottery of CP1.

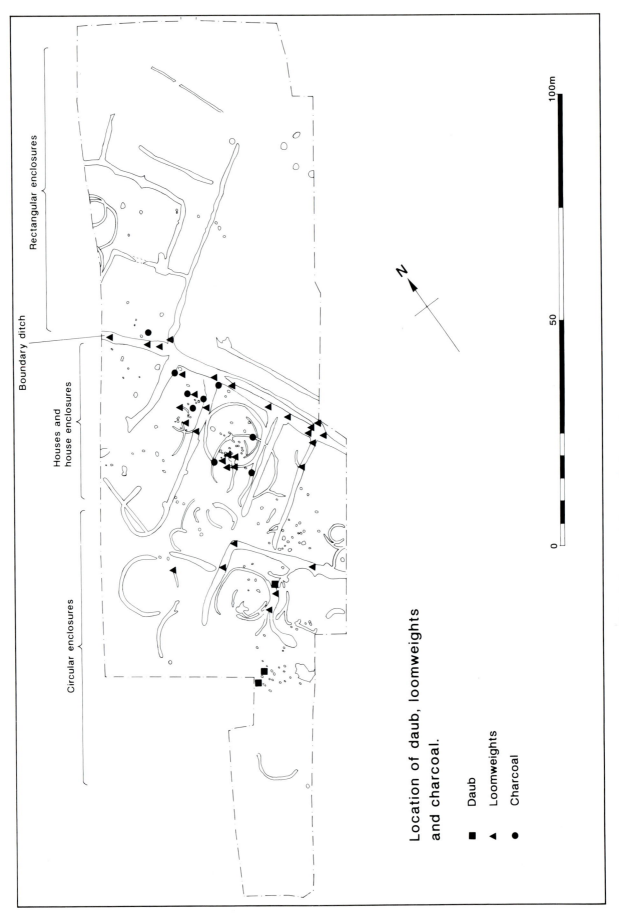

Location of daub, loomweights and charcoal.

■ Daub
▲ Loomweights
● Charcoal

Figure 57 Park Farm, Binfield: distribution of daub, loomweights, and charcoal

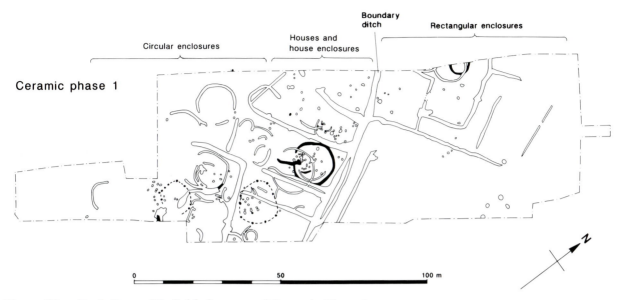

Figure 58   Park Farm, Binfield: features of Ceramic Phase 1

They may be linked by a common orientation, with possible entrances to the north-east (Fig. 51). Daub in pits adjacent to House 4 indicates wattle-and daub construction.

The replacement of post-ring structures, like Houses 3 and 4, by others surrounded by penannular gullies, like Houses 1 and 2, would conform to a pattern observed in the upper Thames Valley at a rather earlier date (Allen *et al.* 1984, 100). At Binfield the gullies themselves were so slight, the larger surviving to at most 0.23 m deep and 0.70 m wide, as to suggest that they demarcated house areas rather than drained them or excluded animals from them, both functions suggested for more substantial house gullies elsewhere (Parrington 1978, 34; Allen 1990, 75).

This may imply that animals were kept away from the houses, as at Mingies Ditch (Allen and Robinson 1993, 97). At Binfield, this function could have been served by a series of rectilinear enclosures formed by the central boundary and the ditches running at right-angles to it, most convincingly for House 1, but also possibly for Houses 2 and 3. Ditch 1002, apparently early Roman, may have formalised a distinction between the domestic area and the area of relatively sterile sub-circular enclosures to the south-west.

Economy

Status
The pottery suggests a low status site. The vessel types are mainly confined to jars; only a few fine wares are present; and the fabrics indicate a limited, largely local, trading area (Booth, this report).

Craft activities
Two of the most interesting aspects of the site are the high frequency of loomweights and the abundance of oak charcoal (Fig. 57). Local comparisons are precluded, since no similar sites have been excavated nearby, although 73 loomweight fragments were found at Ash-

ridge Wood some 3 km to the west (Ford 1987a, 86), perhaps implying that loomweights are abundant in the area.

The unusually high frequency of loomweights and the fact that they were found in features of all types and ceramic phases (Fig. 57) suggests that weaving occupied a special position in the economy of the site throughout its occupation. The loomweights were all of a large, triangular Iron Age type, irrespective of whether they came from Iron Age or Romano-British contexts. Loom-weights are usually found only on the least Romanised sites (Wild 1970, 67), but the pottery from Park Farm suggests that although the site was of low status some Roman influence was present.

It is not known what activity or activities the abund-ance of oak charcoal on the site represents. When burnt, oak produces a high temperature and an even heat; its drawback as fuel is that the wood is very hard and difficult to cut. This generally means that, unless oak is the only fuel available, it tends to be used only in specific craft activities where temperature control is critical. It may represent the deliberate production of charcoal for use in subsequent tasks or the generation of charcoal in the course of other processes. At Binfield oak charcoal was concentrated in large pits with *in situ* burning north-west of House 1 (Fig. 57), and was present in features of all ceramic phases. This may indicate that the charcoal-producing activity was confined to this area.

Farming
The most salient feature of the site plan is its division into north-eastern and south-western sections (Fig. 45). The rectangular enclosures north-east of the boundary ditch contained very few finds and no burnt flint, unlike the circular enclosures south-west of the domestic focus which contained rather more finds. This may, however, simply reflect their proximity to the occupied area. The difference in size and shape of these two groups of enclosures suggests distinct functions. The juxtaposi-tion of circular enclosures and houses echoes the layout

122

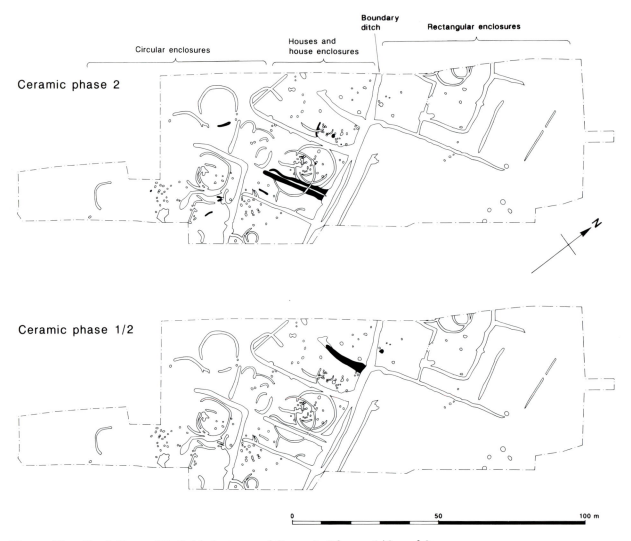

Figure 59   *Park Farm, Binfield: features of Ceramic Phases 1/2 and 2*

of Thornhill Farm, Gloucestershire, an 'unRomanised' settlement of the 1st centuries BC and AD, with sub-circular enclosures adjacent to post-built round-houses and interpreted in terms of stock management (Palmer and Hey 1989, 44). The protection of at least some of the Binfield houses by surrounding ditches suggests that animals were indeed kept on the site. The two groups of enclosures may have served for different aspects of animal management.

The larger, rectangular enclosures may alternatively have surrounded arable plots, although probable granaries and grain storage pits were absent, as was grain-processing equipment, and the spelt and emmer remains from Romano-British levels in the boundary ditch are likely to represent dehusking (Robinson this report) and do not necessarily demonstrate on-site cultivation.

The group of curvilinear gullies within one of these enclosures may be analogous to shallow circular gullies sometimes interpreted as rick-rings. Their position in the area away from the houses would accord with this. At 4.8 m to 9.8 m in diameter, however, they are rather larger than most such features. Those at Thornhill Farm, for example, were approximately 3 m in diameter (Palmer and Hey 1989, 44).

The economy of the site may to some extent be inferred from fuller evidence for contemporaneous farming elsewhere, although most of this is from sites on the Chalk or on valley gravels. This would have been one of the many small, mixed economy farmsteads which predominated in the Middle–Late Iron Age and continued virtually unchanged into the 1st and 2nd centuries AD. The Late Iron Age agricultural intensification documented on the upper Thames gravels (Lambrick 1992, 97–9, 105) may be reflected in the extension of occupation to areas such as this. Grant's (1984, 116) suggestion that sheep were substantially more important on Chalk downland sites than on wetter low-lying ones may apply to other upland areas away from river valleys. If so, it would accord with the frequency of loomweights at Binfield.

The Site and its Surrounding Area

The Iron Age and Romano-British settlement at Park Farm lies on the London Clay between the hillfort at Caesar's Camp and the villa at Wickham Bushes on the Plateau Gravel to the south and the Romano-British temple complex at Weycock Hill on Chalk to the north

Circular enclosures   Houses and house enclosures   Boundary ditch   Rectangular enclosures

Ceramic phase 3

⊟⊟⊟: Phasing uncertain

Ceramic phase 2/3

0   50   100 m

Figure 60   Park Farm, Binfield: features of Ceramic Phases 2/3 and 3

(Fig. 43). Few other sites have been recognised on the London Clay of east Berkshire; the East Berkshire Archaeological Survey (EBAS) identified one site per 2.4 km^2 on this geology, fewer than were found on adjacent geologies (Ford 1987a, 93–5). Outside the EBAS transect the density of identified sites is only one per 19.5 km^2 on the clay as opposed to one per 8.5 km^2 on the Upper Chalk and Reading Beds.

The nearest known site to Park Farm is Cabbage Hill, 1 km to the north-east, where the Berkshire Archaeological Group found a 1st–4th century settlement by fieldwalking, test-pitting, and sieving. At Park Farm, Warfield, 2 km to the east of Park Farm, an evaluation by Thames Valley Archaeological Services identified some Roman ditches. The next nearest Iron Age and Romano-British site was recorded by the EBAS at Ashridge Wood 4 km to the west (SMR no. 3397). This consisted of two discrete finds scatters about 15 m and 25 m across identified by fieldwalking (Ford 1987a, 86). Four more potential sites on the London Clay (SMR nos 260, 261, 669, and 729) are unexcavated (Fig. 43).

Employing criteria applied in other regions for the Iron Age and Romano-British periods, high status

settlements can be identified nearby at Weycock Hill, Wickham Bushes, and Caesar's Camp, although Ford found no evidence for such settlements on the London Clay itself (1987a, 94–5) while the Park Farm settlement would have been near the bottom of the local hierarchy.

It is clear from the experience of Binfield that sites on clay may be extremely difficult to detect. The site was originally identified by the recovery of fewer than three sherds. During the subsequent field evaluation no Iron Age or Romano-British artefacts were recovered from the ploughsoil by shovel test-pitting and the excavated trenches revealed only two ditches and three pits, despite the fact that one of these trenches ran over the nucleus of the settlement; Houses 1 and 2 and the wide boundary ditch were not identified.

On this geology it can be extremely difficult to distinguish features. If a site as extensive as Binfield was so difficult to identify it is quite conceivable that many of the findspots on Figure 43 may also represent Romano-British sites. The pottery and loomweight scatter at Ashridge Wood, for example, was also relatively discrete and may signal the existence of a similar site.

Conclusions

The site at Park Farm, Binfield shows many elements common to Middle Iron Age–early Romano-British settlements. It is possible to see it as a farmstead, going through successive modifications and exhibiting the basic components seen elsewhere, as in the Late Iron Age phase of Barton Court Farm (Miles 1986, fig. 4) or the successive early Roman layouts of Old Shifford Farm (Hey 1990), both in Oxfordshire. A combination of enclosure (piecemeal at Binfield), one or two houses, pits, and subsidiary, non-residential enclosures, recurs through such sites, although in varying forms and configurations.

The frequency of loomweights at Binfield may indicate a specialised economy with an emphasis on textile production. The abundant oak charcoal hints at a craft activity which may perhaps be linked to textile production, although this is not demonstrable.

The discovery of a Middle Iron Age–early Romano-British settlement which produced such meagre surface traces, either in the form of cropmarks or of artefacts, may indicate that further sites on the clay may be represented by finds of one or a few artefacts.

Appendix: The Mesolithic Flint Scatters

The Mesolithic flint scatters (Areas A/M and B) lay west of Park Farm on the east side of the ridge on which modern Binfield is built, sited on the lip of the slope (Fig. 44). Area B sloped steeply, with a drop of 9.0 m from north-west to south-east. Area A/M was rather flatter, highest in the north-west, sloping gently to east and south and steeply to the north. The underlying geology of both was clay.

Methods of Excavation

Area B

A 70 x 70 m area was gridded out from the National Grid with reference to the finds recovered by the East Berkshire Archaeological Survey and the Oxford Archaeological Unit evaluation. It had been ploughed only 10 days before excavation and there was no substantial rainfall to weather the clay and thus aid the recovery of finds.

Four methods of investigation were used:
i.   total collection fieldwalking on a 5 m grid
ii.   0.30 x 0.30 m sieved shovel test-pits on a staggered 5 m grid
iii.   0.5 x 1.0 m sieved shovel test-pits on a stag-gered 10 m grid
iv.   the struck flint collected by all three methods was plotted, brick and tile from the ploughsoil also being plotted as a control. An area equivalent to 30 x 30 m, where the plots showed the struck flint to be densest, was stripped of ploughsoil to reveal any features. The resulting surface was hand-cleaned to clarify any soilmarks. The ploughsoil stripped off was monitored as closely as possible to increase the recovery rate of finds, but could not be monitored consistently because of the shortage of time.

Area A/M

A 70 x 70 m area was gridded out in the same way as for Area B. In the light of the results of the investigation of Area B it was decided not to strip any topsoil, as no significant features had been detected by this means; to dig 0.30 x 0.30 m sieved shovel test-pits rather 0.5 x 1.0 m ones; and not to plot burnt flint, as this had not proved useful in Area B. There was in any case little or no burnt flint in Area A/M, in contrast to a total of over 14 kg from Area B.

The area had been ploughed and power-harrowed only nine days before work started. Substantial rain fell on one day. The power-harrowing greatly increased the ease of sieving the sun-baked clay soil and did not seem to have destroyed or damaged a significant number of artefacts.

Four methods of investigation were employed:
i.   total collection fieldwalking on a 5 m grid
ii.   0.30 x 0.30 m sieved shovel test-pits on a staggered 5 m grid
iii.   the results were plotted and transects of 2 x 2 m shovel test-pits were aligned over the densest concentration of flints. Alternate (east and west) halves of the test-pits were sieved
iv.   the unsieved halves of the large (2 x 2 m) test-pits were monitored to check the results against those of sieving.

Results

A total of 223 pieces of struck flint was recovered from Area B by fieldwalking and shovel test-pitting, and 51 by topsoil monitoring and cleaning the subsoil surface. From Area A/M, 357 pieces were recovered by fieldwalking, and 421 by shovel test-pitting (Table 44; Fig. 61).

Area B: distribution of all struck flint (SU 8470 7040, N↑)

4	2	3		2	1	1	1			1		2
5	1	10	2	3			1	2	1			
2	3	15	2	1	3	2	2			1		2
1	1	2	2	4	1	1	1	1				3
		2	1	2		2	1			1	1	1
	1		1	1	3		3				2	1
	1	2	4	1		4		1	2	1	1	1
	3	1	2	6			6	1	1		1	1
1	1	4			3			2				1
	1		1			1	1	5	2	2		4
	1			1	1	1	1	1	1	1		
	1	1		4			2	3			3	1
2		1		2				3		1	1	1
4	1			1		1			1	3		3

Area B: distribution of struck flint from fieldwalking (SU 8470 7040, N↑)

3	2	2		2	1	1	1				1	
1	1	1	1				1		1			
1	3	5	1		3		1					
	1			1	1	1		1				
	1				1	1					1	
	1		1		3		2					1
		3			2		1	1		1		
3		1				1		1				
	4				2			1				
	1		1				2	2		1		
		1			1	1	1					
1	1		1		2				2		1	
1		1				3			1			
1	1			1		1	3		1			

Area A/M: distribution of all struck flint (SU 8460 7060, N↑)

2	6	8	4	1	6	4	3	3		2	4		1
2	1	18	5	1	7	3	6	5	2		1		1
1	4	23	11	1	1	4		3	3		2		1
6	2	19	2	1	2	1	2	1			1	1	3
2	15	25	30	14	14	16	8	14	5	1		1	
3	6	22	4	4	5	5	1	7	2	1			1
4	2	11		6		4	4	4	2	1		1	
16	18	26	14	18	8	3	7	14	1	6		5	
1	1		3		1	3	6	2	2	1	3	2	
1	2	11			3		2		3		2	1	1
4	2		3	5	8	6	5	3	3	1	3	2	
	5	6		1	1	3	3	3	2	2	2	1	2
	2	3		1	5	1	7	3	5	3	1		1
		3			3	1	6	3	2		5		

Area A/M: distribution of struck flint from fieldwalking (SU 8460 7060, N↑)

1	6	2	4	1	4	4	2	2		2	4		
2	1	4	5		4	3	5	3	1		1		1
1	1	5	11		1	4		2	3		2		1
5	11	4	2		1	1	1				1	1	1
		7	12	3	9	5		2	1			1	
2	2	7	4	1	5	5	1	4	1				
3	1	4		6		2	3	3	2	1			
1	6	5	1	3	5	2	3	7		1			
1	1		2		1	3	2	1	1	1	3	1	
1	1				1		1		3		2		
4	1			2	7	6	2	1	2	1	3	1	
	1			1	1	3	3	3	1	2		1	1
	1			1	5	1	2	2	4	3	1		
				1	1	5	3	1		5			

Figure 61   Distribution of all struck flint in Area B (upper) and Area A/M (lower)

Figure 62   Distribution of struck flint from fieldwalking in Area B (upper) and Area A/M (lower)

When flint from Areas B and A/M and tile/brick from Area B were plotted they formed a grid pattern which followed the field edges and the lines of ploughing outside the investigation area (Figs 62, 64, and 65).

There was a cluster of about 50 pieces in both plough-soil and subsoil in the north-west corner of Area B, centred around SU 84750 70510. A slighter concentration of flint at the bottom of the slope in the south of the area was at least partly due to soil movement. Ploughing had moved the flints to the base of the steep slope, where ploughsoil containing struck flint overlay a substantial layer of colluvium which in turn overlay

slightly plough-disturbed natural clay. The colluvium also overlay a small relict stream which had been canalised to some extent while it was still open in the 19th century.

There was no clear cluster of flint in Area A/M, although material was concentrated in the north-west quadrant (Fig. 62). The results of the EBAS (Ford 1987a) suggest that ploughing may have displaced artefacts from the investigated area, as in Area B, spreading them downslope to the north and to a lesser extent to the south and east.

Table 44   Park Farm, Binfield: number of pieces of struck flint per 5 m² collection unit by method of recovery

No. per collection unit	Area B			Area A/M			
	Field-walking	Test-pits 0.3 x 0.3 m	Test-pits 1 x 0.5 m	Field-walking	Test-pits 0.3 x 0.3 m	Test-pits 2 x 2 m (sieved)	Test-pits 2 x 2 m (not sieved)
0	122	160	5	114	110	–	–
1	49	26	40	52	63	1	5
2	14	6	4	26	11	4	5
3	8	3	–	19	7	5	2
4	1	–	–	13	2	2	3
5	1	–	–	12	–	1	1
6	–	1	–	4	–	1	1
7	–	–	–	4	–	1	–
8	–	–	–	–	–	3	–
9	1	–	–	1	–	–	–
10	–	–	–	–	–	4	–
11	–	–	–	1	–	4	–
12	–	–	–	1	–	1	–
13	–	–	–	–	–	4	–
18	–	–	–	–	–	1	–

Table 45   Park Farm, Binfield: sites used for compositional analysis. Data from Ford (1991)

Site	S	M	B	TA/S	MD	C	Total retouched	Total	Density per m² of denser areas
Binfield A/M	6	3	–	1	6	24	49	357	6.2
EB 340	8	4	–	–	–	35	28	615	4
EB 250	15	1	–	2	–	26	23	266	4.5
EB 480	18	9	1	1	–	90	73	899	9.7
North Stoke ST 150	33	9	6	1	–	68	147	1209	15
North Stoke ST 56	99	17	8	4	8	164	230	2557	20
Wawcott I	4	112	4	8	1	77	247	4662	141
Wawcott III	116	526	30	12	38	195	1279	51,455	990
Wawcott IV	16	19	7	5	1	60	55	1915	145
Fulmer, Bucks	15	6	1	4	–	16	29	589	3.4
Holyport, Berks	85	117	?	4	?	235	206	15,941	large
Thatcham	132	285	61	33	??	283	634	19,282	166
Sandstone, Bucks	8	15	1	1	–	14	26	290	41
Gerrards Cross, Bucks	20	3	1	5	–	27	47	1931	193
Paddington Farm, Surrey	15	25	1	5	–	267	219	3830	29

S = Scrapers; M = Microliths; B = Burins; TA/S = Tranchet axes and sharpening flakes; MD = Micro-denticulates; C = Cores

Flint, by Steve Ford

In total, 1063 pieces of struck flint were recovered, which can be divided into four categories:

1. Material from the detailed investigation of flint scatter Area A/M
2. Material from the detailed investigation of flint scatter Area B
3. Residual material from later archaeological contexts
4. Other unstratified material

Raw Materials

Most of the flintwork is certainly or probably from a good flint source such as the Upper Chalk or the lowest parts of the Reading Beds. The nearest material is available about 8 km to the north (Fig. 43). A small number of pieces are of poor quality material which would have been available locally. This emphasis on Chalk flint caused some difficulty in distinguishing between ancient and recent imports — the latter could have been included with powdered Chalk for liming or with post-medieval building rubble. Pieces of possibly doubtful origin are excluded from the totals. This process of selection is not perfect and the totals here have probably excluded some prehistoric artefacts.

The two flint scatters (Areas A/M and B) were originally identified by the EBAS (Ford 1987a) as sites 470 and 320. Site 470 (Area A/M; SMR 3370) produced 19 items (from a 4% surface sample), albeit from a restricted area, and was thought likely to be of later Neolithic date on the basis of its retouched component. It was noticed at the time that a blade core was present and that 33% of the struck flints were blades. Site 320 (Area B; SMR 3068) produced only 12 items from a wider area. It was undated but again it was noted that 16% of the struck flints were blades.

Area A/M

Total collection while fieldwalking on a 5 x 5 m grid within a 70 x 70 m area produced 357 pieces with an additional 46 spalls, bashed lumps, and core fragments. Three components were used to date the collection as a whole: shape, core type, and retouched types. Struck flints were sorted by eye into shape categories of blade, possible blade, and flake. A distinction was made between broken and intact pieces so that the potential for metrical analysis could be determined. The flake component for the fieldwalked finds was measured and analysed as set out below.

For the whole collection approximately 35% of struck flints were of bladelike proportions, a quantity typical of Mesolithic assemblages (*see* Ford 1987b and the site on St Catherine's Hill, Guildford, Surrey, in Gabel 1976). Similarly, blade cores and possible blade cores account for 76% of all cores, again a Mesolithic characteristic. Finally, the retouched component contains a number of common items such as scrapers and awls (Fig. 66, Nos 4 and 11), but also includes three microliths (two ob-

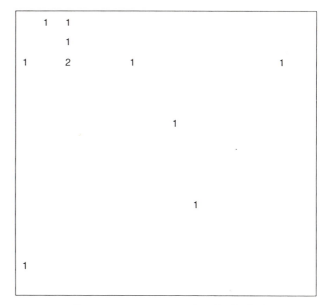

SU 8470 7040 ↑
N

Area B: distribution of cores

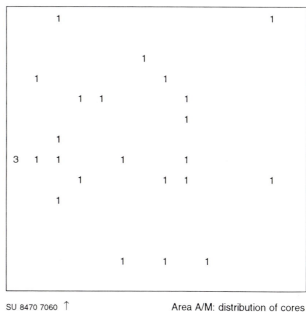

SU 8470 7060 ↑
N

Area A/M: distribution of cores

Figure 63   Park Farm, Binfield: distribution of cores in Area B (upper) and Area A/M (lower)

liquely blunted points and one rod; Fig. 66, Nos 3, 2, and 1). There were no items that were certainly of post-Mesolithic date. This also applies to the finds from the original (EBAS) fieldwalking. The rod microlith dates from the later Mesolithic.

Some 28 flakes and blades had small amounts of retouch including possible notched pieces. Several other examples were noted where there was some doubt as to the origin of the retouch. Some obviously showed recent accidental damage. Two pieces are possible microburins and one broken flake is a possible burin.

Serrated pieces (micro-denticulates) are certainly represented by one broken blade and possibly by a

Table 46 Park Farm, Binfield: retouched pieces

| | Area B | | | Area A/M | | | |
	Field-walking	Test-pits 0.3 x 0.3 m	Test-pits 1 x 0.5 m	Field-walking	Test-pits 0.3 x 0.3 m	Test-pits 2 x 2 m (sieved)	Test-pits 2 x 2 m (not sieved)
Scrapers	5	–	–	3	1	2	–
Awl/scraper	1	–	–	–	–	–	–
Notch/scraper	–	–	–	1	–	–	–
Awl	–	1	–	2	1	1	–
Knife	–	–	–	1	–	–	–
Notched flakes	–	–	–	1	–	2	–
Microliths	–	–	–	2	–	–	1
Microlith tip	–	–	1	–	–	–	–
Retouched fragment	–	–	–	–	1	–	–
Denticulate scraper	–	–	–	1	–	–	–
?Drill bits (aré cou)	–	–	–	2	–	–	–

Includes possibles but excluding flakes/blades with irregular retouch, etc, as in text

second. A further four pieces probably belong to a similar category, as they show very delicate retouch (Fig. 66, Nos 7 and 10). A much larger group of material shows probable or possible utilisation damage but this could not be consistently distinguished from accidental (post-depositional) damage. An awl (Fig. 66, No. 9), a fabricator (Fig. 66, No. 8), and a possible knife were recovered during the original widely spaced fieldwalking.

There are very few items of special note. A single large blade is apparently crested and bears some similarity to pieces found in Upper Palaeolithic–Early Mesolithic long blade industries. Several other crested blades and core rejuvenation flakes were noted but none was exceptionally large. Another feature of note is the presence of two small flakes (spalls) with fine retouch forming a point (Fig. 66, Nos 5 and 6). They may be of

similar function to the drill bits (aré cou) of Indonesia (White and Thomas 1972, 286). One or two of the flakes may have resulted from axe manufacture and one core may be classed as a dubious axe roughout.

Three hundred and nineteen flints from the fieldwalking were subjected to more detailed measurements following the methods set out by Ford (1987b). Of the 98 intact flakes, 25% had a length:breadth ratio equal to or exceeding 2:1. This is a characteristic of Mesolithic/earlier Neolithic assemblages. One problem with length:breadth ratios is that blades are frequently under-represented, presumably because of their proneness to accidental damage and their deliberate selection for tool manufacture (eg, of microliths). To compensate for this, broken pieces were also analysed. Of 221 broken pieces, 41% were broken blades or possible broken

Table 47 Park Farm, Binfield: flint summary

| | Area B | | | Area A/M | | | | |
	Field-walking	Test-pits 0.3 x 0.3 m	Test-pits 1 x 0.5 m	Field-walking	Test-pits 0.3 x 0.3 m	Test-pits 2 x 2 m (sieved)	Test-pits 2 x 2 m (not sieved)	Unstrati-fied
Flakes	30	14	10	87	17	52	2	5
Blades	6	2	–	11	1	10	4	–
Broken blades	49	26	17	135	39	92	19	5
Broken blades/ broken ?blades	17	12	12	87	34	63	11	–
Spalls	14	17	7	35	27	25	4	4
Cores	5	4	1	4	3	2	1	1
Blade cores & possibles	8	1	1	20	1	5	2	–
Core frags/ bashed lumps	6	1	–	11	3	8	2	–

blades, a proportion more strongly characteristic of a Mesolithic date. When the broken and intact totals are combined, 36% are of bladelike proportions, a Mesolithic characteristic.

A second measure of the numbers of blades in an assemblage is the proportion of pieces with dorsal blade scars. For the combined total of broken and intact pieces, 17% had blade scars, which is again a strong Mesolithic characteristic.

Area B

Total collection fieldwalking, again over an area of 70 x 70 m, produced a total of 121 flints with an additional 20 spalls, bashed lumps, and core fragments. Interpretation of this material is problematic. The density and extent of the clustering are very much lower than for Area A/M. Some activity in the area in the Mesolithic is indicated, but whether this was a small occupation site (now dispersed by ploughing) or an 'off-site' activity area (Foley 1981) adjacent to the settlement focus of area A/M is unclear.

The dating of the flintwork is similar to that of the collection from Area A/M. The proportion of bladelike flakes for the whole collection is about 25%. Blade cores and possible blade cores account for 50% of all cores. Eight pieces were retouched or possibly notched. One core may have been used as a hammerstone. The small number of common retouched pieces includes a microlith tip. Again there is no reason to doubt that the collection is largely or wholly of Mesolithic date.

Other flints
In the other contexts a similar range of material was present. The only item of note was a microlith from context 301.

Local Context

The main contribution of this study has been the clarification of the nature and the dating of two possible sites. It has shown that Area A/M is a definite concentration of material, while Area B may be best interpreted as a very small occupation site or an off-site activity area. It is significant that these sites occurred only as scatters of material within the topsoil so that extensive unexamined topsoil stripping would have removed them without trace.

Metrical analysis and more subjective assessment of the remaining flintwork have shown that the collections are largely or wholly of Mesolithic date. Closer dating was more difficult, with insufficient material to demonstrate a clear Early or Late Mesolithic date (Jacobi 1976) or to show affinities to transitional 'Horsham' industries (Clark 1946; Saville 1981). The rod microlith from Area A/M suggests a Late Mesolithic date.

The results of the EBAS (Fig. 67; Ford 1987a) suggested that much of the flintwork on the Tertiary geologies of east Berkshire was of Mesolithic date, and this site is an addition to the small number already recorded. In a wider perspective it helps to enlarge the topographical and geographical range of Mesolithic

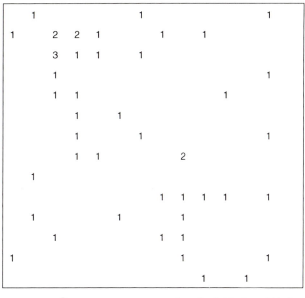

activity. To the north and west the Mesolithic settlement pattern is dominated by the Thames and Kennet valleys, as Clarke's (1976) work would lead one to expect. The site here, along with the others newly identified in east Berkshire, has more affinities with the variably located small, and occasionally larger, sites of Surrey and east Hampshire (Rankine 1954; Gabel 1976; Field *et al.* 1987).

The density and spread of flintwork are slightly greater than, but broadly comparable to, those at two other east Berkshire sites investigated in a similar manner at Hungerford Lane (EB 250) and Easthampstead Park (EB 340; Ford 1988), located respectively on

Figure 64   Park Farm, Binfield: distribution of blades in Area B (upper) and Area A / M (lower)

130

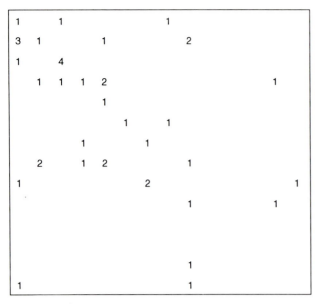

SU 8470 7040 ↑
N

Area B: distribution of retouched pieces

SU 8460 7060 ↑
N

Area A/M: distribution of retouched pieces

Figure 65   Park Farm, Binfield: distribution of retouched pieces in Area B (upper) and Area A/M (lower)

a ridge and knoll. The density is much lower than at the recently fieldwalked site at Paddington Farm, Abinger, Surrey (Field *et al.* 1987), and at sites in the major river valleys of Berkshire such as Whistley Court Farm (EB 480; Harding and Richards 1991–3). It is hard to assess whether these differences are due to the effects of distance on raw material procurement or the nature and extent of the settlements.

Table 45 (Ford 1991) summarises selected characteristics of the Area A/M collection along with those from 15 other sites in the region. Eight of these were investigated by excavation of little disturbed stratified deposits, the remainder were flint scatters discovered

by fieldwalking. The density was calculated by using the surface counts from the more productive parts of the distribution and adjusted upwards, assuming that 2% of material occurs on the surface. This is a coarse measure, taking into account subjective judgements on the extent of the dense parts of a scatter and a variable surface:topsoil ratio. It does, however, show that Area A/M at Binfield falls at the lower end of the range. Assuming that the site has been spread to a greater or less extent by ploughing, it is still not of comparable density to many of the other sites in the table.

Discussion, by Steve Ford and M.R. Roberts

The spread of struck flint within the ploughsoil is all that survives of the Mesolithic activity on this site. Features were uncovered by excavation but these were modern. Both ploughing and slope seem to have had an influence on the observed distributions. This is more obvious in the case of Area B, where the brick and tile form the same pattern as the flint. Only the concentra- tion of flint in the north-west corner is apparent above this 'background noise', creating a discrepancy in the distribution even after topsoil movement (ploughing and hillwash).

The much larger quantity of flint in Area A/M reduces the 'visibility' of concentrations (Fig. 61). The plots of cores and retouched forms (Figs 63 and 65) show the same gridded pattern as in Area B although the distribution plots are affected by the test-pits sieved to bulk up the assemblage. The lack of a single concentration (Fig. 61) may suggest that successive scatters were deposited in almost the same place, creating a dense distribution of flints, such as those shown by Schild (1989, 98) which represent use of a site over thousands of years. Plots of blades (Fig. 64), retouched forms (Fig. 65), and the total finds from the fieldwalking (Fig. 62) hint at many superimposed flint concentrations. The collection procedures complemented each other. Both fieldwalking and shovel test-pitting identified the concentration in the north-west of Area B, but Area A was less susceptible to interpretation by these techniques because of the density of flints.

Many years of ploughing on this site have caused some movement of the flints, although studies of artefact distribution in ploughsoils suggest that such movement may be expected to be minimal (Odell and Cowan 1987, 481). The slope of the sites at Binfield may have had an influence on this observed distribution. Odell and Cowan did not describe the topography of their experimental area nor did their experiment simulate the number of ploughings, which at Binfield may have been carried out annually since enclosure in the early 19th century and may number as many as 200. The effect of ploughing is demonstrated by the hillwash, itself containing struck flint, which buried a 19th century stream/drain in Area B and may have lowered the top of the hill.

The flint is not diagnostic enough to suggest a date within the Mesolithic. The range of retouched forms may indicate that the site had more than one main use, ie, it was not task-specific. This range matches those of large riverside sites interpreted as base camps (Mellars

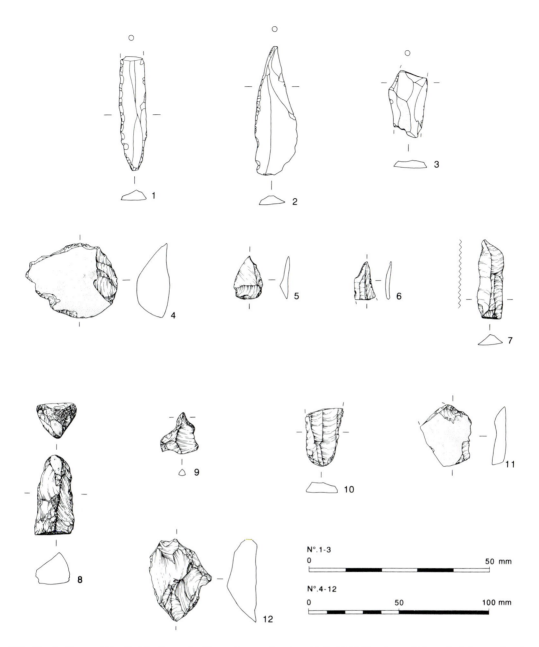

Figure 66 Park Farm Binfield: Struck flint. 1 = rod microlith (2097); 2 = obliquely blunted microlith (1708); 3 = ?microlith; 4 = scraper (1639); 5 = ?aré cou drill bit (1727); 6 = aré cou drill bit (1768); 7 = serrated flake (2001); 8 = fabricator (from EBAS); 9 = awl (from EBAS); 10 = saw (1709); 11 = scraper (1695); 12 = denticulate scraper (1905)

1976, 391). This may signify that smaller groups of people were carrying out the same activities as at large base camps, either independently of large riverside groupings or as part of a dispersal strategy, possibly seasonal, in order to exploit food resources.

Burnt flint found in large quantities at Park Farm, Warfield, c. 1.5 km to the east of the Binfield sites, suggests prehistoric domestic activity. The amount of burnt flint found in Area B at Binfield suggests a similar activity, rather than naturally occurring flints scorched by stubble burning. While burnt flint is generally more usual and more abundant in later prehistoric than in Mesolithic contexts, it may be noted that it occured in alluvial silts containing a Mesolithic industry at

Jennings Yard, Windsor (Healy 1993), and at the Mesolithic occupation site at Thatcham, both in Berkshire (Healy *et al.* 1992, table 2).

Prior to the East Berkshire Archaeological Survey local Mesolithic activity was thought to be focused on the river margins, but the extensive fieldwalking showed a much more extended pattern (Fig. 67). The two Park Farm scatters fit into this pattern as small, low-density sites away from the main base camps by rivers. Their location on a spur overlooking a small valley may be related to the main criteria for location of Mesolithic sites noted by Kvamme and Jochim, namely view, nearness of water, shelter, and landform (not necessarily in this order). The siting of many (seasonal) Mesolithic

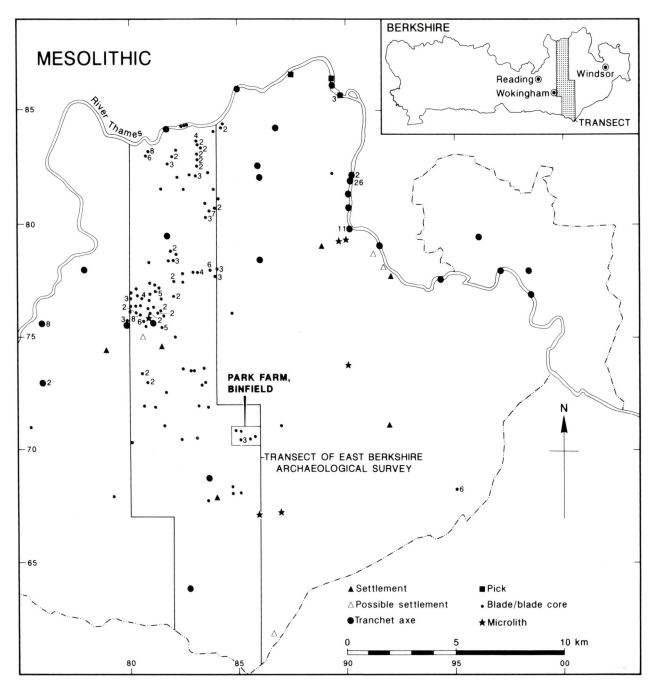

Figure 67   Mesolithic material in east Berkshire

sites on ridges and high places (Kvamme and Jochim 1989, 1) may perhaps be deliberate, in order to provide a vantage point over the surrounding area (Jacobi, cited by Kvamme and Jochim 1989, 2). This may have been a factor in the location of the Binfield sites, although neither the degree of contemporaneous tree cover nor the extent of any clearance (Mellars and Reinhardt 1978, 256) can be determined. Nearness to water may have been a consideration, since a pond, perhaps spring fed, lies to the south-west of the sites, roughly 120 m from Area A/M and 80 m from Area B (Fig. 45). There is no bias towards shelter (Kvamme and Jochim 1989, 8). High ground was preferred but no directional bias is apparent: Area A/M faced north, away from the sun.

The range of natural resources available to Mesolithic hunter-gatherers would have been wide and abundant. Clarke (1976, 475) describes the immense variety of animal and vegetable foodstuffs which would have been available in temperate deciduous forest and would have obtainable through most of the period.

The theoretical planned exploitation of these resources is described by Binford (1980, 18–19), and the sites at Binfield may have been used seasonally to exploit nearby food supplies by a society organised around systematic food-gathering over a large area. It is impossible to tell whether they were part of the population exploiting the river valleys or belonged to a separate social group.

Bibliography

Adkins, L. and Needham, S., 1985, 'New research on a Late Bronze Age enclosure at Queen Mary's Hospital, Carshalton', *Surrey Archaeol. Collect.* 76, 11–50.

Allen, T.G., 1990, *An Iron Age and Romano-British Enclosed Settlement at Watkins Farm, Northmoor, Oxon*, Oxford, Univ. Comm. Archaeol., Thames Valley Landscapes: The Windrush Valley 1.

——, Miles, D. and Palmer, S., 1984, 'Iron Age buildings in the Upper Thames region', in Cunliffe, B.W., and Miles, D. (eds), 1984, 57–71.

—— and Robinson, M.A., 1993, *The Prehistoric Landscape and Iron Age Enclosed Settlement at Mingies Ditch, Hardwick-with-Yelford, Oxon*, Oxford, Univ. Comm. Archaeol., Thames Valley Landscapes: the Windrush Valley 2.

Ames, R.E., 1991–3, 'A Mesolithic assemblage from Moor Farm, Holyport, near Maidenhead, Berkshire', *Berkshire Archaeol. J.* 74, 1–8.

Anderson, A.S., 1980, 'Romano-British pottery kilns at Purton', *Wiltshire Archaeol. Natur. Hist. Mag.* 72/73, 51–8.

Arnold, D.E., 1981, 'A model for the identification of non-local ceramic distribution: a view from the present' in Howard, H. and Morris, E.L. (eds), *Production and Distribution: a Ceramic Viewpoint*, Oxford, Brit. Archaeol. Rep. S120, 31–44.

——, 1985, *Ceramic Theory and Cultural Process*, Cambridge, Univ. Press.

Barnes, I. and Lobb, S.J., 1989, *Dunston Park, Thatcham, Berkshire. Archaeological Evaluation 1988/89*, Salisbury, Wessex Archaeology, unpubl. client report.

Barrett, J.C., 1974, 'Four Bronze Age cremation cemeteries from Middlesex', *Trans. London Middlesex Archaeol. Soc.* 24, 111–34.

——, 1975, 'The later pottery: types, affinities, chronology and significance', in Bradley and Ellison 1975, 99–118.

——, 1980, 'The pottery of the Later Bronze Age in lowland England', *Proc. Prehist. Soc.* 46, 297–319.

——, 1989, 'Food, gender, and metal: questions of social reproduction', in Sørenson and Thomas 1989, 304–20.

——, 1991, 'Bronze Age pottery and the problem of classification', in Barrett, Bradley, and Hall (eds), 1991, 201–30.

—— and Bradley, R.J., 1980a, 'The later Bronze Age in the Thames Valley', in Barrett and Bradley 1980c, 247–69.

—— and ——, 1980b, 'Later Bronze Age settlement in south Wessex and Cranborne Chase', in Barrett and Bradley 1980c, 181–208.

—— and —— (eds), 1980c, *The British Later Bronze Age*, Oxford, Brit. Archaeol. Rep. 83.

——, —— and Green, M., 1991, *Landscape, Monuments and Society; the Prehistory of Cranborne Chase*. Cambridge, Univ. Press.

——, —— and Hall, M.(eds), 1991, *Papers on the Prehistoric Archaeology of Cranborne Chase*, Oxford, Oxbow Monog. 11.

Bersu, G., 1940, 'Excavations at Little Woodbury, Wiltshire, part I: the settlement as revealed by excavation', *Proc. Prehist. Soc.* 6, 30–111.

Binford, L., 1980, 'Willow smoke and dogs' tails', *Amer. Antiq.* 45, 4–20.

Blalock, H.M., 1979, *Social Statistics*, London, McGraw-Hill (2nd edn).

Blankholm, H.P., 1991, *Intrasite Spatial Analysis in Theory and Practice*, Aarhus, Univ. Press.

Boismier, W.A., 1981, *Human Behaviour and Spatial Analysis: A Preliminary Study*, unpubl. MA Thesis, Univ. Southampton.

Booth, P. M. and Green, S., 1989, 'The nature and distribution of certain pink, grog-tempered vessels', *J. Roman Pottery Stud.* 2, 75–84.

Bowden, M. and McOmish, D.S., 1987, 'The required barrier', *Scottish Archaeol. Rev.* 4, 76–84.

——, Ford, S. and Gaffney, V., 1982, 'Excavation of an earthwork on Maidenhead Thicket, 1982', *Berkshire Archaeol. J.* 71, 21–31.

Bowen, C. and Smith, I.F., 1977, 'Sarsen stones in Wessex: the society's first investigations in the evolution of the landscape project', *Antiq. J.* 57, 185–96.

Bowman, S., 1991, 'Radiocarbon chronology', in Barrett, Bradley, and Green 1991, 3–5.

Bradford, J.S.P., 1942, 'An Early Iron Age site on Blewburton Hill, Berks', *Berkshire Archaeol. J.* 46, 97–104.

Bradley, R.J., 1990, *The Passage of Arms; an Archaeological Analysis of Prehistoric Hoards and Votive Deposits*, Cambridge, Univ. Press.

——, and Barrett, J.C., 1991, 'The excavations: South Lodge enclosure, cemetery and field system', in Barrett, Bradley and Green 1991, 144–83.

—— and Ellison, A.B., 1975, *Rams Hill: a Bronze Age Defended Enclosure and its Landscape*. Oxford, Brit. Archaeol. Rep. 19.

——, Lobb, S.J., Richards, J. and Robinson, M., 1980, 'Two Late Bronze Age settlements on the Kennet gravels: excavations at Aldermaston Wharf and

134

Knight's Farm, Burghfield, Berkshire', *Proc. Prehist. Soc.* 46, 217–95.

——, Over, L., Startin, D.W.A. and Weng, R., 1981, 'The excavation of a Neolithic site at Cannon Hill, Maidenhead, Berkshire, 1974–1975', *Berkshire Archaeol. J.* 68, 5–19.

Brown, G., Field, D. and McOmish, D., 1994, 'East Chisenbury Midden complex', in Fitzpatrick and Morris (eds) 1994, 46–9.

Brown, N., 1988, 'A Late Bronze Age enclosure at Lofts Farm, Essex', *Proc. Prehist. Soc.* 54, 249–302.

Buckley, V., (comp.), 1990, *Burnt offerings: International Contributions to Burnt Mound Archaeology,* Dublin, Wordwell

Burgess, C.B., 1980, *The Age of Stonehenge,* London, Dent.

Burstow, G.P. and Holleyman, G.A., 1957, 'Late Bronze Age settlement on Itford Hill, Sussex', *Proc. Prehist. Soc.* 23, 167–212.

Butterworth, C.A. and Lobb, S.J., 1992, *Excavations in the Burghfield Area, Berkshire; Developments in the Bronze Age and Saxon Landscapes,* Salisbury, Wessex Archaeol. Rep. 1.

Calkin, J.B., 1964, 'The Bournemouth area in the Middle and Late Bronze Age, with the 'Deverel–Rimbury' problem reconsidered', *Archaeol. J.* 119, 1–65.

Campbell, G., 1992, 'Bronze Age plant remains', in Moore and Jennings 1992, 103–12.

Carr, C., 1984, 'The nature and organization of intrasite archaeological records and spatial analytic approaches to their investigation', in Schiffer, M.B. (ed.), *Advances in Archaeological Method and Theory* 7, London, Academic, 103–222.

——, 1987, 'Removing discordance from quantitative analysis', in Aldenderfer, M. (ed.), *Quantitative Research in Archaeology: Progress and Prospects,* London, Sage, 185–248.

Carruthers, W., 1992, 'The carbonised plant remains', in Gingell 1992, 143–4.

Carstairs, P., 1986, 'An archaeological study of the Dorney area', *Rec. Buckinghamshire* 28, 163–68.

Castle, S.A., 1978, 'Amphorae from Brockley Hill', *Britannia* 9, 383–92.

Chadwick, S., 1960, 'Early Iron Age enclosures on Longbridge Deverill Cow Down, Wiltshire', in Frere, S.S., (ed.), *Problems of the Iron Age in Southern Britain,* London, Inst. Archaeol. Univ. London Occas. Pap. 11, 18–20.

Chadwick Hawkes, S., 1994, 'Longbridge Deverill Cow Down, Wiltshire, House 3: a major round house of the Early Iron Age', *Oxford J. Archaeol.* 13, 49–69.

Champion, T.C., and Collis, J.R.(eds), in press, *The Iron Age in Britain: Recent Trends,* Sheffield, Univ. Sheffield.

Clapham, A.R., Tutin, T.G. and Moore, D.M., 1989, *Flora of the British Isles* Cambridge, Univ. Press.

Clark, A., 1980, 'Pollen and spores', in Bradley *et al.* 1980, 279–80.

Clark, J.G.D., 1934, 'Derivative forms of the petit tranchet in Britain', *Archaeol. J.* 91, 32–58.

——, 1946, 'The classification of a microlithic culture: the Tardenoisian of Horsham', *Archaeol. J.* 90, 52–77.

Clarke, D.L., 1976, 'Mesolithic Europe: the economic basis', in Sieveking, G. de G., Longworth, I.H., and Wilson, K.E. (eds), *Problems in Economic and Social Archaeology,* London, Duckworth, 449–81.

Coe, D. and Newman, R., 1992, 'Excavations of an Early Iron Age building and Romano-British enclosure at Brighton Hill South, Hampshire', *Proc. Hampshire Fld Club Archaeol. Soc.* 48, 5–21.

Cole, J.P. and King, C., 1970, *Quantitative Geography,* London, Wiley.

Collins, A.E.P., 1947, 'Excavations on Blewburton Hill, 1947', *Berkshire Archaeol. J.* 50, 4–29.

Collins, M., 1975, 'Lithic technology as a means of processual inference', in Swanson, E. (ed.), *Lithic Technology,* The Hague, Mouton, 17–34.

Cotton, M., 1961, 'Robin Hood's Arbour; and rectilinear enclosures in Berkshire', *Berkshire Archaeol. J.* 59, 1–35.

Courty, M.A., Goldberg, P. and Macphail, R., 1989, *Soils and Micromorphology in Archaeology,* Cambridge, Univ. Press.

Cowell, R.W., Fulford, M.G., and Lobb, S., 1978, 'Excavation of a prehistoric and Roman settlement at Aldermaston Wharf 1976–77', *Berkshire Archaeol. J.* 69, 1–35.

Cox, P., 1991, 'The portable stone objects', in Woodward 1991, 95.

Coy, J., 1992, 'Faunal remains', in Butterworth and Lobb 1992, 128–30.

Cunliffe, B.W., 1978, *Iron Age Communities in Britain,* London, Routledge and Kegan Paul (2nd edn).

——, 1984, *Danebury: An Iron Age Hillfort in Hampshire, vol. 2. The Excavations 1969–1978: the Finds,* London, Counc. Brit. Archaeol. Res. Rep. 52.

——, 1990, 'Before hillforts', *Oxford J. Archaeol.* 9, 323–36.

—— and Miles, D. (eds), 1984, *Aspects of the Iron Age in Central Southern Britain,* Oxford, Univ. Comm. Archaeol. Monog. 2.

Cunnington, M.E., 1923, *The Early Iron Age Inhabited Site at All Cannings Cross Farm, Wiltshire,* Devizes, George Simpson.

Dacre, M. and Ellison, A.B., 1981, 'A Bronze Age urn cemetery at Kimpton, Hampshire', *Proc. Prehist. Soc.* 47, 147–203.

Davies, S. M., 1981, 'Excavations at Old Down Farm, Andover, part II: prehistoric and Roman', *Proc. Hampshire. Fld Club Archaeol. Soc.* 37, 81–163.

Dewey, H. and Bromehead, C.E.N., 1915, *The Geology of the Country around Windsor and Chertsey.* London, Mem. Geol. Survey, HMSO.

Done, G., 1980, 'The animal bone', in Longley 1980, 74–9.

Drewett, P., 1982, 'Later Bronze Age downland economy and excavations at Black Patch, East Sussex', *Proc. Prehist. Soc.* 48, 321–409.

Driesch, A., von den, 1976. *The Measurement of Animal Bones from Archaeological Sites,* Harvard, Peabody Mus. Bull. 1.

Driskell, B.N., 1986, *The Chipped Stone Tool Production/ Use Cycle: Its Potential in Activity Analysis of Disturbed Sites,* Oxford, Brit. Archaeol. Rep S305.

Ellison, A., 1987, 'The Bronze Age settlement at Thorny Down: pots, post-holes and patterning', *Proc. Prehist. Soc.* 53, 385–92.

Ehrenreich, R.M., 1990, 'Considering the impetus for the Bronze to Iron transition in prehistoric Britain', *J. Metals,* 42(7), 36–8.

Evans, C. J., 1989, 'Perishable and worldly goods — artifact decoration and classification in the light of wetlands research', *Oxford J. Archaeol.* 8, 179–201.

Farwell, C.A., 1989, *Site E Bray, Berkshire. Archaeological Evaluation,* Salisbury, Wessex Archaeology, unpubl. client report.

Fasham, P.J., 1985, *The Prehistoric Settlement at Winnall Down, Winchester,* Winchester, Hampshire Fld Club Archaeol. Soc. Monog. 2.

——, Farwell, D.E. and Whinney, R.J.B., 1989, *The Archaeological Site at Easton Lane, Winchester,* Winchester, Hampshire Fld Club Monog. 6.

—— and Ross, J.M., 1978, 'A Bronze Age flint industry from a barrow site in Micheldever Wood, Hampshire', *Proc. Prehist. Soc.* 44, 47–67.

Field, D., Graham, D., Thomas, S. and Winser, K., 1987, 'Fieldwalking in Surrey: surveys in Waverley and at Paddington Farm, Abinger', *Surrey Archaeol. Collect.* 78, 79–102.

Fisher, A. R., 1985, 'Winklebury hillfort: a study of artefact distributions from subsoil features', *Proc. Prehist. Soc.* 51, 167–80.

Fitzpatrick, A.P., 1991, 'Everyday life in the Iron Age', unpubl. paper from *Archaeology in Britain* Conference 1991.

—— and Morris, E.L. (eds), 1994, *The Iron Age in Wessex: Recent Work,* Salisbury, Wessex Archaeology.

Foley, R., 1981, 'A model of regional archaeological structure', *Proc. Prehist. Soc.* 47, 1–18.

Ford, S., 1986, 'A newly-discovered causewayed enclosure at Eton Wick, near Windsor, Berkshire', *Proc. Prehist. Soc.* 52, 319–20.

——, 1987a, *East Berkshire Archaeological Survey,* Reading, Berkshire Co. Counc. Occas. Pap. 1.

——, 1987b, 'Chronological and functional aspects of flint assemblages', in Brown, A.G. and Edmonds, M.R. (eds), *Lithic Analysis and Later British Prehistory.* Oxford, Brit. Archaeol. Rep. 162, 67–83.

——, 1988, 'Easthampstead Park Mesolithic site', *Berkshire Fld Res. Group Newslet.* 6(3).

——, 1991, *The Nature and Development of Prehistoric Settlement and Landuse in the Middle Thames Region (8000–500 bc) with Special Reference to the Evidence from Lithic Artefacts,* unpubl. PhD thesis, Univ. Reading.

——, Bradley, R.J., Hawkes, J.W. and Fisher, P., 1984, 'Flint working in the Metal Ages,' *Oxford J. Archaeol.* 3, 157–73.

Foster, J., 1990, 'Other Bronze Age artefacts', in Bell, M., *Brean Down Excavations 1983–1987,* London, English Heritage Archaeol. Rep. 15, 158–73.

Fulford, M.G., 1984, *Silchester: Excavations on the Defences 1974–1980,* London, Britannia Monog. 5.

Gabel, G., 1976, 'St Catherine's Hill Mesolithic site near Guildford', *Res. Vol. Surrey Archaeol. Soc.* 3, 78–102.

Gates, T., 1975, *The Middle Thames Valley: an Archaeological Survey of the River Gravels.* Reading, Berkshire Archaeol. Comm. Publ. 1.

Gent, H., 1983, 'Centralized storage in later prehistoric Britain', *Proc. Prehist. Soc.* 49, 243–67.

Gingell, C.J., 1992, *The Marlborough Downs: a Later Bronze Age Landscape and its Origins.* Devizes, Wiltshire Archaeol. Natur. Hist. Soc. Monog. 1.

—— and Lawson, A.J., 1984, 'The Potterne Project: excavation and research at a major settlement of the late Bronze Age', *Wiltshire Archaeol. Natur. Hist. Mag.* 78, 31–4.

—— and ——, 1985, 'Excavations at Potterne, 1984', *Wiltshire Archaeol Natur. Hist. Mag.* 79, 101–8.

Grant, A., 1984, 'Animal husbandry in Wessex and the Thames Valley' in Cunliffe and Miles (eds), 1984, 102–19.

Green, H.S., 1980, *The Flint Arrowheads of the British Isles,* Oxford, Brit. Archaeol, Rep. 75.

Green, M., Bradley, R.J. and Barrett, J.C., 1991, 'The excavations: Down Farm enclosure and cemetery', in Barrett, Bradley and Green 1991, 183–214.

Greene, K., 1978, 'Imported fine wares in Britain to AD 250: a guide to identification', in Arthur, P., and Marsh, G.(eds), *Early Fine Wares in Roman Britain*, Oxford, Brit. Archaeol. Rep. 57, 15–30.

Greep, S., 1987, 'The bone objects', in Sparey Green, C., *Excavations at Poundbury Volume I: the Settlements*, Dorchester, Dorset Natur. Hist. Archaeol. Soc. Monog. 7, 112–13.

Grieg, J.R.A., 1991, 'The botanical remains', in Needham 1991, 234–61.

Guilbert, G., 1981, 'Double-ring roundhouses, probable and possible, in prehistoric Britain', *Proc. Prehist. Soc.* 47, 299–317.

——, 1982, 'Post-ring symmetry in roundhouses at Moel y Gaer and some other sites in prehistoric Britain', in Drury, P.J., (ed.), *Structural Reconstruction: Approaches to the Interpretation of the Excavated Remains of Buildings,* Oxford, Brit. Archaeol. Rep. 110, 67–86.

Haigh, J.G.B., forthcoming, 'A new issue of AERIAL — Version 4.20', *AARG News* 7.

Halstead, P. and O'Shea, J., 1982, 'A friend in need is a friend indeed: social storage and the origins of social ranking' in Renfrew, A.C. and Shennan, S. J.(eds), *Ranking, Resource and Exchange,* Cambridge, Univ. Press, 92–9.

Hanworth, R. and Tomalin, D.J., 1977, *Brooklands, Weybridge: the Excavation of an Iron Age and Medieval Site 1964–65 and 1970–71*, Guildford, Res. Vol. Surrey Archaeol. Soc. 4.

Harding, D.W. and Blake, I. M., 1963, 'An early Iron Age settlement in Dorset', *Antiquity* 37, 63–4.

——, —— and Reynolds, P.J., 1993, *An Iron Age Settlement in Dorset: Excavation and Reconstruction*, Edinburgh, Univ. Edinburgh Dept Archaeol. Monog. 1.

Harding, P.A., 1991, 'The worked stone', in Woodward 1991, 73–87.

——, and Richards, J.C., 1991–3,' Sample excavation of a Mesolithic flint scatter at Whistley Court Farm', *Berkshire Archaeol. J.* 74, 145.

——, 1992, 'The flint', in Gingell 1992, 123–33.

Healey, E. and Robertson-Mackay, R., 1983, 'The lithic industries from Staines causewayed enclosure and their relationship to other earlier Neolithic industries in southern Britain', *Lithics* 4, 1–27.

Healy, F., 1993, 'Lithic material', in Hawkes, J., and Heaton, M., *Excavations at Jennings Yard, Windsor*, Salisbury, Wessex Archaeol. Rep. 3, 9–15.

——, Heaton. M., and Lobb, S.J., 1992, 'Excavations of a Mesolithic site at Thatcham, Berkshire', *Proc. Prehist. Soc.* 58, 41–76.

Heaton, M. Montague, R., Mepham, L. Healy, F. and Barnes, I., 1991, *Stubbings House, Burchett's Green, Maidenhead Berkshire: Archaeological Assessment,* Salisbury, Wessex Archaeology, unpubl. client report.

Hey, G., 1990, 'Aston, Bampton and Shifford, Old Shifford Farm', *South Midlands Archaeol.* 20, 86–8.

Hietala, H. (ed.), 1984, *Intrasite Spatial Analysis in Archaeology,* Cambridge, Univ. Press.

—— and Stevens, D.E., 1977, 'Spatial analysis: multiple procedures in pattern recognition studies', *Amer. Antiq.* 42, 539–59.

Hill, J.D., 1993, 'Can we recognise a different European past?; a contrastive archaeology of later prehistoric settlements in southern England', *J. European Archaeol.* 1, 57–75.

Hill, P. H., 1982, 'Towards a new classification of prehistoric houses', *Scott. Archaeol. Rev.* 1, 24–31.

——, 1984, 'A sense of proportion; a contribution to the study of double-ring roundhouses', *Scot. Archaeol. Rev.* 3, 80–6.

Hingley, R.C., 1990, 'Domestic organisation and gender relations in Iron Age and Romano-British households', in Samson, R., (ed.), *The Social Archaeology of Houses*, Edinburgh, Univ. Press, 125–47.

—— and Miles, D., 1984, 'Aspects of Iron Age settlement in the Upper Thames Valley', in Cunliffe and Miles (eds), 1984, 52–71.

Hodder, I. R., 1984, *Wendens Ambo: the Excavation of an Iron Age and Romano-British Settlement*, London, Passmore Edwards Mus., Archaeology of the M11 1.

Hoffmann, M., 1964, *The Warp–weighted Loom: Studies in the History and Technology of an Ancient Implement*, Oslo.

Holgate, R., 1988, *Neolithic Settlement of the Thames Basin*, Oxford, Brit. Archaeol. Rep. 194.

Jacobi, R., 1976, 'Britain inside and outside Mesolithic Europe', *Proc. Prehist. Soc.* 42, 67–84.

Jarvis, M.G., Allen, R.H., Fordham, S.J., Hazelden, J., Moffat, A.J. and Sturdy, R.G., 1984, *Soils and their Use in Southern England*, Harpenden, Soil Survey.

Jennings, D., 1992, 'Small finds', in Moore and Jennings 1992, 93–7.

Johnson, B., 1975, *Archaeology and the M25: 1971–1975*, Guildford, Surrey Archaeol. Soc.

Johnston, J., 1987, 'Excavations at Pingewood', *Berkshire Archaeol. J.* 72, 1983–85, 17–52.

Jones, M.K., 1984, 'Regional patterns in crop production', in Cunliffe and Miles (eds), 1984, 120–5.

——, 1986, *England before Domesday*, London, Batsford.

——, 1991, 'Down Farm, Woodcutts: the carbonised plant remains', in Barrett, Bradley and Hall 1991, 49–53.

Kendall, M.G., 1970, *Rank Correlation Methods*, London, Griffin (4th edn).

Kvamme, K.L., and Jochim, M.A., 1989, 'The environmental basis of Mesolithic settlement', in Bonsall, C., (ed.), *The Mesolithic in Europe*, Edinburgh, John Donald, 1–12.

Lambrick, G., 1992, 'The development of late prehistoric and Roman farming on the Thames gravels', in Fulford, M., and Nichols, E.(eds) *Developing Landscapes of Lowland Britain. The Archaeology of the British Gravels: a Review*, London, Soc. Antiq. London Occas. Pap. 14, 78–105.

——, and Robinson, M., 1979, *Iron Age and Roman Riverside Settlements at Farmoor, Oxfordshire*, London, Counc. Brit. Archaeol. Res. Rep. 32.

Lawson, A. J., 1994, 'Potterne', in Fitzpatrick and Morris (eds), 1994, 42–6.

Legge, A.J., 1991, 'The animal remains from six sites at Down Farm, Woodcutts', in Barrett, Bradley and Hall 1991, 54–100.

Lobb, S.J., 1986–90, 'Excavations and observations of Bronze Age and Saxon deposits at Brimpton, 1978–9', *Berkshire Archaeol. J.* 73, 1986–90, 43–53.

Longley, D., 1980, *Runnymede Bridge 1976: Excavations of the Site of a Late Bronze Age Settlement*, Guildford, Res. Vol. Surrey Archaeol. Soc. 6.

——, 1991, 'The late Bronze Age pottery', in Needham 1991, 162–212.

Lowther, A.W.G., 1939, 'Bronze Age and Iron Age', in Oakley, K.P., Rankine,W.G., and Lowther, A.W.G. (eds), *A Survey of the Prehistory of the Farnham District*, Guildford, Surrey Archaeol. Soc. Spec. Vol., 153–217.

Lyne, M.A.B. and Jefferies, R.S., 1979, *The Alice Holt / Farnham Roman Pottery Industry*, London, Counc. Brit. Archaeol. Res. Rep. 30.

Mallouf, R.J., 1982, 'Analysis of plow-damaged chert artefacts: the Broken Creek Cache (H1HI86), Hill County Texas', *J. Field Archaeol.* 9, 79–98.

Marsh, G., and Tyers, P., 1978, 'The Roman pottery from Southwark', in *Southwark Excavations 1972–74* vol. 2, London, Middlesex Archaeol. Soc. and Surrey Archaeol. Soc. Joint Publ. 1, 533–82.

McMinn, R.M.H. and Hutchings, R.T., 1985, *A Colour Atlas of Human Anatomy*, Wolfe Medical Pub.

McOmish, D. S., 1989, 'Non-hillfort settlement and its implications', in Bowden, M., Mackay, D. and Topping, P. (eds), *From Cornwall to Caithness; Some Aspects of British Field Archaeology*, Oxford, Brit. Archaeol. Rep. 209, 99–110.

Mellars, P., 1976, 'Settlement patterns and industrial variability in the British Mesolithic', in Sieveking, G. de G., Longworth, I.H. and Wilson, K.E. (eds), *Problems in Economic and Social Archaeology*, London, Duckworth, 375–99.

——, and Rienhardt, S., 1978, 'The patterns of Mesolithic landuse in southern England: a geological perspective' in Mellars, P., (ed.), *The Early Postglacial Settlement of Northern Europe*, London, Duckworth, 243–93.

Mepham, L.N., 1992, 'The pottery' in Butterworth, C.A. and Lobb, S.J., 'Excavations at Field Farm, Burghfield, Berkshire', in Butterworth and Lobb 1992, 40–8.

Middleton, A.P., 1987, 'Technological investigation of the coatings on some 'haematite-coated' pottery from southern England', *Archaeometry* 29, 250–61.

Miles, D. (ed.), 1986, *Archaeology at Barton Court Farm, Abingdon, Oxon*, London, Counc. Brit. Archaeol. Res. Rep. 50.

Millett, M., 1979, 'An approach to the functional interpretation of pottery', in Millett, M., (ed.), *Pottery and the Archaeologist*, London, Univ. London Inst. Archaeol. Occas. Publ. 4, 35–48.

Moore, J. and Jennings, D., 1992, *Reading Business Park: a Bronze Age Landscape,* Oxford, Oxford Univ. Comm. Archaeol., Thames Valley Landscapes: the Kennet Valley 1.

Morris, E.L., 1991, 'Ceramic analysis and the pottery from Potterne: a summary', in Middleton, A. P. and Freestone, I.C. (eds), *Recent Developments in Ceramic Petrology*, London, Brit. Mus. Occas. Pap. 81, 277–87.

——, 1992, 'The pottery', in Coe and Newman, 1992, 13–23.

——, in press, 'Artefact production and distribution' in Champion and Collis, in press.

Needham, S.P., 1987, 'The Bronze Age', in Bird. J. and Bird, D.G.(eds), *The Archaeology of Surrey to 1540*, Guildford, Surrey Archaeol. Soc., 97–137.

——, 1991, *Excavation and Salvage at Runnymede Bridge, 1978: the Late Bronze Age Waterfront Site,* London, Brit. Mus. Press/English Heritage.

Newcomer, M.H. and Karlin, C., 1987, 'Flint chips from Pincevent', in Sieveking, G., de G., and Newcomer, M.H. (eds), *The Human Uses of Flint and Chert: Proceedings of the Fourth International Flint Symposium,* Cambridge, Univ. Press, 33–6.

Newman, R., Adam, N. and Lancley, J., 1991, *Archaeological Investigations at Maidenhead Thicket, Maidenhead, Berkshire: August 1990 to April 1991,* Salisbury, Wessex Archaeology, unpubl. client report.

——, Tatler, S. and Trott, M., 1990, *Maidenhead Thicket, Berkshire: Archaeological Evaluation,* Salisbury, Wessex Archaeology, unpubl. client report.

Nyberg, G.G., 1990, 'Spinning implements of the Viking Age from Elisenhof', in Walton, P. and Wild, J.P. (eds), *Textiles in Northern Archaeology: North European Symposium for Archaeological Textiles III: Textile Symposium in York, 6–9 May 1987*, London, 73–84.

O'Connell, M., 1986, *Petters Sports Field, Egham; Excavation of a Late Bronze Age / Early Iron Age Site,* Guildford, Res. Vol. Surrey Archaeol. Soc. 10.

138

Odell, G.H. and Cowan, F., 1987, 'Estimating tillage effects on artifact distributions', *Amer. Antiq.* 52, 456–584.

Over, L.J., 1973, 'A Belgic occupation site at Knowl Hill, Berks.', *Berkshire Archaeol. J.* 67, 63–70.

Oxford Archaeological Unit 1989, *Archaeological Assessment Park Farm, Binfield. SU 855705*, Oxford, Oxford Archaeol. Uniut, unpubl. client report.

Palmer, R. and Cox, C., 1993, *Uses of Aerial Photography in Archaeological Evaluations,* Birmingham, Inst. Fld Archaeol. Tech. Pap. 12.

Palmer, S., and Hey, G., 1989, 'Thornhill Farm, Fairford', *Glevensis* 23, 43–5.

Pals, J.P. and Dierendonck, M.C., van, 1988, 'Between flax and fabric: cultivation and processing of flax in a mediaeval peat reclaimation settlement near Midwoud (Prov. Noord Holland)', *J. Archaeol. Sci.* 15, 237–51.

Parker-Pearson, M., in press, 'Food, fertility and front doors in the first millennium B.C.', in Champion and Collis, in press.

Parrington, M., 1978, *The Excavation of an Iron Age Settlement, Bronze Age Ring-ditches and Roman Features at Ashville Trading Estate, Abingdon 1974–76*, London, Counc. Brit. Archaeol. Res. Rep. 28.

Prehistoric Ceramics Research Group, 1992, *The Study of Later Prehistoric Pottery: Guidelines for Analysis and Publication,* Oxford, Prehist. Ceramics Res. Group Occas. Pap. 2.

Pearson, G.W. and Stuiver, M., 1986, 'High-precision calibration of the radiocarbon time scale, 500–2500 BC', in Stuiver, M. and Kra, R.S. (eds), 'International 14C conference, 12th Proceedings', *Radiocarbon* 28, 839–62.

Petersen, F.F., 1981, *The Excavation of a Bronze Age Cemetery on Knighton Heath, Dorset,* Oxford, Brit. Archaeol. Rep. 98.

Pitt Rivers, A.L.F., 1898, *Excavations in Cranborne Chase,* Vol. IV, privately printed.

Pitts, M.W., 1978, 'Towards an understanding of flint industries in post-glacial England', *Bull. Inst. Archaeol. Univ. London* 15, 179–97.

—— and Jacobi, R.M., 1979, 'Some aspects of change in flaked stone industries of the Mesolithic and Neolithic in southern Britain', *J. Archaeol. Sci.* 6, 163–77.

Pryor, F.M.A., 1980, 'The flints', in Pryor F.M.A., *Excavations at Fengate, Peterborough, England: the Third Report*, Northampton, Northamptonshire Archaeol. Soc. Monog. 1/ Roy. Ontario Mus. Archaeol. Monog. 6, 106–25.

Rankine, W.F., 1954, 'Mesolithic research in east Hampshire', *Proc. Hampshire Fld. Clb. Archaeol. Soc.* 15, 157–72.

Reynolds, P.J., 1979, *Iron Age Farm: the Butser Experiment,* London, Brit. Mus. Press.

Richards, J., 1978, *The Archaeology of the Berkshire Downs: An Introductory Survey,* Reading, Berkshire Archaeol. Comm.

——, 1990, *The Stonehenge Environs Project,* London, English Heritage Archaeol. Rep. 16.

Rigby, V., 1989, 'Pottery from the Iron Age cemetery', in Stead, I.M. and Rigby, V., *Verulamium: the King Harry Lane Site*, London, English Heritage Archaeol. Rep. 12, 112–210.

Riley, D.N., 1987, *Air Photography and Archaeology,* London, Batsford.

Robertson-Mackay, R., 1987. 'The Neolithic causewayed enclosure at Staines, Surrey: excavations 1961–63', *Proc. Prehist. Soc.* 53, 23–128.

Robinson, M., 1980, 'The environmental evidence from Knight's Farm Site 1', in Bradley *et al.* 1980, 277–82.

Rowlands, M.J., 1976, *The Organisation of Middle Bronze Age Metalworking,* Oxford, Brit. Archaeol. Rep. 31.

Salter, C.J., 1989, 'The scientific investigation of the iron industry in Iron Age Britain', in Henderson, J. (ed.), *Scientific Analysis in Archaeology*, Oxford, Univ. Comm. Archaeol. Monog. 19/Univ. College Los Angeles Archaeol. Res. Tools 5, 250–73.

Saunders, C., and Havercroft, A.B., 1977, 'A kiln of the potter *Oastrius* and related excavations at Little Munden Farm, Bricket Wood', *Hertfordshire Archaeol.* 5, 109–56.

Schild, R., 1989, 'The formation of homogeneous occupation units (Kshemenitsas) in open air sandy sites and its significance for the interpretation of Mesolithic flint assemblages, in Bonsall, C. (ed.), *The Mesolithic in Europe*, Edinburgh, John Donald, 89–98.

Seager Smith, R. and Davies, S.M., 1993, 'Roman pottery', in Woodward, P.J., Davies, S.M. and Grahame, A, *Excavations at the Old Methodist Chapel and Greyhound Yard, Dorchester, 1981–4*, Dorchester, Dorset Natur. Hist. Archaeol. Soc. Monog. 12, 202–89.

Shepherd, W., 1972, *Flint: its Origins, Properties and Uses,* London, Faber.

Smith, I.F., 1965, *Windmill Hill and Avebury: Excavations by Alexander Keiller 1925–1939,* Oxford, Clarendon.

Smith, K., 1977, 'The excavation of Winklebury Camp, Basingstoke, Hampshire', *Proc. Prehist. Soc.* 43, 31–129.

Sørensen, M.L.S. and Thomas, R. (eds), 1989, *The Bronze Age–Iron Age Transition in Europe,* Oxford, Brit. Archaeol. Rep. S484.

SPSS Inc., 1986, *SPSSX Users Guide,* London, McGraw-Hill (2nd edn).

Stace, C., 1991, *New Flora of the British Isles,* Cambridge, Univ. Press.

Stacey, L. and Walker, K.E., forthcoming, 'Worked bone objects', in Smith. R.J.C., *Excavations Along the Route of the Dorchester By-Pass 1986–8*. Salisbury, Wessex Archaeol. Rep.

Stone, J.F.S., 1941, 'The Deverel–Rimbury settlement in Thorny Down, Winterbourne Gunner, south Wilts', *Proc. Prehist. Soc. 7*, 114–33.

Strang, A., 1991, 'Towards a functional classification of round-houses', *Bull. Board Celtic Stud. 37*, 159–66.

Thomas, R., 1989, 'The Bronze–Iron transition in southern England', in Sørensen and Thomas (eds), 1989, 263–86.

Thompson, I., 1982, *Grog-tempered 'Belgic' pottery of South-eastern England*, Oxford, Brit. Archaeol. Rep. 108.

Thompson, J. and Manning, W.H., 1974, 'The pottery from enclosures I and II', in Manning, W.H., 'Excavations on the late Iron Age, Roman and Saxon sites at Ufton Nervet, Berkshire, in 1961–1963', *Berkshire Archaeol. J. 67*, 24–39.

Timby, J., 1989, 'The pottery', in Fulford, M.G., *The Silchester Amphitheatre*, London, Britannia Monog. 10, 80–124.

Turnbull, A. L., 1984, *From Bronze to Iron: the Occurrence of Iron in the British Later Bronze Age*, Unpubl. Ph.D. thesis, Univ. Edinburgh.

VCH, 1923, *Victoria County History of the Counties of England: Berkshire Vol. 3*.

Ware, B., 1980. 'Pollen', in Bradley *et al.* 1980, 245–6.

Webster, P.V., 1984, *Roman Samian Ware*, Cardiff, Univ. College, Dept Extra-Mural Stud., (2nd edn.).

White, D.A., 1982, *The Bronze Age Cremation Cemeteries at Simon's Ground, Dorset*, Dorchester, Dorset Natur. Hist. Archaeol. Soc. Monog. 3.

White, H.J.O., 1907 *The Geology of the Country Around Hungerford and Newbury*, London, Mem. Geol. Survey, HMSO.

White, J.P. and Thomas, D.H., 1972, 'What mean these stones? Ethno-taxonomic models and archaeological interpretations in the New Guinea Highlands', in Clarke, D.L. (ed.), *Models in Archaeology*, London, Methuen, 275–308.

Whittle, A.W.R., 1977, *The Earlier Neolithic of Southern England and its Continental Background*, Oxford, Brit. Archaeol. Rep. S35.

——, 1987, 'Ebbsfleet pottery', in Robertson-Mackay 1987, 90.

Wild, J.P., 1970, *Textile Manufacture in the Northern Roman Provinces*, Cambridge, Univ. Press.

——, and Jørgensen, B.J., 1988, 'Clothes from the Roman Empire, barbarians and Romans' in Jørgensen, L.B., Magnus, B. and Munkagaard, E. (eds), *Archaeological Textiles: Report from the 2nd North European Symposium for Archaeological Textiles Symposium 1–4 V 1984*, Copenhagen, 65–98.

Woodward, A.B., 1992, 'Discussion [of the urns]', in Lobb, S.J., 'Excavation at Shortheath Lane, Abbotts Farm, Sulhamstead', in Butterworth and Lobb 1992, 75–7.

Woodward, P.J., 1991, *The South Dorset Ridgeway: Survey and Excavations 1977–1984*, Dorchester, Dorset Natur. Hist. Archaeol. Soc. Monog. 8.

Wymer, J.J., 1977, *Gazeteer of Mesolithic Sites in England and Wales*, London, Counc. Brit. Archaeol. Res. Rep. 20.

Young, C.J., 1977, *Oxfordshire Roman Pottery*, Oxford, Brit. Archaeol. Rep. 43.

Zvelebil, M., Moore, J., Green, S. and Henson, D., 1987, 'Regional survey and the analysis of lithic scatters: a case study from southeast Ireland', in Rowley-Conway, P., Zvelebil, M. and Blankholm, H.P. (eds), *Mesolithic Northwest Europe: Recent Trends*, Sheffield, Dept Archaeol. Prehist., 9–32.

Index

by *Lesley and Roy Adkins*

Entries are largely in alphabetical order, but sub-entries follow a chronological order of entry where appropriate (for example, Middle Bronze Age, Late Iron Age). Microfiche tables are referred to as Mf1–9.